Based on a True Story

Latin American History at the Movies

Edited by
Donald F. Stevens

SR Books

Lanham • Boulder • New York • Toronto • Oxford

Published by SR Books
An imprint of Rowman & Littlefield Publishers, Inc.
A wholly owned subsidiary of The Rowman & Littlefield Publishing Group, Inc.
4501 Forbes Boulevard, Suite 200
Lanham, MD 20706

PO Box 317
Oxford
OX2 9RU, UK

Illustrations

Frame enlargements in Chapter 7 were provided by John Mraz.
All uncredited photographs were provided by Donald F. Stevens.

Library of Congress Cataloging-in-Publication Data

Based on a true story : Latin American history at the movies /
   edited by Donald F. Stevens.
      p.   cm. — (Latin American silhouettes)
   Includes bibliographical references.
      ISBN 0-8420-2582-0 (cloth : alk. paper). — ISBN 0-8420-
2781-5 (pbk. : alk. paper)
      1. Latin America in motion pictures. 2. Latin Americans in
motion pictures. 3. Historical films—History and criticism.
I. Stevens, Donald Fithian, 1953–   . II. Series.
PN1995.9.L37B37   1997
791.43'628—DC21   97-10742
                                                                 CIP

♾ The paper used in this publication meets the minimum requirements
of the American National Standard for permanence of paper for printed
library materials, Z39.48, 1984.

For Nathaniel,

who has his own ideas

about the movies

Contents

Acknowledgments

I am grateful to my department head, Eric Dorn Brose, and to Dean of the College of Arts and Sciences Thomas L. Canavan for their support in making this book possible, and to the students in my Latin American history classes at Drexel University, whose enthusiasm made it worthwhile. As I expanded my use of feature films to teach history, I benefited from countless discussions with colleagues. When I was unable to convince anyone else to edit a book like this at the 1992 meeting of the Conference on Latin American History in Washington, DC, I decided that I would have to do it myself. Portions of the manuscript were presented at meetings of the Latin American Studies Association (1995), the Conference on Latin American History (1996), and the fifth Studies in Latin American Popular Culture Conference (1996). Without the opportunity for real interaction that such occasions permit, scholarship in general would be diminished and, certainly, this book might not have been possible. Thank you to all who offered advice, suggestions, criticism, and encouragement.

I am sure that no editor ever had a more congenial group of authors with whom to work. I am grateful to Jim Saeger for showing me an early draft of his work on *The Mission* and to the editorial board of *The Americas* for permission to reproduce it here with minor amendments and corrections. All of the other chapters are previously unpublished, and their authors usually had to take time to write them amid the claims of more traditional obligations. Nearly all of their essays were written specifically for this volume. I cannot thank them enough.

From the beginning, Editorial Director Richard Hopper and Latin American Silhouettes series editors William Beezley and Judith Ewell made SR Books the natural publisher for such a collection. At the other end of the process, Linda Pote Musumeci cheerfully and efficiently took charge of turning the manuscript into a book. It has been a real pleasure to work with all of them.

For their support and assistance with videos, film stills, and assorted computer paraphernalia I thank Terry Geeskin of the Museum of Modern Art, Peter Bartscherer of Nesbitt College of Design Arts, Richard Binder of Drexel's Hagerty Library, and the staff of Instructional Media Services at Drexel University.

Finally, I am grateful to Judith Silver for all of the unusual reasons.

D.F.S.

Philadelphia
June 1997

Introduction

"Based on a true story" is an expression seen frequently in advertisements for films and television programs that deliberately blend fact and fiction. At the same time that it makes a claim of authenticity, it contains a caution that changes have been made. The two messages are not communicated at the same volume. "Based on a true story" proclaims a promise of veracity while whispering a discreet warning that mere "facts" alone are not sufficient.

In 1915 one of filmmaking's most innovative pioneers, D. W. Griffith, predicted that "moving pictures" would quickly replace book writing as the principal way to communicate knowledge about the past. In the first essay in this volume, Donald F. Stevens looks at the promise, problems, parallels, and paradoxes of visual presentation of the past both in the movies and in professional history. Each of the remaining chapters examines one or two of the best available feature films on Latin America from a historian's perspective.

The essays are arranged in rough chronological order, beginning with Sonya Lipsett-Rivera and Sergio Rivera Ayala's illuminating view of Christopher Columbus in Ridley Scott's *1492: The Conquest of Paradise*. Thomas H. Holloway digs into the elusive story of the sixteenth-century conquistador Lope de Aguirre in Werner Herzog's *Aguirre, the Wrath of God*. María Luisa Bemberg's film *Yo, la Peor de Todas (I, the Worst of All)* evokes Mexico's celebrated seventeenth-century poet, Sor Juana Inés de la Cruz. Susan E. Ramírez traces what we know about her life and her thoughts through Octavio Paz's biography, other historical works, and, ultimately, Sor Juana's own writing. James Schofield Saeger exposes the common cultural preconceptions in both written history and in Roland Joffé's spectacular film, *The Mission*, about Jesuit missionaries' attempts to transform Guaraní Indian lives and beliefs in eighteenth-century Paraguay.

Nineteenth-century Argentina provides the setting for Bemberg's *Camila*, which Stevens describes as a brilliant critique of romantic passion and patriarchal terror. John Mraz compares divergent viewpoints in two Cuban films on slavery: Sergio Giral's *The Other Francisco* and Tomás Gutiérrez Alea's *The Last Supper*. Barbara Weinstein examines how Cuban women's history has changed since Humberto Solás made *Lucía*, a film divided into three segments, one in the 1890s, one in the 1930s, and one in the 1960s, each focusing on a different woman named Lucía. Bruno Barreto's *Gabriela*, based on the novel by the celebrated Brazilian author Jorge Amado, provides a contrasting perspective on the modernization of sexual relationships in Brazil. James D. Henderson considers it "the best feature-length film depicting elite culture and mentality in early twentieth-century Latin America."

Barbara A. Tenenbaum explains what foreigners find confusing about Mexican culture when they read Laura Esquivel's *Like Water for Chocolate* or see Alfonso Arau's cinematic version of the novel. Mark D. Szuchman examines how historical debates on the family and politics are addressed in Argentine films, especially Bemberg's *Miss Mary* (set in the late 1930s and early 1940s) and Luis Puenzo's *The Official Story* (which takes place during the collapse of the military dictatorship in 1983). In this volume's final chapter, Robert M. Levine exposes the elusive interplay of fiction and reality in Héctor Babenco's *Pixote*, which tells the prescient story of a child living on the streets of São Paulo and Rio de Janeiro, Brazil.

Each of these essays addresses the past, both as we see it at the movies and as we imagine it in traditional historical research. *Based on a True Story* is not a complete, panoramic view of Latin American history but rather a series of windows through which we can catch glimpses of men, women, and children from the late fifteenth century to the present, as well as watch the historians and filmmakers whose work behind the scenes makes these visions possible.

CHAPTER ONE

Never Read History Again?
The Possibilities and Perils of Cinema as Historical Depiction

DONALD F. STEVENS

The time will come, and in less than ten years, when the children in the public schools will be taught practically everything by moving pictures. Certainly they will never be obliged to read history again.

—D. W. Griffith, March 28, 1915[1]

The nineteenth century was profoundly optimistic about the possibilities of recording objective reality in both words and images. The invention of photography in the 1820s, and its improvement by Louis Daguerre and George Eastman later in the century, coincided with the development of the profession of historian. Both history and photography promised accurate descriptions of objective reality. As photographers recorded images of places, objects, and people unmediated (it was thought) by the artist's style, scholars believed that they could write history, in Leopold von Ranke's essential phrase, "as it really was."[2]

Both history and photography became more methodologically and technically sophisticated. Further mechanical improvements made sequential photography possible, then kinetoscopes and peep shows. Finally, in 1895, the first true motion picture flashed on a theater screen. As the movies, television, and videotape reached ever-larger audiences, the written products of the historical profession became increasingly specialized. Visual images became more attractive and pervasive; history became more disciplined, compartmentalized, and marginalized from the broader culture.

1

These technological innovations and market conditions were the basis for D. W. Griffith's optimism that filmmaking would quickly replace book writing as the basis for presenting the past to mass audiences. He continued:

> Imagine a public library of the near future, for instance. There will be long rows of boxes or pillars, properly classified and indexed, of course. At each box a push button and before each box a seat. Suppose you wish to "read up" on a certain episode in Napoleon's life. Instead of consulting all the authorities, wading laboriously through a host of books, and ending bewildered, without a clear idea of exactly what did happen and confused at every point by conflicting opinions about what did happen, you will merely seat yourself at a properly adjusted window, in a scientifically prepared room, press the button, and actually see what happened.
>
> There will be no opinions expressed. You will merely be present at the making of history. All the work of writing, revising, collating, and reproducing will have been carefully attended to by a corps of recognized experts, and you will have received a vivid and complete expression.[3]

Today, many historians would consider Griffith's (and Ranke's) idea of "what did happen" to be an antiquated and naive notion, a quaint vestige of outmoded positivism. Griffith did hold some simple ideas about the past. He assumed that history was shaped by the lives of great men and that knowledge of the past was encapsulated in "episodes" in the lives of the powerful. Few professional historians today would share those assumptions. The days of heroic history are past. Movies, though, still lend themselves to action and heroes. Griffith believed that history was important and interesting but he thought that professional historians were not. He assumed without question both an interest in the past and the value of teaching and learning history. But Griffith also was certain that "wading laboriously through a host of books" and "consulting all the authorities" would only result in conflict, frustration, and confusion.

Griffith's vision of a future video library of historical episodes neatly avoids those problems because all of the difficult work is performed by unseen forces. His inquiring mind encounters passive constructions that, at the push of a button, miraculously provide the desired historical commodity ready to be consumed uncritically. The construction of the past is carried on out of sight; it is implied but not explained. Who is it who locates and frames that window into the past? Who "scientifically prepared" the room? Who determines when the window is "properly adjusted"? Even if we could frame and locate an accurate and unobtrusive window on the past, will this single, fixed point of view suffice for every occasion? What happens when the scene changes? If time moves as slowly in these re-creations as it does in real life, the process of observing the past from this fixed perspective could become exceedingly tedious. Do we really have time to watch three hundred years of Spanish colonial administration or even five and one-half years to spend sitting in front of the window to see the Cuban Revolution from Castro's attack on the Moncada barracks to the fall of Batista? Stories of wars and battles remain among the most popular subjects of interest in the past, if one judges by the number of texts offered for sale by the History Book Club or national bookstore chains. Yet even warfare has been described as endless tedium "punctuated with moments of sheer terror and exhilaration."[4] Perhaps Griffith's window is equipped with another button as well, a fast-forward to skip through the monotony.

Once we begin to hit the fast-forward button, we have taken another crucial step away from the notion of objective reality. We have begun to edit what we see through the window. We can no longer avoid noticing the heroic efforts that are necessary to make the past presentable. Who is doing all that traditional labor of "writing, revising, collating, and reproducing"? Just who are those "recognized experts," how were they trained, and who accredited them? What power assures us that no opinions are ever expressed? What technical wizardry has transformed the bewildering chaos of conflicting historical interpretations into "a vivid and complete expression"?

It is, of course, ironic (in at least three distinct ways) that Griffith himself should portray the future of the past in this way. The content, the technique, and the reception of his most famous film ensured that we could never see the past through a perfect window. First, look at his own great contribution to putting the past on movie screens. Griffith's *The Clansman* opened in February 1915 (just before the interview I have quoted from appeared). Later retitled *The Birth of a Nation*, the film was not so much a window on the past as it was a mirror of particular stereotypes and prejudices.[5] Second, it demonstrated tremendous innovations in filmmaking technique. *The Birth of a Nation* first unlocked the motion picture camera from its previously fixed position. Griffith put the window on the past in motion, panning from a mother comforting her children amid the devastation of war, to Sherman's troops passing in the distance, and back to the pathetic, huddled figures again, and later cutting dramatically back and forth between scenes of a distraught young white woman menaced by a mulatto suitor and the Ku Klux Klan galloping to save her. Griffith's innovations in cinematography and editing ensured that cinematic art would never again be as static as his metaphorical view through a window implied.[6] Third, even the view through Griffith's window did not remain unchallenged or unchanged. *The Birth of a Nation* was reedited many times over the years both by Griffith himself and by others who contested his version of the Civil War and Reconstruction. History is not obvious and inert but challenged and ever changing.

For all a professional historian may balk at the intellectual weaknesses of his vision of history's future, Griffith was probably more accurate than we might like to think. More people today get their history in movie theaters, from broadcast and cable television, and on prerecorded videocassette tapes than from reading print.[7] During the nineteenth century, historical narratives by William H. Prescott, George Bancroft, and Thomas Carlyle were widely read. Today, history is more likely to be interpreted by Roland Joffé, Bernardo Bertolucci, or Oliver Stone. Carl Sandburg is said to have remarked that Hollywood was a more effective educational institution than Harvard.[8] The products of Hollywood, Buenos Aires, São Paulo, and Churrubusco are more economical and popular as well.

Despite, and perhaps in part because of, the evident popularity of motion pictures, most historians have been slow to take film and television seriously as a way of depicting the past.[9] Justification abounds for intellectual suspicion and emotional resentment. Movies are relatively short. They can deal with only a relatively small amount of information. Even a full-length feature film is seldom more than two hours long and may contain only about as much information as a chapter or an article. Hence, films seem superficial to professionals who spend years immersed in the details of a particular subject and time. Filmmaking appears to be nothing like book writing. Movie making is a gregarious activity; it seems glamorous, expensive, and lucrative. Historians generally work on their own, in relative solitude, on restricted budgets for small audiences. But many of these ideas and attitudes will not stand up to scrutiny. As Robert Rosenstone has pointed out, a short work is not inherently less historical than a long one any more than an article is worse than a book or a 200-page book less historical than five heavy volumes.[10] Brevity can be a virtue, and film has other merits of immediacy and emotional impact that make it more accessible to the wide audiences that somehow are not attracted to professional historical writing. Most period movies nevertheless rely on historians' labor of one sort or another. Robert Brent Toplin has noted that filmmakers generally do not have a complete grasp of the appropriate scholarly literature, but they do "frequently operate under the influence of specific works in print."[11] Historians have, for the most part, repaid this attention by neglecting films, leaving the analysis of visual media to scholars trained in cinema studies, literature, and communications.[12]

Even as film and television are increasingly important as interpreters of history, most professional historians have seen filmmakers as outsiders who need not be addressed.[13] A small minority began using films in class nearly thirty years ago. Those scholars who broke ranks undoubtedly paid a price. There was little to protect the ones who first brought films into the history classroom from the suspicion of their older, tenured colleagues that they were involved in some dubious experiment to attract more of the visually oriented (and therefore, by definition, less literate) students. They appeared to be risking their professional integrity through some untoward pact with the purveyors of slick, seductive, and misleading images. Many of these historians, such as Robert Sklar, gravitated toward the new field of cinema studies.[14]

Recently, the availability of videotape seems to have increased the use of films in history classes, but the intellectual obstacles to films in the classroom may well have been greater than the technological ones.[15] As Rosenstone has written, "Let's face the facts and admit it: historical films trouble and disturb (most) professional historians. Why? We all know the obvious answers. Because, historians will say, films are inaccurate. They distort the past. They fictionalize, trivialize, and romanticize important people, events, and movements. They falsify history."[16] And some filmmakers are relatively immature, unreflective, disingenuous, even callous about the past. Joffé's *The Mission*, for example, ignores the conventional, institutional racism of the Jesuit missionaries in eighteenth-century Paraguay and turns centuries of historical certainty upside down to provide a dramatic and heroic ending for favored characters, as James Schofield Saeger demonstrates in his essay in this volume. Such distortions are even more disturbing when the movie begins with a conspicuous appeal to authenticity. *The Mission* claims that "the historical events represented in this story are true and happened in Paraguay and Argentina in 1758 and 1759."[17]

Even the films that are most congruent with professional history require certain liberties that historians find troubling.[18] They may complain that filmmakers concretize what is not known, that too much imagination is involved in making historical texts into visual representations and reenactments. But many of the same objections could be made to written history. Do we not do the same thing in our own minds (that is, visualize an imagined past based on the evidence) when we read traditional historical documents or narratives? Is there a clear distinction between trying to imagine what seventeenth-century peasant households looked like from reading inventories postmortem and assembling words or images to convey that knowledge?[19] Hayden White argues that the process is the same: "Every written history is a product of processes of condensation, displacement, symbolization, and qualification exactly like those used in the production of a filmed representation. It is only the medium that differs, not the way in which messages are produced."[20] E. Bradford Burns goes even further, considering the clear communication of visual images a potential advantage of filmmaking over traditional historical writing. In his words, "thus, the historian should note that in at least this respect the film could be less subjective than the written word since it transfers the image directly to the mind rather than requiring, as the written description does, the mind to create an image, one that naturally varies with each person. Thus, the film leaves less to the imagination, requiring perhaps less interpretation than other forms of communication."[21]

While the public hungers for something beyond a diet of dry facts, historians have a voracious appetite for scraps of paper hidden away in previously unexplored places. One of the wonders of historical research and writing is the way the sources both discipline and delight us. The past is a strange land, far more peculiar than we can imagine on our own.[22] Yet, even the most traditional approach to "facts" and "what really happened" cannot proceed without inspiration, assumptions, and questions. Imagination shapes the questions we ask about the past and helps us guess where appropriate sources might be found.[23] Films and filmmaking can encourage historical imagination. Natalie Zemon Davis found that the process of putting the story of Martin Guerre's disappearance and reappearance on film provoked questions that would not have occurred to her if she had only tried to tell the story in words. Making the movie led her to ask new questions not only about appearances but also about motivations: "I felt I had my own historical laboratory, generating not proofs, but historical possibilities."[24]

Films can serve as an introduction to the past and an incentive to study history. Werner Herzog's *Aguirre, the Wrath of God* is a cinematic marvel with striking visuals of actors portraying sixteenth-century Spanish conquistadors descending from the mists of the Andes into the steamy jungles of the Amazon. Yet, those who know something of the historical Lope de Aguirre will find the cinematic version disappointing. Aguirre's own story is stranger and more compelling than fiction, as Thomas H. Holloway demonstrates in Chapter Three.

Here is the crucial point: Where filmmakers and their mass audiences may be looking for the present and the familiar in the past, historians are attracted to its distinctiveness, its "otherness," and its peculiarities. As Davis puts it, "I wanted to shake people up, because I feel that is what history is about. It is not about confirming what you already know, but about stretching it and turning it upside down and then reaffirming some values, or putting some into question."[25] The best history allows the past to speak to us in its own strange way.

Because historians refuse to give imagination and invention free rein, they may perceive that what are called documentaries are closer to their stylistic preconceptions of how history should be portrayed on film. Even the term itself is reassuring and almost tranquilizing. "Documentary" sounds very much like the documents and manuscripts we usually study. The documentary style flatters historians while it relies on their authority as arbiters of the past; historians regularly appear as "talking heads" in this sort of movie. Constructed out of "actuality footage" to distinguish them from re-creations, these films have the advantage of showing students actual people, places, and sounds from the past.[26]

Documentary films, though, are also mediated by our imaginations and can suffer from falsification through juxtaposition and problems of connecting images with texts.[27] Most of these difficulties are inherent even in the use of simple photographs. Were the photos spontaneous or posed? For most of the nineteenth century, subjects had to remain motionless for long periods. Even the minimum time under exceptional circumstances, about five seconds, was probably too long for spontaneous or candid photography. As late as the 1870s, studio portraiture required the subject to remain motionless from fifteen seconds to more than a minute.[28] Long exposure times made it nearly impossible not only to capture action but also even to record unaffected poses on film. Thus, Matthew Brady's Civil War battlefield views show the ideal photographic subjects of his time, corpses. Dead bodies did not move and blur the image. Even when faster film speeds made stop-action photography possible, anticipation, preparation, and even rehearsal were essential to successful images. The famous, dramatic photograph of Pancho Villa galloping on horseback at the head of his cavalry during the Mexican Revolution of 1910 could only have been carefully staged after the filmmaker was sent out ahead to a suitable location and given ample time to prepare.[29] Robert M. Levine has also pointed out that, as much as early photographers thought of themselves as scientists rather than artists, they "were first and foremost businessmen and could not afford to take [unflattering or bluntly realistic] pictures which could not be sold."[30]

Photographs do not speak for themselves; they must be spoken for.[31] Connecting text to image is not a self-evident process. Portraits of individuals used in traditional documentary films seldom show how they looked when the words, actions, or ideas attributed to them in the narration occurred. Even a photograph of someone seated at a desk, pen in hand, apparently in the act of writing, may bear no connection to the words read in the voice-over narration. We are inclined simply to accept the filmmaker's juxtaposition as accurate. Even when that narration contains the actual words, another fiction is created. The letters written by real Civil War soldiers to loved ones and family were some of the most emotionally evocative moments in Ken Burns's *The Civil War*. In listening to them, we imagine a voice from the past, but we are listening to the intonations and enunciations of professional actors hired to read lines.

The boundary between dramatic re-creation and documentary can be clouded. In some of the best historical feature films, dialogue comes from the same sort of documentary sources. In María Luisa Bemberg's *Camila*, a cinematic melodrama set in midnineteenth-century Argentina, the actor playing the family patriarch reads chilling words actually written by Camila's father nearly a century and a half ago.[32] The blurred boundary between documentary and feature or fictional film can also be a matter of interpretation as filmmakers attempt to tell the truth in spite of political interference. Héctor Babenco began to make a documentary about Brazil's juvenile detention system. When official obstruction made that project impossible, he told the story through fiction, writing and directing *Pixote*, a haunting and realistic vision of a child's life on the streets of São Paulo and Rio de Janeiro. As Levine documents in Chapter Twelve of this volume, the film was not only a powerful condemnation of Brazil's social crisis but also an international financial and critical success and a foretelling of the tragic death of the film's own star, Fernando Ramos da Silva.

Certainly those who know Latin American and postmodern culture are familiar with the juxtaposition of what Julianne Burton has called "art and actuality, fabrication and found objects, the fictional and the factual."[33] Tomás Gutiérrez Alea's *Memories of Underdevelopment* (1968) mixed historical fiction with documentary footage in a complex and contradictory visual structure.[34] Burton herself has pointed out that, even earlier in the century, after the Mexican Revolution of 1910, "feature filmmakers, motivated by economy rather than by any will to authenticity, inserted actual documentary battle footage from the great unassembled 'archive' of the revolution into their fictional films."[35]

Privileging the empirical, however, is what historians have to do. One of the historian's fundamental propositions is that "the past does exist and that, contrary to some notion that the past is only in our minds, it has an existence independent of our knowledge of it."[36] What would we be if we stopped trying to distinguish the factual from the purely imaginative? I do not know, but surely we would cease to be historians.

Nevertheless, the idea that "fact" and "fiction" are clearly distinguishable categories creates another dichotomy redolent of nineteenth-century polarities, one that smells a bit stale to our postmodern noses. If it seems that the boundaries are not as clear as they once were, perhaps they were never all that distinct to begin with.[37] E. Bradford Burns reminds us of the words of Louis Gottschalk, first published in 1950:

> It might be well to point out again that what is meant by calling a particular credible is not that it is actually what happened, but that it is as close to what actually happened as we can learn from a critical examination of the best available sources. This means verisimilar at a high level. It connotes something more than merely not being preposterous in itself or even than plausible

and yet is short of meaning accurately descriptive of past actuality. In other words, the historian establishes verisimilitude rather
than objective truth.[38]

The subtitle to this chapter also partakes of this nineteenth-
century rhetorical technique of polarizing. Just as fact and imagination are not always clearly separable, the advantages and
disadvantages of using film to study history are not necessarily distinguishable either. Films have an emotional impact and a popular
appeal that is usually missing from professional scholarship. Is this
a disadvantage and reason to exclude them from classrooms and
professional discussion, or an opportunity to reduce the marginaliza-
tion that has accompanied the professionalization of historical research? The possibilities and the perils are not discrete items; they
are valuations attributed to the same conditions. It is not a case of
either/or, but of both and more at once. Neither book writing nor
filmmaking provides a perfect window on the past. Neither is "true"
and complete in itself. Both are "based on a true story," and their
efforts to make the past presentable, for all their apparent differences, are rather similar. People are interested in the past, and historians, plodding empiricists though we may be, have something
important to say to a postmodern culture.

Suggested Readings

Burns, E. Bradford. *Latin American Cinema: Film and History*. Los Angeles: UCLA Latin American Center, University of California, 1975. A
classic work by one of the first Latin Americanists to use films in teaching history.
Levine, Robert M. *Images of History: Nineteenth- and Early Twentieth-
Century Latin American Photographs as Documents*. Durham, NC: Duke
University Press, 1989. Not only a guide to the current literature on
photography in Latin America but an essential discussion of images as
documents.
Novick, Peter. *That Noble Dream: The "Objectivity" Question and the
American Historical Profession*. Cambridge, England: Cambridge University Press, 1988. A fascinating look at the professionalization of history and the debate on the ideal of "what really happened."
O'Connor, John E., ed. *Image as Artifact: The Historical Analysis of Film
and Television*. Malabar, FL: R. E. Krieger, 1990. Essays analyzing film
and television as a series of "frameworks" including: representations
of history; evidence of facts, events, and culture; and the development
of the motion picture industry.

Rosenstone, Robert A. *Visions of the Past: The Challenge of Film to Our Idea of History*. Cambridge, MA: Harvard University Press, 1995. Promotes the idea of film as a distinct way of expressing ideas about the past but discusses films that are mostly obscure.

Rosenstone, Robert A., ed. *Revisioning History: Film and the Construction of a New Past*. Princeton: Princeton University Press, 1995. A collection of essays that includes John Mraz on *Memories of Underdevelopment* (1968) and Rosenstone on *Walker* (1987).

Sklar, Robert, and Charles Musser, eds. *Resisting Images: Essays on Cinema and History*. Philadelphia: Temple University Press, 1990. All of the contributors to this volume are associated with film studies or communications rather than traditional history departments.

CHAPTER TWO

Columbus Takes On the Forces of Darkness,
or Film and Historical Myth in *1492: The Conquest of Paradise*

SONYA LIPSETT-RIVERA
SERGIO RIVERA AYALA*

1492: The Conquest of Paradise (1992); produced by Ridley Scott and Alain Goldman; directed by Ridley Scott; written by Roselyne Bosch; color; 149 minutes. Touchstone Pictures. The familiar story of the stalwart navigator Christopher Columbus (Gérard Depardieu), who overcomes obstacles to find his way across the Atlantic Ocean to the New World.

For most people growing up in the Americas, Columbus is not just a historical personage. He is also a cultural icon who carries many burdens. He is alternately a hero for his voyages of exploration, the founder of a new race by inaugurating colonialism, and the person who initiated the devastation of native civilizations. Columbus Day in the United States and Día de la Raza in many Latin American countries serve as reminders of these contradictory depictions. The recent quincentennial of Columbus's landing in the Caribbean provoked a flurry of cultural, scholarly, and artistic projects. Riding this wave of commemoration, Ridley Scott directed *1492: The Conquest of Paradise.*

*The authors would like to thank David Dean, Ann Blum, and Donald F. Stevens for their comments.

Any film on this subject, like any historical work, has to negotiate many preconceptions about Columbus, national myths as well
as legends. Because documentary information on Columbus is not
abundant, historians often make leaps of interpretation that reflect
contemporary sensibilities, and thus any film on this same topic
must make similar choices. Scott's film begins in Spain where Columbus (played by Gérard Depardieu) seeks the support of Queen
Isabela. He finally gains her approval for his first voyage, and the
film portrays two of his four trips, although clearly incidents from
the later (unrepresented) voyages are condensed into those that form
part of the film. The chronology gets increasingly fuzzy as the film
progresses. The difficulty of covering such a long and eventful period means that strict historical veracity would be daunting for the
filmmakers, and errors are easy to pinpoint. Yet, on the surface,
Scott's account does not seem so far-fetched. Despite many distortions of convenience, it remains close enough to a mainstream understanding of the "facts," and thus this illusion gives the film an
air of historical authenticity that is deceptive. These misrepresen-
tations are easy to spot for those familiar with the literature,[1] but
the portrayal of Columbus through the choice of scenes and cinematographic language is of greater concern since these elements
are most important in shaping our understanding of him. Therefore, instead of dwelling on the details of the film, we will examine
its interpretation of Columbus as a historical figure.

Although the number of works on Columbus is extensive, the
store of documentary information on him has not increased since
the nineteenth century, so recent works provide innovative interpretations rather than new data. The primary sources for any study
of Columbus the man remain the biography written by his illegitimate son, Fernando Colón, and his logbook, transcribed by
Bartolomé de las Casas, a Dominican missionary and a defender of
native rights. Las Casas reproduced the journal from the first voyage with some annotations and deletions, and the account written
by Columbus's son is not available in the original but rather in an
Italian translation. These sources, as well as Columbus's writings,
the accounts of contemporaries such as Peter Martyr, Dr. Chanca,
Michele de Cuneo, and Gonzalo Fernández de Oviedo, as well as
the narratives of people involved in some lawsuits regarding the
voyage and thus less enamored of the Admiral, remain less than
satisfactory but essential to any historical study.[2]

Scott inscribes his vision of Columbus within the familiar nineteenth-century ideological construction of Columbus as hero. In this sense, he is a product of American ideology. The mainstream portrait has been of a visionary, the man who did not believe in the flat world, the man who broke the shackles of superstition and chicanery. Although some historians have unabashedly admired Columbus,[3] this depiction has been debunked many times over in the scholarly and less scholarly literature.[4] In the past few decades, this denunciation of the traditional image has gone to extremes, portraying Columbus as an evil genius responsible for all the acts of genocide, environmental destruction, and cultural devastation that followed in his wake.[5]

These versions are also inscribed in a larger historical debate in Latin American history; in essence, they are part of the tug-of-war between white-legend and black-legend interpretations of the conquest of the Americas. In the white legend, the excesses of Spanish colonialism are redeemed by the boon of Christianity and the consequent saving of souls. In a more recent and secular rendering of this school of thought, the redemption is further accentuated by the benefits of democracy and capitalism that are said to be the eventual results of this conquest.[6] Black-legend historians dwell on the plight of the native civilizations of the Americas and their persecution by the Spanish or other colonial powers. They document the atrocities committed by Europeans, the devastating effects of diseases imported by the colonists, the enforced conversion to Christianity, and other such outrages of colonialism. Any work on Columbus must be inscribed in one or another of these schools of thought in order to negotiate the differences between the mainstream and the academic view.

Not simply the subject of scholarly debates, Columbus is also one of the heroes who became a symbol of nation in nineteenth-century America. It is this popular understanding of the man, derived from textbooks and pictorial representations, that forms the mainstream thinking on Columbus and probably is closer to the film's representation of the historical character.[7] The film portrays a Columbus familiar to Americans and therefore is primarily directed to a U.S. audience. Its depiction uses a set of events that are derived from the American mythology of Columbus as hero. The film also shares certain preconceptions about Columbus with the American public. After the Revolution, he was embraced as a symbol of nation—first as a female icon, Columbia, and then increasingly as a masculine, romantic hero familiar to all through Washington Irving's dramatic, if inaccurate, rendition of his life.[8] Columbus became not only an American icon through glowing accounts in textbooks, but he also became all things to all people. To nineteenth-century Progressives fighting the control of religion in society, he represented the man of science who defied the obscurantism of the Church, while to the Knights of Columbus he was a saint, and they campaigned for his canonization.[9] The popular understanding of Columbus is based on several myths, and these interpretations are extremely hard to dismiss.

The heroic version is obvious in *1492: The Conquest of Paradise* even though the film does not subscribe to many of the erroneous anecdotes associated with the Columbus story.[10] Essentially, the man portrayed by Depardieu reflects many nineteenth-century impressions that have been formulated into the mainstream notion of the historical figure. Columbus, within this plot structure, is the ultimate Renaissance man who rejects a backward Spain of Inquisition, scholasticism, and superstition. He is a man of vision, an intellectual, a humanitarian, and an individualist. This rendering was created by nineteenth-century Americans as a role model. Yet, Scott's Columbus does have a few more complexities: he is not an elitist; rather, he is a man of the people, a democrat who does not mind helping out the common workers or associating with "inferior" natives, and he even talks to the queen of Spain in a totally ordinary manner. This added dimension reflects modern sensibilities and the corollary to the white-legend interpretation of Latin American history as conquest redeemed by democracy.

This portrait of Columbus is conveyed in a number of ways. The film opens with a statement that sets the tone. Across the screen, we read, "500 years ago Spain was a nation gripped by fear and superstition ruled by the Crown and a ruthless Inquisition that persecuted men for daring to dream. One man challenged this power. Driven by his sense of destiny, he crossed the sea of darkness in search for honor, gold and the greater glory of God." Already, the film contrasts Columbus the dreamer and the Spain of the Inquisition. This opposition is further reinforced by the use of the phrase "the sea of darkness," which implies that Columbus not only crossed the Atlantic but also broke through the barrier of obscurantism.[11] Throughout the film, we are presented with such oppositions. Dark and light compete not only in the chiaroscuro cinematography, which uses a high level of contrast in most scenes, but also in content. Columbus is constantly given opposites who embody all the defects that he must fight. In this way, while he is a more completely formed character with many attributes and qualities, most of those around him are devoid of any features other than those that pit them against him.

A tender scene takes place in which Columbus, seated by the ocean, tells his son to watch a ship disappearing across the horizon. He uses this exercise to explain to Fernando that the Earth is round, pointing to an orange in his hand and saying, "It is round like this." This scene feeds into the common understanding that most of Columbus's contemporaries believed that the world was flat. The film does not state that fifteenth-century Europeans believed this and anachronistically uses a globe in one scene.[12] Yet, by opening with such an explanation, the film evokes this widespread belief and brings the audience into a cozy relationship with Columbus. Along with Fernando, the viewer will also be guided into the New World within this father-son relationship. In fact, few, if any, believed that the Earth was anything but round, but this myth has been propagated since the nineteenth century largely in response to the struggle between Progressives and traditionalists, evolutionists versus creationists, and religious versus secularizing tendencies. The error that people of past ages believed in a flat Earth is one of the hardest myths to demolish and is found in all sorts of works, both academic and otherwise.[13] Yet this scene serves another purpose, and that is to reinforce the old nineteenth-century notion of Columbus as a man of science and a visionary, the only European who rejected the superstitious fears of those around him in favor of scientific fact. The reality is much more banal; Columbus's understanding of the world was neither extraordinary for his time nor particularly advanced.[14] He was a man of his time rather than ahead of it.

The opposition between Columbus and the backwardness of Spain is portrayed in several scenes. When his son breaks away from him in the city streets to follow the crowds and ends up watching an execution, presumably an auto-da-fé (act of faith) of the Inquisition, Columbus's revulsion at the display is clear to us. The crowd seems impressed with the grandeur of the scene, but he turns away in disgust. The execution scene is designed to make us think of the persecution of witches; the wild grey hair of one of the two female victims is blown about in the wind, and she is old and wizened. Although anxiety over witches and sorcery was not absent from Spain, widespread execution of accused witches was more common in northern Europe. Indeed, for all its faults, the Inquisition at least adhered to regular procedures and recognized stringent standards of proof. It was unlikely to put someone to death on mere accusation, nor did it tolerate the mobs that operated in other countries.[15] Nonetheless, this scene serves as an easily grasped shorthand for the barbarism of Spain, the persecution of innocents, and Columbus's principled rejection of such acts.

Columbus is also shown to be a man of learning in a couple of other scenes. For instance, when he appears before a committee of scholars to argue the feasibility of his plan to sail west to Asia, they ridicule his idea. Because the viewer knows that he was successful, the joke is on those laughing in this scene, and the viewer sympathizes with the beleaguered Columbus who must face such ignorance.[16] Actually, the scholars were correct in their dismissal of these plans, because his strategy was based upon a notion that the distance between Europe and Asia was quite short. His calculations of the circumference of the Earth were off by 32 percent.[17]

Columbus consults cosmographer Antonio de Marchena as a shaft of light enters the window. *Courtesy Museum of Modern Art*

This scene, however, is founded upon several historical inventions that have been repeated over the years. The Catholic monarchs did seek advice on the practicability of Columbus's plan but not from scholars at the University of Salamanca. Rather, they met privately with a committee of their own choosing. This image of Columbus facing a barrage of intellectuals at Salamanca comes from Irving's imagination.[18] He invented this scene for dramatic purposes, and it has remained part of a mainstream understanding of Columbus that pits him against the forces of obscurantism. The film emphasizes this interpretation by its treatment of the Spanish clerics and intellectuals. In particular, the leading cleric demonstrates his intolerance (and thus Spain's intolerance) for free thought by stating that he has "always found such independent men dangerous" and calls the navigator a heretic. This aspect is also alluded to in the scene in which Columbus practices his presentation with the monk Marchena. When he mentions the name of a Jewish scholar, Marchena warns him against the use of such experts because "men have been burned for less." When Columbus meets the mariner Pinzón, at first he does not talk because he has to remain silent as a penance. The film again tells the viewer that men of vision are silenced by religion. The opposition—already hinted at—between religion and superstition and between science and reason is clearly established as is Columbus's rejection of both religion and superstition.

The viewer is reminded of the Columbus with whom we are familiar, and Scott uses the play of light to accentuate this interpretation. At the beginning of the film the scenes in Spain are mostly in darkness. Many settings are interiors, but the viewer sees Columbus going chiefly from darkness to darkness with the light surrounding him like an aura. Even the burning of heretics is inaccurately set at night and in the city rather than on its outskirts.[19] The only scenes of light are those that feature Columbus with his son or beginning to prepare for his voyage. The contrast between Columbus, the man of light, and Spanish society, which is in darkness and seething with corruption and superstition, is clearly drawn. The use of light is replicated in other parts of the film and in a sense reinforces the message of Columbus's struggle to redeem the colonial enterprise in the face of the immorality of many of his compatriots.

On Columbus's first voyage, one of the most cited incidents is his quelling of an onboard mutiny. By the force of his personality, he is able to persuade the sailors to continue west despite their fears. There is considerable historical debate about whether this incident actually happened and who indeed rallied the crew. In a lengthy lawsuit between various parties involved in the first voyage, the recollections of sailors and captains who were present for this mutiny diverge starkly. Some blamed Columbus and credited Pinzón with the courage to continue. Others maintained that it never happened. Still others supported the traditional account.[20] But in this film the scene is important because it reinforces the image of Columbus as a man of reason battling the forces of darkness.

The viewer is given to understand that the sailors are afraid because of their superstitious natures and lack of scientific rationality. One sailor states that he does not like the smell of the sea in these parts and declares the enterprise cursed by God. Pinzón comes aboard and attempts to persuade Columbus to turn back and accuses him of lying about the distance already traveled. An earlier scene that had showed the measurement of the speed of the ships by throwing logs into the sea already hinted at this deception, as did Columbus's preboarding confession that he lied about the distance between Spain and Asia. These depictions feed into another common accusation that Columbus falsified the distance to pacify his nervous crews. William Phillips, Jr., and Carla Rahn Phillips believe that the alternate numbers recorded in his logbook, which are the source of this accusation, are simply the result of two different units of measurement that were misunderstood by Las Casas when he transcribed the account. Other historians believe that Columbus did indeed lie but do not credit him with fooling experienced mariners.[21]

So, was Columbus barely in control of an unruly mob of fearful sailors as the film depicts? Were they really ignorant of navigational techniques as Scott's interpretation suggests? Whether Columbus did rally his crew or not, as historians suspect, the reasons for a reluctance to continue probably had nothing to do with superstition. Rather, the Phillipses argue that the sailors worried quite rightly about the journey home and whether their supplies would be sufficient while they battled contrary winds and currents to return to Spain.[22] Whichever account of the famous mutiny is true almost does not matter because this story has become a component in the construction of Columbus as hero and man of science. Its reproduction in the film only inscribes this ideological interpretation within that tradition.

When the Spaniards land on an island that Columbus names San Salvador but that its inhabitants call Guanahaní, they encounter the Arawak Indians for the first time. Scott's vision of this moment includes a lot of mist. This clouding of the scene makes the island seem mysterious and dangerous but also dark. The ship advances toward the island through a kind of cloud, and then suddenly Columbus shouts "There!" The mist clears, and a verdant, lush land awaits. Once on shore, after a few formalities, such as the reluctant, slow-motion hero taking possession of this island, the Spaniards advance into the forest. It is dark, mysterious, misty, a primeval forest marked by shafts of light that pierce the dense foliage. Once again, the use of light and dark reinforce the message about Columbus as the carrier of light and wisdom. The natives are suddenly spotted in the mist; they seem sullen and they are armed. One Spaniard calls out "Musket!" but Columbus immediately stops the action. He moves forward, and the natives begin to touch Juanito's cleft palate, his beard, and finally they laugh and welcome the newcomers. The scene is dramatic and suspenseful, but it also continues the thread of construction of Columbus the hero.

Columbus and his men make their first landing on a mist-shrouded island. *Courtesy Museum of Modern Art*

How does this representation differ from the historical record? The entry in the Admiral's journal tells a very different story. The Arawak came onto the beach; they did not lurk in the woods. They were not at all threatening, they were carrying no weapons of any kind, and Columbus stresses their docility. He does not see them at all as enemies; in fact, his description emphasizes their status as exploitable entities. He mentions that the men wore their hair long, which to a sixteenth-century Spaniard represented feminization and therefore subservience.[23] They were naked. When they were shown steel swords, they cut themselves on the blades. Columbus portrays them as a blank slate; they have no language, no religion, and they repeat everything that is said to them.[24] In fact, he immediately suggests that they would make good slaves. The historical record is clear but does not conform to the ideal presented by Scott. Earlier interpretations of Columbus might not have shied away from this side of his character,[25] but at the end of the twentieth century, for Columbus to maintain his status of hero, he undoubtedly had to become the protector of natives in addition to his many other heroic qualities.

After landfall at San Salvador-Guanahaní and meeting with the Arawak, Columbus led his ships through some explorations of various islands in the Caribbean. He hoped to locate either Cipangu (Japan) or the Great Khan of China. Failing that, he wanted to justify the expedition in financial terms and so secure access to valuable trading goods such as spices or other plants but most particularly gold. This aspect of Columbus's exploration is almost absent from the film as is any sense of the exploration of different islands and the meeting with several native peoples. In fact, although Scott goes to some pains to try to portray the natives in a sympathetic light, to him, they are undifferentiated. They are not Arawak, Carib, or Siboney but rather the generic native.[26] The individual attributes of their society are missing; their social structure, urban life, art, and agriculture are all ignored. The viewer sees them as simple creatures who laugh a lot. It seems almost incomprehensible that they are able to present Columbus with such a fine piece of craftsmanship as the gold mask that he accepts before his return to Spain. Apart from a headdress and an air of authority, there is no distinction among the on-screen natives to indicate rank or status. The historian can only guess that the man with the headdress is Guacanagri, the cacique who assisted Columbus continually and remained his loyal ally, but the film audience is not entrusted with this information.

In general, the natives have no identity other than that of objects of Spanish cruelty or pity. The plot places them in a position of secondary importance. For a film about the conquest of the Caribbean, it is peculiar that the fighting seems to happen mostly among the Spaniards. The violence directed at the Arawak appears as a minor incident in the larger theme of the Spaniards fighting other

Spaniards for power. The only time that Columbus is involved in a battle with the natives, they are suddenly wearing masks and have become frenzied beings who make strange, animalistic screechings. These dehumanized beings are contrasted with Columbus's family in Spain in a series of flashbacks before a native assailant is run through with a sword. There are no flashbacks to this man's family.

In the film, Columbus leaves some men on Hispaniola (the present-day island of Haiti and the Dominican Republic) at the end of the first voyage, but there is an interesting omission here. The viewer is not told that the *Santa María* ran aground and sank. Scott not only deletes this episode from his version, but he even shows three ships departing for the return voyage to Spain. Perhaps the whole question of Columbus's maritime competence is too contrary to the film's heroic portrayal.

After a triumphal visit to Spain where he is given the title "Admiral" by Ferdinand and Isabela, Columbus returns to Hispaniola to find the ruins of the fort he had built at the end of his first trip because of the destruction of the *Santa María*. The film's portrayal of the second voyage compresses elements of the other three that Columbus undertook for the Spanish monarchs. This time, the intention clearly was to set up a colony and to begin the economic exploitation of Hispaniola. In the film, this second arrival contrasts with the first landing. Soldiers line up on the beach, a cannon is fired several times, and one Spaniard whirls about on his horse in a very menacing manner. The Spanish sailors whom Columbus had left on Hispaniola to await his return were, in fact, killed. According to historical records, the cacique Guacanagri sent people to the ship who slowly broke the news of the deaths to the sailors.[27]

Columbus resisted the easy solution of killing natives in revenge for his men's lives, but not for long. Immediately, he has to stave off the hostility of his fellow colonists, in particular a sinister character called Moxica. In introducing this character, the film departs from the historical record, and it is not clear whom this character is meant to represent. Columbus mentions a certain Adrián, whom Consuelo Varela identifies as Adrián de Múgica, in a letter addressed to Doña Juana de la Torre in 1500. This person was a member of the group of Spaniards who revolted against Columbus under the leadership of Roldán, but his role was minuscule, and he is only mentioned in passing, if at all, in most historical studies.[28] The film's Moxica, always dressed in black (in a costume that might have been designed by Michael Jackson's tailor), oozes evil and seems to have been created as the archetype of Spanish malevolence. He provides the contrast with Columbus's humanitarian impulses. Moxica becomes the embodiment and the scapegoat for all of the iniquities of Spanish colonialism in the Caribbean so that Columbus will not be held responsible. He resolves the problem that Scott's interpretation would have run into because the portrayal of Columbus as hero could not be reconciled with the destruction of the native civilization and the cruelties that followed.

From the arrival at the destroyed fort at La Navidad, the action moves to the founding of a city at Isabela and the beginning of the collection of gold. Columbus is shown trying to create a new civilization by the construction of a city and a church. Yet the existing civilization, the Arawak cities, and their religion do not appear in the film. The viewer is given the erroneous impression that building a city is totally new in the Americas and that no urban centers existed before the arrival of the Spaniards. In the film, Columbus seems unconcerned with the mining operations that were also begun at this time, employing the forced labor of natives. Naturally, Moxica is in charge of this aspect of colonization. Thus, while Columbus builds, Moxica destroys—again, the light versus the forces of darkness. In essence, the message is that Columbus is not responsible for the abuses of colonialism, that he wanted to build a new society in the Americas but was thwarted by Moxica.

In one of the scenes most emblematic of this construction, Columbus sees a cordon of native slaves being taken away. His downcast expression presages the destruction by hurricane of the city that he built. In fact, Columbus envisaged the enslavement of natives as one of the financial underpinnings of the colonial endeavor from the start.[29] The film portrays Utepa, the interpreter, as an individual who latched onto the Spaniards and voluntarily learned their language. Actually, Columbus and his men regularly took natives prisoner to force them into the role of interpreter; this convenient omission as well as the increasing commodification of natives is entirely secondary, if not ignored, in the film. It is true that Columbus was not involved in the day-to-day running of the gold-mining operations set up on Hispaniola, but this was not because of any moral qualms. Rather, he was exploring the surrounding area on the quest for Asia. He delegated authority to his brother. Both Columbus and his brother, however, were directly responsible for the colony and the treatment of natives.

In the film, Columbus is shown as the urban and colonial planner who is thwarted in his constructive aims by the lazy, brutish Spaniards. In fact, his involvement in the planning for the colony was disastrous. He brought far too many people without any skills and then tried to found a city, Isabela, in a totally inappropriate place. The results of such decisions meant that the Spaniards were dependent on the goodwill of the Arawak to feed them between arrivals of supply ships from home. When the Arawak tired of this role and Spaniards such as Alonso de Hojeda began to attack them systematically, they withdrew their support and tried to eject the Spaniards. In the film, the first hostilities between natives and Spaniards are presented as the result of a disagreement over the provision of gold.[30] According to available historical accounts, the first incident was caused by Hojeda, who decided to punish some Arawak for stealing clothes. He cut off the ears of one of the cacique Pontón's men and sent the cacique, his brother, and his nephew as prisoners to Isabela. Instead of horror at this conduct, Columbus had first planned to execute these men by beheading them, but another cacique interceded and he relented.[31]

The film, however, portrays Columbus as the friend and protector of the natives. In the long sequence that pits Moxica against Columbus, it is clear that the motivation for the Admiral's initial decision to imprison Moxica, and later their duel, is concern for the native population. In the culmination of their fight, fearful natives, half hidden in the bushes, point out to Columbus the direction taken by Moxica. The film's natives understand intuitively that the Admiral is on their side. They are also portrayed as passive and incapable of facing up to Moxica, their persecutor, so they must depend on Columbus to defeat the forces of darkness. This passage as well as the fight in the monastery that comes earlier in the film make no pretensions to historical accuracy and, in fact, seem to satsify some Hollywood minimum of fight or action scenes per film. Columbus seems like some sort of Renaissance Rambo.

Despite the film's pretensions, Columbus was never the protector of natives. After the first period of good relations, when Spaniards began to lop off native body parts, Columbus joined in a campaign to capture and execute the Arawak caciques. After the initial establishment of the colony, he did not censure those who abused the hospitality of the Arawak, nor did he try to alter the type of master-slave relationship that was emerging. By 1494, only two years after the first Spanish landfall, the Arawak launched their first uprising; they did not depend on Columbus to protect them. In fact, even before this turn of events, he had begun to think in terms of good Indians and bad Indians: those who were peaceful were good, and those who resisted, the Caribs or "cannibals," were bad. This logic justified the enslavement of the native population.

The animosity between Columbus and Moxica also serves an important role in the film. It pits Columbus the democrat against Moxica the aristocrat. This construction is another element of the nineteenth-century idealization of Columbus and part of the white legend of Latin American history's new corollary: conquest redeemed by democracy. Even before the introduction of the character Moxica, this thread of the movie was developed in the fencing scene and the condescending manner of the bureaucrats and nobles toward Columbus. Then, once in the Caribbean, Columbus gets involved in building, orchestrating the lifting of a magnificent bell into the church tower to a choral accompaniment. At one point, he directs the work as a maestro would an orchestra. In contrast, Moxica prances around on his horse and lazes about with his pal, leering at seminude native women.[32] These opposing attitudes are brought into high contrast when Columbus tells Moxica that his horse is needed for the raising of the bell. Moxica answers with a sneer that his horse does no work. This scene as well as the persecutions that the Admiral is portrayed to suffer in the last gasps of the film complete this image of the victimized Columbus whose plebeian origins were never forgiven by the haughty Spaniards. The image of Columbus as martyr, deprived and unfairly ignored, is part of the mainstream American understanding of these events. But the film's concentration on this strand of the story means that the deprivation and despoliation of the Arawak, Siboney, and Carib are lost in the fray.

Despite its many pretensions and its lush cinematography, Scott's *1492: The Conquest of Paradise* does not reach any cinematic milestones. Like earlier movies on this subject, the film reflects some contemporary concerns (such as the plight of native peoples), but its portrayal of the native peoples of the Caribbean is halfhearted and superficial. In one of the final scenes in the Caribbean, Utepa "goes native" once more, stating to the uncomprehending Columbus, "You never learned my language." This criticism is the only reproach that the film offers of the colonial enterprise, and it falls far short. Essentially, the film stays within the safe boundaries of the traditional Hollywood quest of good versus evil and even uses the symbolism of light against darkness and the oppositional thrust of Columbus against a series of bogeymen to advance the story. The interpretation remains a mainstream version familiar to most American audiences from the textbooks they read in school, and it uses stereotypical characters to trigger this understanding of the Columbus story. The forces of darkness finally do conquer Columbus in this film, but the historical record cannot be altered so easily. For thousands of native peoples, Columbus, rather than the "carrier of light," was one of the harbingers of darkness.

Suggested Readings

Bushman, Claudia. *America Discovers Columbus: How an Italian Explorer Became an American Hero*. Hanover, NH: University Press of New England, 1992. A study of the process by which Columbus became an important and mythical figure in the United States.

Columbus, Christopher. *Textos y documentos completos: Relaciones de viajes, cartas y memoriales*. Prologue and notes by Consuelo Varela, ed. Madrid: Alianza, 1982. A transcription of the available documentation written by Columbus with extensive annotation.

———. *The Voyages of Christopher Columbus, Being the Journals of His First and Third, and the Letters Concerning His First and Last Voyages, to Which Is Added the Account of His Second Voyage*. Trans. Cecil Jane. London: Argonaut Press, 1930. An English translation of the logs of Columbus's first voyages. The text was taken from the version transcribed by Fray Bartolomé de las Casas.

Colon, Fernando. *The Life of the Admiral Christopher Columbus by His Son Ferdinand*. Translated, annotated, and with a new introduction by Benjamin Keen. 2d ed. New Brunswick, NJ: Rutgers University Press, 1992. The translation of the biography written by Columbus's younger son. Although an important source, it is not an eyewitness account.

Henige, David P. *In Search of Columbus: The Sources for the First Voyage*. Tucson: University of Arizona Press, 1991. An exploration of Columbus's first voyage based upon an intensive examination of the sources.

Morison, Samuel Eliot. *Admiral of the Ocean Sea: A Life of Christopher Columbus*. Boston: Little, Brown, 1942. A classic work. Morison is often criticized for an overly adulatory portrait of Columbus, but his approach from the point of view of sailing is useful.

Phillips, William D., Jr., and Carla Rahn Phillips. *The Worlds of Christopher Columbus*. New York: Cambridge University Press, 1992. A good general overview of the Columbus literature as well as the context in which the Admiral operated.

Russell, Jeffrey Burton. *Inventing the Flat Earth: Columbus and Modern Historians*. New York: Praeger, 1991. Russell traces the origins of the prevailing myth that medieval Europeans believed that the Earth was flat. He places the creation of this idea within the context of the mythification of Columbus and U.S. political currents.

Sale, Kirkpatrick. *The Conquest of Paradise: Christopher Columbus and the Columbian Legacy.* New York: Alfred A. Knopf, 1990. A critical portrait of Columbus, which provides a counterpoint to the work of Morison.

Sauer, Carl Ortwin. *The Early Spanish Main.* Berkeley: University of California Press, 1966. A classic work of historical geography. Sauer painstakingly recreates the voyages of Columbus as well as the peoples, places, and environmental settings that were part of the saga.

CHAPTER THREE

Whose Conquest Is This, Anyway?

Aguirre, the Wrath of God

THOMAS H. HOLLO

Aguirre, der Zorn Gottes *(1972), or* Aguirre, the Wrath o: God; *produced by Werner Herzog; directed by Werne; Herzog; written by Werner Herzog; color; 90 minutes Werner Herzog Filmproduktion/New Yorker. Sixteenth century explorer Lope de Aguirre (Klaus Kinski) rebel: against Spanish authority, takes charge of an expeditior into the Amazon basin looking for gold, and leads it dowr the Amazon River.*

The Werner Herzog film *Aguirre, the Wrath of God* is based n mally and loosely on a true story, a history that, despite existence of several independent accounts left by participants the preservation of extended statements by Aguirre himself, ; forever remain elusive. All versions left by eyewitnesses participants, as well as the interpretive positions developed ir twentieth-century renewal of interest in the Aguirre story, mar them heavily researched, have a vested interest in one or anc interpretation among the several possible. Furthermore, the Ag; story has become the subject of numerous fictionalized or lite accounts, some of which themselves are based to a consider extent on histories and chronicles but which add yet another v one deliberately creative even as it seeks to develop a view o: "true" Aguirre through such imaginative embellishment.

Herzog's film, on the other hand, is no docudrama attem; embellish the historical record in a way that remains true to wh known while filling in the blanks for dramatic interest and narrative continuity. The film is inspired more by the legends that have built up around the story of the Ursúa expedition and Aguirre's mutiny as well as the filmmaker's imaginative extension of general myths and stereotypes regarding the Spanish conquistadors, native peoples, and the luxuriant tropical environment of the Amazon region. Its basis in history aside, it is a tale of obsessive fixation on fortune and fame, jealousy and lust, honor betrayed and defended, and, ultimately, paranoid delusions. The film suggests that such an intense mix, stripped of the inhibitions and restrictions of civilized society, immersed in the power of nature, can lead to brutal and deadly strife, delirium, and destruction. As Herzog himself has said, "This film, I think, is not really a narrative of actual happenings or a portrait of actual people. At any level it is a film about what lies behind landscapes, faces, situations, and works."[1]

Such an approach, of course, is well within the prerogative of the filmmaker. But just as Herzog is free to do with the story whatever his creative urges dictate, it is also legitimate, even worthwhile, for historians and students of history to examine the film from their own point of view. Those who seek a historical version of these events can approvingly comment on many of the images Herzog evokes: the grimy coarseness of the ragtag band of would-be conquerors of yet another rich indigenous kingdom; bits and pieces of dented and rusty armor over the tattered remains of once-fine costumes rotting in the tropical humidity; stubble beards and stringy hair and wild looks; the dense, dripping foliage and precipitous paths of the eastern Andes; the mighty river, alternately roiling through rapids that toss huge rafts like toy boats or so calm and vast as to induce lethargy and despair. This is no Technicolor swashbuckler reconstructed on a sanitized Hollywood backlot, and the film is well worth seeing for these cinematographic aspects alone.

At the same time, however, any historical commentary must also point to several egregious examples of creative license that go far beyond allegorical symbolism and surreal images of caravels in treetops. First, the priest Carvajal, voice-over narrator and recurring foil for Aguirre's excesses in the Herzog film, was not a member of the expedition, did not write about it, and had nothing to do with it. He was, instead, the chronicler of the *first* Spanish expedition down the Amazon from Peru, that of Francisco de Orellana in 1542, nineteen years before the Ursúa-Aguirre trip. There are six eyewitness chronicles extant by participants in the latter expedition,[2] which together provide a rich if unavoidably biased narrative, but none of these authors figures as an important character in the film. Second, all the chroniclers agree that the murder of Ursúa by a gang of mutineers was a swift and definitive surprise attack. In the film version he is first only wounded, then lingers in convalescence, is given a pardon by his successor Guzmán, and later is surreptitiously taken into the forest and hanged by the plotters. Finally, the film suggests that the orgy of internecine strife and suicidal obstinacy, culminating in the fiendish delirium of Aguirre himself, leads to the complete destruction of the entire company, lost in the midst of the Amazon river-sea.

In the historical accounts, the mutiny and murder of Ursúa during the trip down the river and the subsequent assumption of command by Aguirre set the stage for considerable give-and-take between the rebels and forces loyal to the crown, over several months, once the survivors made it back to the island of Margarita and the adjacent mainland of what is today Venezuela. While they were in that region the mutineers terrorized several towns and vainly schemed to move overland and reconquer Peru for themselves, but many defected to the royalist side in return for clemency, further isolating the ringleaders. While in Venezuela, Aguirre wrote and dispatched several letters, the texts of which have been preserved, and killed his own daughter before being shot dead by one of his former comrades. None of this appears in Herzog's film, and consequently anyone aware that there was a historical Aguirre might wonder how any account of the trip survived, if all involved perished in the jungle.[3]

This essay provides a descriptive outline of the career of Lope de Aguirre, focusing on his role in the ill-fated Ursúa expedition into the Amazon (called the Marañon at the time, from which the veterans of the trip called themselves Marañones). It then takes up briefly the various explanations of those events that have been developed in recent times and concludes with a historical interpretation—that is, one that attempts to understand the events in their context and to take Lope de Aguirre on his own terms.

Chronology

Lope de Aguirre was born in the town of Oñate, in the Basque province of Guipúzcoa, probably in 1514 or a little earlier.[4] As a youth and later in Peru he worked at breaking horses—the only vocation other than soldier associated with him. He shipped out of Seville probably in 1534, appeared in Cartagena de Indias in 1536, and spent a career in the service of arms, always on the royalist side as far as has been determined, through the most turbulent period of the post-conquest civil wars in Peru between Pizarristas and Almagristas and subsequent efforts of royal agents Blasco Núñez Vela and Pedro de la Gasca to impose royal authority on the new colony. He fought in the 1555 battle of Chuquinga against the last of the great rebels, Francisco Hernández Girón, receiving a leg wound from which he limped ever after. In 1560, nearing age fifty, long in the royal service but enjoying few lasting personal rewards for his efforts, he responded to the call to join a new expedition in search of the land of El Dorado, the Gilded One, an Indian kingdom to the east of Peru where gold was said to be so plentiful that it was thrown into a sacred lake in an annual ritual.[5]

Lope de Aguirre seeks fortune and fame but finds envy and despair as he and his dwindling expedition drift down the Amazon River. *Courtesy Museum of Modern Art*

The appointed leader of the expedition was Pedro de Ursúa (or Orsúa), a Navarrese of the lesser nobility from near Pamplona, born about 1525, who had arrived in Cartagena in 1546 in the entourage of his uncle, the Visitador Armendáriz, and subsequently commanded several other expeditions of exploration and campaigns against Indian uprisings. His reputation for decisive and ruthless action grew when, after putting down a slave rebellion in Panama, he turned over several of the captured Africans to his mastiffs to kill and eat, as an example to others. This successful military and administrative career put Ursúa, at age thirty-five, in a position to take the governorship of the province of Omagua, yet to be consolidated in eastern Peru, and command of the expedition to search there for the land of gold. Although there is some suggestion that one purpose of such expeditions, or *entradas*, into unexplored territory was to rid the consolidating core areas of the Spanish colonies of surplus adventurers and fortune seekers as the era of conquest wound down, the successes of the previous few decades had shown the potential that came along with the risk. Joining such an expedition was well within the rational choices available to those men of arms who had yet to achieve the secure rewards that had accrued to a minority of their comrades through division of the spoils of conquest, encomienda grants, and administrative sinecures.

The company was assembled in the eastern foothills of the Andes, where a makeshift boatyard was set up along the Huallaga River to build the necessary vessels for the river trip east. The expedition took to the water in late September 1560 on numerous rafts and keelboat-like brigantines, with some three hundred soldiers (nearly twice the number that had accompanied Francisco Pizarro on his original *entrada* into the Peruvian interior in 1532) along with a large entourage of African slaves, Indian bearers, horses, munitions, equipment, and supplies. Among the party were several women, including Ursúa's creole mistress, Inés de Atienza, and Aguirre's mestiza daughter, Elvira, a girl in her early teens from a now-forgotten liaison with an Indian woman. River rapids and faulty construction with unseasoned timber soon took their toll on the heavily laden vessels, costing supplies and horses. As word passed along the shore that the immense expedition was approaching, the Indians faded into the jungle, leaving abandoned communities where the Spaniards had hoped to obtain information about what lay ahead, and empty storage bins where they might have resupplied. Delays on shore for rest, repairs, and the building of new boats were interspersed by periods of the river sweeping them inexorably eastward, farther from familiar bases and into the unknown heart of the continent. In the sweltering heat, as endless miles of jungle passed by, morale began to sag.

Any assessment of the subsequent internecine strife must accept the versions of one or another of the chroniclers, all of whom had very personal reasons for laying blame in certain quarters and exonerating others, but through the maze of charges and innuendo the basic outline of events emerges fairly clearly. None of the surviving accounts clarifies the specific cause of the original mutiny, but Ursúa's leadership seemed wanting, lax, or ruthless by turns, whether because he was ill, depressed, or spending too much time in the arms of his mistress. He delayed in appointing officers from among the ranks, but slowly the table of organization was filled. Among those placed in positions of authority were Fernando de Guzmán, a nobleman from Seville in his midtwenties, and the veteran Lope de Aguirre. But from the continued drift, real or imagined offenses, or jealousy over the fair Inés, grumbling discontent coalesced into a plot to eliminate Ursúa and replace him with Guzmán. Ursúa was killed on New Year's Day 1561, surprised in his tent by a gang of thirteen heavily armed conspirators, one of whom was Aguirre, who subsequently made a speech bluntly laying out the alternatives: either they return to the realm of royal authority and assume responsibility for their acts, or they "denaturalize" themselves from Spain and assume responsibility for themselves.

The group took the latter course by subsequently swearing allegiance to Guzmán as their "prince, lord, and rightful king" and cowing or killing the few men who dared to stand in their way. Jockeying for control and defensive intrigues persisted, with Aguirre emerging as the most outspoken and decisive of the several faction leaders. In May 1561, during another extended shore encampment, Aguirre ordered his men to kill Inés de Atienza, "King" Fernando de Guzmán, and several of their allies and followers. In the wake of this new round of murderous strife, Aguirre made an impassioned speech in which he gave himself the titles "Wrath of God, Prince of Liberty, and of the kingdom of Tierra Firme and the Provinces of Chile"—in other words, ruler of all of Spanish South America. In a high-risk game of kill-or-be-killed in which more than sixty people met a violent end at the hands of erstwhile comrades-in-arms or protectors, Aguirre and those loyal or submissive to him were the eventual survivors. Others not murdered outright were lost to disease and to the river or never returned from reconnaissance forays.

In two new brigantines constructed en route, the remnants of the expedition sailed on down the Amazon, proceeded up the coast—

abandoning their now superfluous Indian servants on shore along the way—and reached Margarita Island on July 20, 1561. There the small Spanish outpost was overwhelmed by the sudden appearance of some two hundred desperate and heavily armed outlaws ravaged by their experiences of the previous ten months. There followed an inconclusive near encounter with Friar Francisco de Montesinos, provincial of the Church in Santo Domingo and captain general of the subordinate zone on the Spanish Main, whose ship coincidentally arrived offshore. The party which Aguirre sent to confer with Montesinos defected to the royalist side, but the military force thus under the Dominican friar's command, though formidable, was still no match for Aguirre's remaining legion. Aguirre sent a letter to Montesinos laden with ironic references to the standoff, reminding the turncoats now siding with the friar that their signatures were on various documents implicating them in their actions while on the Amazon, and with subtle menace suggesting that "we now live in a state of grace, after being threatened with death by the river, the sea, and hunger, and thus any who challenge us are coming to fight the ghosts of dead men. . . . By fate we only know how to make ball and sharpen lances, which is the coin that circulates among us. If where you are there is need of such change, we will provide you with some of what we have."[6] Montesinos thought it better to return to Santo Domingo and spread the word of the threat of the Marañones than to post a direct challenge.

Aguirre's party, now numbering about 160 men, left Margarita at the end of August, coasted westward, and arrived on the mainland on September 12. They struggled inland as far as Valencia by early October, where Aguirre paused to dictate his famous letter to Philip II of Spain, of which more will be said. He gave the letter to a priest being held by the party, Father Alonso Contreras, forcing him on bended knee to swear to deliver the missive to the Audiencia in Santo Domingo, from where it was to be delivered to the king. Several versions, differing only in minor grammatical points that suggest that the letter was copied several times at the time of drafting, have come down to the present day, although no manuscript that can be called original is now extant.[7]

During this period increasing numbers of the Marañones defected, either fading into the hills to fend for themselves or going over to the loyalist forces who waited for an opportune moment to challenge the dwindling band of intruders. Recognizing their position as hopeless, Aguirre and his close supporters persisted in their

vain dream of forging overland to Peru. They burned Valencia behind them and pushed on to the town of Barquisimento, which the
inhabitants had abandoned in advance. Local governor Pablo
Collado made an offer of clemency to any of the rebels who would
surrender peacefully, and more responded to this call. The end came
on October 27, 1561, when Aguirre and his immediate party were
surrounded by loyalist troops, including several former Marañones.
Among his last acts was to call his daughter Elvira to his side and
stab her to death, telling her that this fate was preferable to living a
life of infamy as the child of a traitor and becoming the sexual
victim of whichever soldier claimed her after her father and protector was gone. He then faced the arquebus balls of the encircling
soldiers, two of which brought him down. His corpse was beheaded
and quartered, and parts were put on public display or given to
towns that his party had passed through as trophies of their involvement in the affair.

Interpretations

One Aguirre is the insolent and murderous traitor who had dared to
"denaturalize" himself and his followers from allegiance to Spain
and its king during a period when centralized royal authority was
bound on overtaking the contractual forms of reciprocal obligation
and responsibility on which medieval allegiance had been based,
particularly in the tradition of armed bands of the military recon-
quest of Iberia that had spread over the preceding half-millennium.
The latter tradition still formed the political culture of the independent Spanish soldier-hidalgo that Aguirre and hundreds of his fellow conquistadors shared and were motivated by. It conflicted
sharply with the bureaucratic imperatives of the centralizing state,
the new mode of governance that heavily depended on the earlier
one to accomplish its ends in acquiring new territory and consolidating the far-flung Spanish empire. Compounding the specific of-
fense was the general threat that any successful challenge to royal
control might have posed in situations similar to the Ursúa-Aguirre
expedition, in remote and isolated corners of the expanding empire
where the principles of monarchical authority necessarily had to be
mitigated by a considerable measure of independent initiative in
response to specific and changing local circumstances. Such a bra-
zen challenge to constituted authority, once eliminated, was better

ignored as completely and for as long as possible among defenders of Spanish legal tradition, creating what might well be called the "suppressed" version of Aguirre's story.

This suppressed Aguirre is in many ways consistent with the "cruel tyrant" version of the self-interested chroniclers themselves, the "insane" version of Spanish nationalists, the "brave resister of Castillian authority" of the Basque nationalists, and the "first freedom fighter" of the Venezuelans and other modern Latin American writers. Such interpretations either deny the validity of Aguirre's actions and the principles on which they were based, calling them illegal at best and the evil actions of a deranged mind at worst, or they anachronistically appropriate the memory of Aguirre and his band for political causes relevant in times and places different from the world in which he lived and died.

A view shared in some measure among these interpretations of the Aguirre story, and the film version by Herzog, is that Aguirre was crazy or at least irrational and mentally unbalanced. Such a view is perpetuated by modern writers who take Aguirre to task for not making his various letters to authorities more coherent and transparent to those who, four and one-half centuries after the events, presume to know how Aguirre should have acted to survive in the conditions of the expedition in which he took part, and who take the self-serving tirades of the several chroniclers uncritically, as simple descriptions of events. But accusations of insanity or irrationality are too often the refuge of those who have no basis for, or who refuse to consider, an interpretation that is more sensitive to the moment and circumstances in question and is more true to the memory of historical actors who cannot defend themselves from such ahistorical vilification.

Lope de Aguirre should not be made into a tragic but misunderstood hero, nor should one excuse, defend, or glorify his remarkable life, much less the Spanish conquest of America generally. Nor should it be denied that he killed people. If the latter were a criterion for insanity, then much historical interpretation would be the study of psychopathology. But in an attempt at historical understanding, it is only fair to the memory of Aguirre and those whom his actions affected to put the story in its own context and take him at his own word. Such an approach listens to one of the few voices of the rank and file of the hundreds who shared a vision of brave action and loyal service, for which they expected rewards that

accrued to only a small minority. Their initial shares of booty, tribute, and conquered land were already in his lifetime being eroded
by the encroachment of grasping royal agents, corrupt bureaucrats,
and venial priests. Aguirre was representative of the resentful late
arrivals among the rank and file of the conquistador generation;[8]
he toiled for years and risked his life with little compensation and
found himself forsaken in an ill-fated expedition during which the
situation deteriorated from bad to worse to desperate. Survival required that someone take charge, despite the eventual reckoning of
jurists, bureaucrats, and, more important, the judgment of God.
Aguirre did, and paid the price.

Knowing that his cause was lost, he took a last opportunity to
make a statement. While taking responsibility for his actions of the
previous few months, he tried to put them in the context of an expedition falling apart. He decided to go beyond the particulars of
the situation to vent the frustrations of his career, which he felt that
many of his comrades-in-arms shared. He took the trouble to recall
the names of several former conquistadors whom he thought had
been unjustly treated and concluded with a list of those in solidarity with him. By example and by citing principle, he indicted the
entire administrative apparatus of the colonies and the responsibility of the monarch for it. By his own word he was a soldier of
fortune, not one of the *letrados* (men of letters) he took to task, and
he may be forgiven if in the press of the circumstances the letter
lacks some of the polish and orderly structure that a final editing
might have provided. We do not have to agree with what Aguirre
did nor approve of his worldview to conclude that this letter is not
the raving of a madman. Some of the tone of sardonic and not-so-
subtle turn of phrase of this letter appears in earlier missives to
Friar Montesinos and Governor Collado, but they were intermedi-
aries. Some interpreters have taken too literally the ironic and sar-
castic references scattered throughout the document, and they have
failed to see the bemused resignation behind the officious bluster
in some passages. The general tone is the one of outrage and despair that comes from an aging soldier of the conquest who felt
betrayed by what today is called "the system" and who, denying
nothing of the accusations directed against him, persisted in the
hope that his position would receive a hearing. I urge modern readers to ponder the voice of Lope de Aguirre as, facing certain death,
he directed his message to the highest authority he could hope to
reach in this world.

LOPE DE AGUIRRE'S LETTER TO
KING PHILIP II OF SPAIN, SEPTEMBER 1561[9]

To King Philip, native of Spain, son of Charles the Invincible:

From Lope de Aguirre, your lesser vassal, old Christian, of middling parents but fortunately of noble blood, native of the Basque country of the kingdom of Spain, citizen of the town of Oñate.

In my youth I crossed the sea to the land of Peru to gain fame, lance in hand, and to fulfill the obligation of all good men. In twenty-four years I have done you great service in Peru, in conquests of the Indians, in founding towns, and especially in battles and encounters fought in your name, always to the best of my power and ability, without requesting of your officials pay or assistance, as can be seen in your royal records.

I firmly believe, most excellent King and lord, that to me and my companions you have been nothing but cruel and ungrateful. I also believe that those who write to you from this land deceive you, because of the great distance.

I demand of you, King, that you do justice and right by the good vassals you have in this land, even though I and my companions (whose names I will give later), unable to suffer further the cruelties of your judges, viceroy, and governors, have resolved to obey you no longer. Denaturalizing ourselves from our land, Spain, we make the most cruel war against you that our power can sustain and endure. Believe, King and lord, we have done this because we can no longer tolerate the great exactions and unjust punishments of your ministers who, to make places for their sons and dependents, have usurped and robbed us of our fame, life, and honor. It is a pity, King, the bad treatment done to us.

I am lame in the right leg from the arquebus wounds I received in the battle of Chuquinga, fighting with Marshal Alonzo de Alvarado, answering your call against Francisco Hernández Girón, rebel from your service as I and my companions presently are and will be until death, because we in this land now know how cruel you are, how you break your faith and your word, and thus we in this land give to your promises less credence than to the books of Martin Luther.

Your viceroy the marquis of Cañete hanged Martín de Robles, a man distinguished in your service; and the brave Tomás Vásquez, conquistador of Peru; and the ill-fated Alonso Días, who worked more in the discoveries of this kingdom than did the scouts of Moses

in the desert; and Piedrahita, a good captain who fought many battles
in your service. In Pucara they gave you victory; and if they had
not, Francisco Hernández would now be the king of Peru. Don't
give much credence to the claims your judges make of services
performed, because it is a great myth, unless they call a service
having spent 800,000 pesos of your royal treasury for their vices
and evil deeds. Punish them as evildoers, as such they certainly
are.

Look here, King of Spain! Do not be cruel and ungrateful to
your vassals, because while your father and you stayed in Spain
without the slightest bother, your vassals, at the price of their blood
and fortune, have given you all the kingdoms and holdings you
have in these parts. Beware, King and lord, that you cannot take,
under the title of legitimate king, any benefit from this land where
you risked nothing, without first giving due gratification to those
who have labored and sweated in it.

I am certain that very few kings go to Hell because there are
few kings, but if there were many of you, none could go to Heaven.
Even in Hell you would be worse than Lucifer, because you all
thirst after human blood. But I don't marvel nor make much of
you, who are like children, and any man naively innocent of this is
crazy. For certain, I and my two hundred arquebus-bearing Marañones, conquistadors and hidalgos, swear solemnly to God that we
will not leave a minister of yours alive, because I already know
how far your clemency reaches. Today we consider ourselves the
luckiest men alive because we are in these parts of the Indies, with
faith in God's commandments full and uncorrupted as Christians,
maintaining all that is preached by the Holy Mother Church of
Rome; and we intend, though sinners in life, to achieve martyrdom
through God's commandments.

Upon leaving the Amazon river, called the Marañon, on an island inhabited by Christians called Margarita, I saw some reports
from Spain regarding the great schism of Lutherans there, which
caused us to be frightened and surprised. In our company there was
a German named Monteverde, and I ordered him cut to pieces.
Destiny rewards the prudent. Believe this, excellent Prince: Wherever we are, we ensure that all live perfectly in the Christian faith.

The dissoluteness of the priests is so great in these parts that I
think it would be well that they feel your wrath and punishment,
because there is now none among them who sees himself as less
than governor. Look here, King, do not believe what they might

tell you, because the tears that they shed before your royal person is so that they can come here to take command. If you want to know the life they lead here, it is to deal in merchandise, seek and acquire temporal goods, and sell the Sacraments of the Church for a price. They are enemies of the poor, uncharitable, ambitious, gluttonous, and arrogant, so that even the lowest of the priests tries to command and govern all these lands. Correct this, King and lord, because from these things and bad examples faith is not impressed upon nor instilled in the natives. Furthermore, if this dissoluteness of the priests is not stopped, there will be no shortage of scandal.

If I and my companions, by the correct position we have taken, are determined to die, for this and for other things that have happened, singular King, you are to blame, for not duly considering the labor of your vassals and for not thinking of what you owe them. If you do not look out for your vassals, and your judges do not take care of this, you will never succeed in government. Certainly there is no need to present witnesses, but simply to point out that each of your judges has 4,000 pesos in annual salary, 8,000 pesos in expenses, and after three years in office each has 60,000 pesos saved, along with properties and possessions. Despite all this, we would be willing to serve them as we do, except that for our sins they want us to drop to our knees wherever we meet and worship them like Nebuchadnezzar. This is intolerable. Just because I am an unfortunate man made lame in your service (and my companions long and weary in the same), I should not fail to advise you never to trust your conscience to these learned persons. It is in your royal interest to watch out for them, as they spend all their time planning the marriages of their children, and care for nothing else. The common refrain among them is: "To the left and to the right, I possess all in my sight."

The friars do not want to bury poor Indians, and they are lodged in the best estates in Peru. The life they lead is bitter and burdensome, as each one has as a penance a dozen young women in his kitchen, and as many boys engaged in fishing, hunting partridges, and bringing fruit! They get a share of everything. In Christian faith I swear, King and lord, that if you do not remedy the evils of this land, divine punishment will come upon you. I tell you this to let you know the truth, even though I and my comrades neither expect nor want mercy from you.

Oh, how sad that a great Caesar and Emperor, your father, should conquer with the power of Spain great Germany, and should spend

so much money from these Indies discovered by us, and that you should not concern yourself with our old age and weariness enough to assuage our hunger for a day.

You know that we know in these parts, excellent King and lord, that you conquered Germany with arms, and Germany has conquered Spain with vices. We over here are more content with just corn and water, to be far removed from such a bad irony. Let those who have fallen into such a situation keep their reward. Let wars spread where they may, and where men make them; but never, no matter what adversity might come upon us, will we cease to be subject to the teachings of the Holy Mother Church of Rome.

We cannot believe, excellent King and lord, that you would be so cruel to such good vassals as you have in these parts. Your judges must be acting this way without your consent. I say this, excellent King, because two leagues from the City of Kings [Lima], there was discovered near the sea a lake where there were some fish God permitted to exist there. Your evil judges and officials, to profit from the fish for their pleasures and vices, leased them in your name, giving us to understand, as though we were fools, that this was done by your will. If this is so, lord, let us catch some of the fish, because we worked to discover it, and because the King of Castile has no need for the 400 pesos they leased it for. Illustrious King, we are not asking for grants in Córdoba or Valladolid, nor in any part of Spain, which is your patrimony. Deign to feed the weary and poor with the fruits and proceeds from this land. Remember, King and lord, that God is the same for all, and the same justice, reward, Heaven and Hell.

In the year 1559 the marquis of Cañete entrusted the expedition of the river of the Amazons to Pedro de Ursúa, Navarrese, or rather, a Frenchman. He delayed the building of the boats until the year 1560 in the province of the Motilones, in Peru. The Indians are called Motilones because they wear their heads shaved. These boats were made in the wet country; and, upon launching, most of them came to pieces. We made rafts, left the horses and supplies, and took off down the river at great risk to our persons. We then encountered the most powerful rivers of Peru, and it seemed to us to be a fresh-water sea. We traveled in the first phase 300 leagues from the point of launching.

This bad governor was so perverse and vicious and miserable that we could not tolerate it, and it was impossible to put up with his evil ways. Since I have a stake in the matter, excellent King and lord, I will say only that we killed him; a very swift death, for sure. We then raised a young gentleman of Seville named Don Fernando de Guzmán to be our king, and we made an oath to him as such, as your royal person will see from the signatures of all those who were in this, who remain on the island of Margarita, in these Indies. They appointed me their field commander, and because I did not consent to their insults and evil deeds, they tried to kill me; and I killed the new king, the captain of his guard, the lieutenant-general, his majordomo, his chaplain, a woman in league against me, a knight of Rhodes, an admiral, two ensigns, and six other of his allies. It was my intention to carry this war through and die in it, for the cruelties your ministers practice on us, and I again appointed captains and a sergeant major. They tried to kill me, and I hanged them all.

We went along our route down the Marañon river while all these killings and bad events were taking place. It took us more than ten and a half months to reach the mouth of the river, where it enters the sea. We traveled a good hundred days, covering 1,500 leagues. It is a great and fearsome river, with 80 leagues of fresh water at the mouth. It covers vast lowlands, and for 800 leagues along its banks it is deserted, with no towns, as Your Majesty will see from the true report we have made. Along the route we took, there are more than six thousand islands. God only knows how we escaped from such a fearsome lake! I advise you, King and lord, not to attempt nor allow a fleet to be sent to this ill-fated river, because in Christian faith I swear, King and lord, that if a hundred thousand men come, none will escape, because the stories are false and in this river there is nothing but despair, especially for those newly arrived from Spain.

The captains and officers with me at present, and who promise to die in this demand like pitiful men are: Juan Jerónimo de Espínola Ginovés, admiral; Juan Gómez, Cristóbal García, captain of infantry, both Andaluz; mounted captain Diego Tirado, Andaluz, from whom your judges, King and lord, with great injury, took Indians he had earned with his lance; captain of my guard Roberto de Sosaya and his ensign Nuflo Hernández, Valencian; Juan López de Ayala, from Cuenca, our paymaster; general ensign Blas Gutiérrez, conquistador for twenty-seven years; Juan Ponce, ensign, native of Seville; Custodio Hernández, ensign, Portuguese; Diego de Torres, ensign, Navarrese; sergeant Pedro Gutiérrez Viso and Diego de Figueroa; Cristóbal de Rivas, conquistador; Pedro de Rojas,

Andaluz; Juan de Saucedo, mounted ensign; Bartolomé Sánchez Paniagua, our lawyer; Diego Sánchez Bilbao, supply; García Navarro, inspector general; and many other hidalgos of this league. We pray to God our Lord that your fortune ever be increased against the Turk and the Frenchman, and all others who wish to make war on you in those parts. In these, God grant that we might obtain with our arms the reward by right due us, but which you have denied.

    Son of your loyal Basque vassals, I rebel until death against you for your ingratitude.

Lope de Aguirre, the Wanderer

Suggested Readings

Historical Treatments and Document Collections

Aguilar y de Córdova, Diego de. *Libro primero del Marañon, año de 1578.* Manuscript in the British Museum, MSS Add. 17,616. The earliest known extant copy of Aguirre's letter to Philip II is in Chapter 2 of Book 3 of this document, produced seventeen years after the events.

Bayo, Ciro. *Los Marañones: Leyenda aurea del nuevo mundo.* Madrid: Bailly-Baillière, 1913. Narrative based primarily on the Vásquez and Almesto eyewitness chronicle.

Caro Baroja, Julio. *El Señor Inquisidor y otras vidas por oficio.* Madrid: Alianza, 1968. Includes (chaps. 2 and 3) insightful interpretive essays on the careers of both Aguirre and his nemesis, Pedro de Ursúa.

Jos, Emiliano. *La expedición de Ursúa al Dorado y la rebelión de Lope de Aguirre y el itinerario de los "Marañones," según los documentos de Archivo de Indias y varios manuscritos inéditos.* Huesca, Spain: V. Campo, 1927. One of the first major modern treatments, based on exhaustive research during which the author concluded that there is probably no original copy of Aguirre's letter to Philip II in the Archive of the Indies: "We are inclined to believe that if the letter arrived in Philip II's hands he would have taken measures so that no one could read its contents, but because Lope permitted and even sought that his writings were known among his soldiers, some of the latter made copies, by which the famous document has survived to our day" (111). The version of the letter Jos used, which has subsequently been reprinted in various forms, is based on that included in the Vásquez and Almesto chronicle. It differs only slightly from the version in the 1578 Aguilar manuscript in the British Museum, listed above.

———. *Ciencia y osadia sobre Lope de Aguirre el Peregrino, con documentos inéditos.* Seville: Escuela de Estudios Hispano-Americanos, 1950. Largely a critique of other authors, whom Jos maintains distorted or plagiarized his fundamental 1927 study, that reiterates the basic conclusion of the earlier work—that Aguirre was insane—with "confirmation" from psychohistorical analyses of his career.

Lope de Aguirre descuartizado. San Sebastián: Auñamendi, 1963. A collection of papers given at a meeting of the Basque "Academia Errante" in October 1961, marking the four-hundredth anniversary of the death of Aguirre—who had become a figure of admiration among Basque nationalists—beginning with the revisionist writings of Segundo de Ispizua in his multivolume *Los Vascos en América, 1914–1918.* The title evokes the usual execution method for rebels in an earlier age, drawing and quartering, here referring ironically to an analytical dissection of the case.

Lowry, Walker. *Lope de Aguirre, the Wanderer.* New York: Bookman Associates, 1952. A brief (74 page) narrative of the excursion, competent in description but short on interpretation.

Mampel González, Elena, and Neus Escandell Tur. *Lope de Aguirre: Crónicas, 1559–1561.* Barcelona: 7 1/2, 1981. An indispensable compilation of the accounts of Gonzalo de Zúñiga, Toribio de Hortiguera, Pedro de Monguia, Custodio Hernández, Vásquez and Almesto, and an unidentified chronicler, with historical/historiographical prologue, additional documents, extensive bibliography, and selected maps, photographs of manuscript pages, and signatures.

Southey, Robert. *The Expedition of Orsúa; and the Crimes of Aguirre.* London: Longman, Hurst, Rees, Orme, and Brown, 1821. An early version of the story in English, by a major English historian of the Romantic era.

Fictionalized and Literary Versions

Acosta Montoro, José. *Peregrino de la ira: Narración dramática sobre la aventura de Lope de Aguirre.* San Sebastián: Auñamendi, 1967. A drama presented in bilingual form, with Spanish and Basque on facing pages.

Arciniega, Rosa. *Dos rebeldes españoles en el Perú.* Buenos Aires: Sudamericana, 1946. Separate narrative accounts of the careers of Gonzalo Pizarro, "el gran rebelde," and Lope de Aguirre, "el cruel tirano." Frontispiece is a photographic reproduction of Aguirre's signature from his letter to Friar Montesinos.

Funes, Jorge Ernesto. *Una lanza por Lope de Aguirre.* Buenos Aires: Platero, 1984. An imagined interview of Aguirre by a time-traveling "chronicler."

López, Casto Fulgencio. *Lope de Aguirre, el Peregrino: Primer caudillo de América.* Madrid: Plon, 1977. First published in Venezuela in 1947, this novelistic re-creation of the Ursúa-Aguirre story is based on considerable archival and bibliographical research. It presents a heavily embellished account favorable to Aguirre, as the issuer of the first "cry of freedom" of Spanish America.

Minta, Stephen. *Aguirre: The Re-creation of a Sixteenth-Century Journey across South America*. New York: Henry Holt, 1994. A modern travelogue retracing the route of the Ursúa-Aguirre expedition interspersed with historical rumination and commentary on the events of the earlier trip, perpetuating the consensus that Aguirre was deranged and that his letter to Philip II "is not the work of a rational mind" (210).

Otero Silva, Miguel. *Lope de Aguirre, Principe de la Libertad*. Barcelona: Seix Barral, 1979. Novelized version of the story by a distinguished Venezuelan writer.

CHAPTER FOUR

I, the Worst of All
The Literary Life of
Sor Juana Inés de la Cruz

Susan E. Ramírez

Yo, la Peor de Todas *(1990), or* I, the Worst of All; *produced by Gilbert Marouani and Lita Stantic; directed by María Luisa Bemberg; written by María Luisa Bemberg and Antonio Larreta based on* Sor Juana, or, The Traps of Faith *by Octavio Paz; color; 105 minutes; GEA Cinematográfica. Sor Juana Inés de la Cruz (Assumpta Serna), the famous seventeenth-century Mexican nun, writes poetry and plays under the patronage of the viceroy (Hector Alterio) and his wife (Dominique Sanda) until they are recalled to Spain. Then a misogynistic archbishop tries to restrict Sor Juana's activities to more humble and traditionally religious pursuits.*

Despite a growing number of books and articles on her life and times, Sor Juana Inés de la Cruz remains an enigma in many respects. Assiduous searches by scholars in archives and libraries all over the world have been unable to find many sources on her life other than those that she herself wrote. And many of these are poems and plays and other literary works which, although they reflect her life and concerns, do not and were not meant to provide facts on or explain her existence. Nevertheless, what remains of her work (because much of it has been lost) allows her to retain much of the power of description, even centuries after her premature death from the plague in 1695. Her writings provide the bare outlines of a self-portrait and representation. Hence, it is largely her own creation that historians, poets, filmmakers, and the many others interested in this seventeenth-century woman and nun have attempted to synthesize and analyze.

The interpretation of Argentine director María Luisa Bemberg follows closely the Mexican Octavio Paz's masterful biography, *Sor Juana, or, The Traps of Faith.*[1] Each leaves some of the questions about Sor Juana's life unresolved. Both show her to have been a woman of strength who chose the cloistered life of a convent to gain the freedom to pursue her art. She is shown as a forceful, willful, intelligent, even gifted individual who could not escape the political, economic, and social conjuncture that surrounded her. Bemberg carefully reconstructs these larger circumstances, especially the conflicts between the church and the state, to explain the trajectory of her singular and exemplary life.

Juana Inés

Bemberg's story focuses on Sor Juana's life during the viceregal reign of the marquis de la Laguna (1680–1686), during which she wrote some of her most memorable work, and the increasingly sad and crisis-ridden years that followed his return to Spain. The film opens with a brief, darkly shadowed scene in which a new viceroy toasts the archbishop. The two promise to save New Spain from license and irreligiosity by governing together. We then see the sunny courtyard of the Convent of San Jerónimo in Mexico City, where nuns and novices are playing and singing. Inside her contrastingly quiet cell, Sor Juana, surrounded by books, scientific instruments, and oddities, is busy at her desk. Thus, we encounter an adult Sor Juana, already a professed nun, writing for an audience.

About her early childhood we know very little. Throughout the film and not necessarily in chronological order, using flashbacks and other devices, Bemberg provides the viewer with the salient points in young Juana Inés's life. Late in the film, Bemberg reminds viewers of her illegitimate birth as Juana Ramírez or Juana Ramírez de Asbaje in Chimalhuacán, in the scene set in 1688 in which she tries to find out who her father was as her mother (Isabel Ramírez de Santilla) lays dying. This interpretation is consistent with Paz's belief that this girl never knew her father, who was from Vizcaya (Spain) and may have been the local priest. Based on a baptismal record and Isabel Ramírez's will, Paz believes that Juana Inés was one of six illegitimate children whom her mother bore:

Surrounded by her books and other possessions, Sor Juana writes at her desk in the privacy of her room.

the first three by Pedro Manuel de Asbaje y Vargas Machuca and the last three by Captain Diego Ruiz Lozano. Juana Inés was the youngest of the first set of children. Given these origins, she always relied on and lived with her maternal relations.

It was there in Chimalhuacán that, as Juana says in her *Respuesta a Sor Filotea de la Cruz*, she learned to read when she was three years old with the help of a teacher of an older sister.[2] By age six or seven, by her own account, she could read and write. Then it occurred to her to ask her mother to send her to the university. Because the seventeenth-century university was open only to males, she promised to dress as a man. When the response was negative, Juana consoled herself by reading and studying in the library of her maternal grandfather on the Hacienda Panoayán. When her grandfather died in 1656, eight-year-old Juana was sent to Mexico City to live with a maternal aunt, Doña María Ramírez, and her wealthy husband, Juan de Mata.

In her aunt's home, she learned Latin from Martín de Olivas and developed into a lovely young lady. Perhaps because her relatives decided that they did not want the responsibility for the ultimate fate of a pretty, virginal, and wayward relative or because the court might give her a better context for developing herself, her relatives presented her to the just-arrived Doña Leonor Carreto, the marquise de Mancera, who accepted Juana Inés as a favored lady-in-waiting.

The court of Viceroy Antonio Sebastián de Toledo, the marquis de Mancera, must have been stimulating to a precocious adolescent such as Juana Inés. Her four years there left a lasting impression on her. The marquise was ingenious, vivacious, and, like her husband, a lover of pomp and pageantry. The Manceras were known for their prodigality: they spent lavishly, arrived late to Mass, and loved literature. Undoubtedly, the opportunities to attend receptions, parties, and dances and to see processions and ceremonies contributed to Juana Inés's reputed liveliness, joviality, narcissism, and flirtatious nature.

However, while at court she also became known for her learning. At one point the marquis assembled forty professors, professionals, and other learned men, among them theologians, writers, philosophers, mathematicians, historians, and poets, to test her knowledge. As Bemberg's film shows, Juana Inés answered the questions of this scholarly assemblage with aplomb and to the satisfaction and even astonishment of those present.

The young and gifted Juana Ramírez examines a botanical specimen as her erudition is tested by a panel of learned men.

It is after this point in her life, in 1667, that she first tried the religious life. At age nineteen she became a novice at the Convent of San José de las Carmelitas Descalzas.[3] The order proved too severe for Juana Inés and she abandoned this attempt soon after she entered. A year and one-half later she professed at the Convent of San Jerónimo, known for the laxity of its discipline. At age twenty-one, in 1669, she took her final vows.

The Convent of San Jerónimo, in contrast to that of San José, was a very good choice for Juana Inés. Unlike many other convents in Mexico at the time, the rule at San Jerónimo was often observed more in the breach. In San Jerónimo, the sisters followed a "private life." Instead of living and eating together communally, each nun lived separately in her own cell where she took meals, worked, prayed, and received other nuns. Sor Juana's cell, or apartment, was a duplex with one large room divided into bedroom and study, another that served as salon and library, a bath, and a kitchen. Where poverty was the rule at other convents, in San Jerónimo nuns had their own possessions. Sor Juana was able to maintain a library of some four thousand volumes,[4] reputed to be the largest in New Spain at the time. Nearby, she kept a disparate array of prized objects such as her telescope, astrolabe, obsidian mirror, and feather headdress. Although the sisters were forbidden to accept gifts, Sor Juana received many presents, especially from the viceroy's wife.

The convent, furthermore, was known as a center of culture and learning. It was celebrated for its classes in music, dance, and theater. Sor Juana was a natural to assume the task of music mistress. Over the years she wrote songs and lyrics for dances and participated in musicals and plays. We see one of these theatrical events in the opening scenes of the motion picture.

The only rule that was observed was that of cloister, which restricted the visits of friends and acquaintances and prohibited nuns from leaving the convent except under extraordinary conditions, such as the death of a mother.[5] When visitors were permitted, they were usually separated from the sisters by wooden bars. Viceroys and their followers visited often. The Manceras often heard Vesper prayers in the chapel and then went to the parlor to talk with Sor Juana. They were joined by other clerics and literary people for a lively exchange and debate. The nuns also received guests in the sacristy, usually with their faces uncovered. In San Jerónimo, says Paz, there was conversation, debate, poetry recitals, and musical performances—both secular and sacred.

Sor Juana

The main focus of the film is a conflict between church and state
and the political intrigues and personal animosities that eventually
catch Sor Juana in their webs, defeat her passion for literature, and
speed the end of her life. The script of the movie starts sometime
after November 1680, emphasizing the years that New Spain was
governed by Viceroy don Tomás Antonio de la Cerda, the third
marquis de la Laguna and the younger brother of the eighth duke of
Medinaceli—that is, a member of the highest nobility of Spain.[6]
He is accompanied by his wife, the *virreina*, also a well-born lady,
María Luisa Manrique de Lara y Gonzaga, the condesa de Paredes.
Both loved the arts, poetry, theater, and music. Even before the
new viceroy arrived, he had heard of Sor Juana, whom he called
the *decíma musa* (the tenth Muse), an allusion to the nine sister
goddesses in Greek mythology who presided over song, poetry, and
the arts and sciences.

According to the movie, after don Tomás's arrival and at the
performance of one of Sor Juana's plays at the convent, the de-
lighted viceroy and his wife, although acknowledging that it was
"crazy" for a woman to want to think and write, decide to adopt

Sor Juana directs a performance of her own play to entertain the new viceroy and his wife.

her. In reality, Sor Juana met the new viceroy as the result of a commission from the town council to write a poem for one of the arches erected to honor him upon his arrival in late 1680. Nevertheless, the outcome was the same; she would work thereafter under his patronage and favor. This episode initiates one of the most fecund times in her literary life, during which she composed the poems *El divino narciso* and *Primero sueño*. A foreshadowing that the proverbial storm clouds were already gathering around her is the attitude of the archbishop of Mexico, Francisco de Aguiar y Seixas, who clearly does not share the viceroy's delight, as he mumbles something about the convent as bordello. The archbishop leaves already thinking of revenge.

In the scenes that follow, we see the life of Sor Juana up close. Unlike a woman living the stereotypical life of a nun, Sor Juana spends her days thinking, reading (sometimes books prohibited by the Inquisition), and writing. (At this time, she was working on her famous *Primero sueño*.) She watches the heavens through her telescope, plucks her lyre, and splashes on perfume and gazes into a mirror to adjust her veil and jewelry before receiving visitors, an allusion to her vanity and narcissism.

One of her most frequent visitors (according to Bemberg) is the *virreina*. In a long conversation in an early scene, the two discuss their lives. Sor Juana lists the advantages of her chosen path. The convent allows her to write and think. In response to a question about loneliness, she says that she has been alone since she was a child—a reference undoubtedly to her early life: to an absent father, to her dead grandfather, and to a mother and aunt who sent her away. The *virreina* sees the parallels with her own life; both are locked in by either a rule (of the convent) or a protocol (of the diplomat's wife). Both have a circumscribed world. They become the best of friends. The *virreina* thereafter comes frequently to Sor Juana's cell. They talk of books. They acknowledge the potential for problems with the Holy Inquisition because of the "dangerous" volumes that Sor Juana reads by Gassendi, Kircher, Kepler, Copernicus, and Descartes. The *virreina* brings her gifts in return for her laudatory poems and admires Sor Juana's "children": her telescope, sundial, astrolabe, and magnets.

Another frequent visitor is her confessor, the Jesuit father Antonio Núñez de Miranda. He was a theologian, philosopher, professor, preacher, and instrument of the Inquisition. He served as confessor to viceroys and as spiritual director to nuns. Bemberg accepts his reputation for having convinced or influenced Juana Inés to profess thirteen years earlier, going so far as to arrange for don Pedro Velásquez de la Cadena to pay her 3,000-peso dowry.[7] We see him rebuking Sor Juana for her vanities. She writes praises for viceregal authorities. He asks, "What about God?"

In contrast to these light and happier scenes are those that allude to the growing adversity that Bemberg inserts, ever more often, as the film progresses in dark and muted colors. Already, in one of the first scenes, we know that Mother Nature is not cooperating. In the same scene in which the abbess announces the first visit of the viceroy de la Laguna to the convent, we are told that there is a drought in Mexico that makes the convent's rent collections slow and difficult. The nuns are admonished to work harder.

The archbishop reappears complaining about the lax rule in the convent. He is a fanatically religious man who hates women. So fearful of temptation is he that he will not sit at a table with one. The archbishop begins meddling with the upcoming secret elections for the new abbess. He wants a stricter nun to govern the sisters, even if it means using influence and promises to win the needed additional votes. Subsequently, a scene shows nuns clandestinely copying the *Primero sueño* in the depths of the night and the members of a divided Inquisition tribunal discussing its merits and demerits. But as long as the marquis de la Laguna rules Mexico, Sor Juana and her creations are safe. Orders to give up some books go nowhere as long as the *virreina* is at Sor Juana's side.

Once Medinaceli is recalled and leaves Mexico at the end of 1688, the conjuncture of forces and the vicissitudes of nature combine to doom Sor Juana and the products of her quill pen.[8] Paz reminds us, "After María Luisa and her husband left, Sor Juana must have felt abandoned. To live without protectors in a world that was a web of alliances, friendships and reciprocal favors was like being in deep water without a lifebuoy to cling to."[9]

Perhaps in seeking to please another protector, the bishop of Puebla, Sor Juana makes a fatal mistake. Manuel Fernández de Santa Cruz, the bishop of Puebla, had a personal grudge against the archbishop of Mexico and had asked Sor Juana to write a critique of a sermon by one of the archbishop's favorite Portuguese theologians. This writer, Father Antonio Vieyra, had refuted the opinions of three saints (Augustine, Thomas Aquinas, and John Chrysostom) about Christ in his last days. Bemberg's film suggests that Sor Juana accepted the assignment to show her erudition in a field that was

As religious pressure to obey increases, Sor Juana learns that her patrons must return to Spain.

the exclusive preserve of men, and that she ignored repeated warnings about the power of the Inquisition in New Spain.[10] In Bemberg's film, Sor Juana accepts the challenge despite stories of Spanish autos-da-fé in which hundreds were burned at the stake to amuse the populace and take people's minds off larger socioeconomic problems. Furthermore, Bemberg suggests that Sor Juana could not resist the opportunity to attack a man who hated women, who had initiated an era of austerity and prohibited friends' visits to the convent parlor, and who damned public spectacles such as plays, bullfights, and cockfights. Paz suggests that Sor Juana regarded the archbishop with a mixture of fear and repugnance. She may have thought that his rejection of the theater and poetry was a condemnation of her life and work. In this one instance, Sor Juana's pride in her accomplishments and her abilities led her to abandon her heretofore extreme prudence and reserve when it came to the Inquisition and the power of the church—as epitomized by the archbishop of Mexico.

Although declared not heretical, Sor Juana's critique was condemned in Mexico. Dorothy Schons explains why: the Jesuits were all powerful. They were practically in control of the Inquisition. Father Vieyra was a Jesuit, and it was thought that the critique was an attack on that order. To attack Vieyra or the order was to attack Aguiar y Seixas himself. Worse, when confronted by the archbishop and asked for the name of the person behind the critique, she responded with the pseudonym Sor Filotea (really the bishop of Puebla, Fernández de Santa Cruz) under which it was published. Paz sums up the situation, saying that "Sor Juana intervened in the quarrel between two powerful Princes of the Roman Church and was destroyed in the process."[11] Only a few months later, she dictated another treatise (*Respuesta a Sor Filotea de la Cruz*, March 1, 1691) to defend the right to study and write.[12]

In the end, her confessor not only did not defend her but also abandoned her. So did the cautious Fernández de Santa Cruz, an origin of her troubles. Envy, fear, hatred of women, and suspicion prevailed under the guise of orthodoxy.

Meanwhile, Mexico was afflicted by unceasing rains, from the summer of 1691 into 1692, and disease, both of which were seen as a sign of God's condemnation of the immorality of society. Social upheaval broke out in June 1692 in Mexico City, where Indians rioted and attacked the viceregal palace. Trouble erupted too in

Tlaxcala, Guadalajara, and elsewhere. Processions and prayers did little to assuage the scarcity of provisions that continued into 1693.

At this point, Bemberg makes Sor Juana look worn and aged (notice that she wears spectacles for the first time). Paz says that she felt culpable. Subsequently, we see her washing floors in the medical ward. Such self-sacrifice in the service of God brought the peripatetic confessor back to her side. Her renunciation of the material world and her self and her art began. Paz believes that she had lost her faith in herself. With no protectors, she needed to find refuge. The only option in such a situation was one of submission. Núñez de Miranda told her that God wanted a different Juana, so Sor Juana renounced her books, her fame, her vanity, her "satanic" ideas, and as penance gave up all her worldly effects. She presented a petition to the Holy Tribunal in which she pleaded for pardon from her sins. Father Juan Oviedo, S.J., states that "she rediscovered how to be 'alone with her Husband [Jesus Christ], and considering Him nailed to the cross for the sins of men, her love gave her inspiration to imitate Him, trying with all her might to crucify her passions and her appetites with such rigorous fervor in the penitence, that she needed the prudent advice and attention of Father Antonio to hold her back, lest her fervor would end her life. And Father Núñez used to say, praising God, that Juana Inés was not running, but flying to perfection.' "[13]

Her first biographer, the Jesuit Diego Calleja, reports much the same story.[14] In February 1694, Sor Juana signed in her own blood another text, entitled *Docta explicación del misterio, y voto que hizo de defender la Purísima Concepción de Nuestra Señora*, in which she pledged to defend that mystery and announced a special devotion to the Virgin Mary and the Immaculate Conception.[15] She sold her books to provide for the poor. She became humble and pious, and she began to scourge her own flesh. In short, the renunciation was so complete that she lost her spirit and came to believe that she was "the worst of all."[16]

Film as Interpretation

Bemberg succeeds admirably in portraying many of the known details of Sor Juana's life. In so doing, her interpretation touches on several themes that have attracted scholarly attention in the last few years. One of these debates concerns the reasons why Juana

Inés originally professed. Bemberg emphasizes the relative freedom that cloistered life promised to continue her studies. Sor Juana
complained, after twenty-two years of religious life, that the spiritual duties and expectations of the community of sisters robbed her
of some of her time (she served as archivist and secretary of San
Jerónimo),[17] yet it was still her best option. Thus, love of learning
is one answer to the question of why she professed. The film also
alludes to her aversion to marriage and children. Sor Juana admits
the "total antipathy I felt for marriage" and her lack of domestic
aptitude.[18] In the scene where Sor Juana holds the *virreina*'s newborn son, the baby elicits a reflection from her instead of a caress.
Once again the role of Núñez de Miranda as confessor is highlighted.
Indirectly, too, there are quick allusions to Juana's illegitimacy, the
absence of a father, her probable relative poverty, and the consequent lack of the dowry necessary for a suitable marriage. But
Bemberg makes no reference to the popular belief that she professed as a reaction to a failed love affair, a point that Paz energeti-
cally rejects, in part based on Sor Juana's own words:

> and so, belovèd of so many,
> I took not one into my heart.[19]

Bemberg fails to put Juana's profession into historical context.
A woman need not have a true vocation to enter a convent; one
only had to be a sincere, orthodox Catholic. Women might choose
the convent for other reasons. Families frequently disposed of unmarried daughters by putting them in a convent. Asunción Lavrin
states, "She professed knowing that life in a convent entailed certain conditions 'most repugnant to my nature; but . . . conventual
life was the least unsuitable and most desirable I could elect.' "
Becoming a nun was seen as a career or occupation, a means to
earn a living and maintain social respectability. To remain a spinster was not an option. Paz concludes a long analysis of this question: "It was a prudent decision consistent with the morality of the
age and the habits and convictions of her class. The convent was
not a ladder toward God but a refuge for a woman who found herself alone in the world."[20]

Another issue left somewhat underdeveloped and unresolved
by Bemberg is whether or not Sor Juana exhibited homosexual tendencies, especially toward the wives of the two viceroys whom she
encountered during her adult life. Sor Juana did not have a high

opinion of men: recall the *Hombres necios* (Foolish men) poem recited in the film.[21] In contrast, many point to her poetry as clear evidence of the love she felt for the condesa de Paredes. For example:

> There is no obstacle to love
> in gender or in absence,
> for souls, as you are well aware,
> transcend both sex and distance.[22]

Bemberg features their relationship in several scenes from quiet contentment and formal familiarity in the adoption scene, to declarations of protection in the court scene in which the pregnant condesa faints, to the close intimacy in the scene in which the condesa asks Sor Juana to loosen her bodice.

Paz explains away the lesbian suggestions, reminding us that of 216 known poems penned by Sor Juana, 52 (or one-quarter) were dedicated to the Manceras and that more than half of her works were *piezas de ocasión* (occasion pieces)—homages, epistles, felicitations, verses to commemorate the death of an archbishop or the birthday of a magnate. Most are written between 1680 and 1688, coincident with the stay in Mexico of Viceroy de la Laguna, and almost all are dedicated to him, his wife, or his son, José María (born in 1683). Paz argues that it makes no difference that these expressions and adulations grew ever more familiar and friendly, ever more exaggerated and exalted. He reminds us that New Spain, in the late seventeenth century, was regimented by a very strict social order, a chain of powers, loyalties, and subordinations. Sor Juana's work reflected the position she held in society. One had to seek support of another power, which she learned to do well at a young age, given the circumstances of her birth and upbringing. She became a friend and confidant of the condesa de Paredes, a woman only one year her junior. Her ever more fervent works of praise to her protectors were natural in that era, an expression of her subordinate and (in some ways) dependent status. Paz concludes that "the sensual expressions and amatory images could be accepted and read as metaphors and rhetorical figures of two true sentiments: appreciation and an inferior's devotion to her superior. . . . In Sor Juana's poems to the Countess of Paredes we find all the motifs of traditional amatory poetry transformed into metaphors of the relationship of gratitude and dependence that united the nun with her Vicereine."[23]

Sor Juana's first book of poetry, a volume published at the behest of the condesa in Spain, was "an homage to her and to the
house of Laguna."[24] Most of the poems were written to accompany
presents or to thank the giver for one. Paz concludes that modern
readers confuse eroticism with feudal submission, reminding us that
"an unmarried girl, especially one in Juana Inés's peculiar circumstances, who displayed her love for a man in public would have
lost her reputation immediately; on the other hand, a loving friendship between women was permissible if they were of elevated rank
and their sentiments idealized."[25]

Bemberg differs from Paz in leaving the issue ambiguous. On
the one hand, she acknowledges that many of Sor Juana's poems
are in homage to the viceroy and his wife—an argument against
claims of homosexuality. Yet later, Bemberg directs the condesa to
say that she does not want to hear of another viceroy's wife from
the lips of her favorite nun (an indication of jealousy?). Meanwhile,
Sor Juana's confessor warns her of "excessive loves" (*amores
excesivos*). And, finally, the viceroy's wife wants to know the details of Sor Juana's solitary life and requests that she take off her
veil. The script continues with phrases such as "Juana is mine, only
mine" coming from the condesa's lips, followed by a deep kiss so
that she will remember. Bemberg is not convinced by Paz's reasoned arguments to the contrary and by his reconstruction of the
past.[26]

Another issue that recent studies have raised is whether or not
Sor Juana was a feminist. If among feminists one includes those
persons who use their abilities to defend and advance the position
and power of women, then there can be no doubt about Bemberg's
interpretation of Sor Juana. In one scene, music teacher Sor Juana
tells her students that women are intelligent and that intelligence
has no gender. Her students must keep their eyes and ears open to
perceive everything. This viewpoint is coincident with Sor Juana's
own words. In her *Respuesta a Sor Filotea* she reiterates these beliefs. Paz states, "She scoffs at the idea, current in her day, that
women are intellectually inferior. As stupidity is not confined to
women, neither is intelligence an attribute only of men."[27]

Already mentioned are her thoughts about men. Who is to blame,
Sor Juana asks, "she who sins and takes the pay,/or he who pays
her for the sin?"[28] She lashes out at the double standard and the
hypocrisy of the male-dominated culture and society. Hers, says
her biographer, was a "resolute feminism."[29] Although the concept

of feminism (as such) did not exist in her day, there can be no doubt that this freethinker was one of the movement's precursors.

Finally, we might ask whether or not Sor Juana was a typical nun, a topic mentioned in passing above. Lavrin states that she was both atypical and typical at different times of her life. She was unlike Isabel de la Encarnación, a discalced Carmelite in the Convent of Puebla, who had felt a religious vocation since the age of nine. She did not live the life of a nun from the time she was a little girl, like Sor María Josefa Lino de la Canal, who founded the Convent of La Concepción in San Miguel Allende.[30] As seen in the film, she does not spend long hours on her knees either praying or scrubbing floors; she does not seem overly inclined to charity, sewing, or other "sisterly" pursuits. In short, she did not have a strong vocation for the religious life. Her motives for moving into the convent were opportunistic.

Her writing was also atypical. Many other nuns wrote autobiographies, usually at the instigation of a confessor.[31] Lavrin says that the "confessional character" of the latter condemned these works to oblivion.[32] They were regarded as a means of achieving self-perfection and were not meant to be literary works of art, as were Sor Juana's. Nuns also wrote biographies, histories of convents, plays, poetry, and personal letters, but few of these are known.

It is only during the last years of her life that we know she practiced asceticism and repented for her worldliness.[33] Sor Juana was not humble, meek, and self-effacing like other nuns. Lavrin remarks that not until her "final spiritual transformation" in 1693 do expressions of humility find their way into her writings. She quotes from the *Petición causídica*: "I, Juana Inés de la Cruz, the most insignificant of the slaves of the Blessed Mary," and "Juana Inés de la Cruz, the most unworthy and ungrateful creature of all created by your Omnipotence."[34] Sor Juana admitted having lived a religious life without religion.[35] Bemberg, fittingly, portrays her death after self-sacrificing scenes of her aiding the ailing. One suspects, though, that she died "although virgin, pregnant with divine concepts."[36]

Suggested Readings

Juana Inés de la Cruz, Sister. *A Sor Juana Anthology.* Trans. Alan S. Trueblood. Cambridge, MA: Harvard University Press, 1988. This collection of Sor Juana's writings is helpful for an English-reading audience.

Juana Inés de la Cruz, Sor. *Obras completas.* 4 vols. Mexico: Fondo de Cultura Económica, 1951. A popular edition of Sor Juana's known writings.

————. *Sor Juana Inés de la Cruz: Sus mejores poesías.* Mexico: Gómez Hermanos Editores, 1980. A collection of some of Sor Juana's best poems in a single volume.

Franco, Jean. *Plotting Women: Gender and Representation in Mexico.* New York: Columbia University Press, 1989. This interesting book focuses attention on women in Mexico. Chapters mention individuals such as Sor Juana and Frida Kahlo, as well as whole classes of women such as the deluded women of colonial times.

Lavrin, Asunción. "Unlike Sor Juana? The Model Nun in the Religious Literature of Colonial Mexico," *University of Dayton Review* 16, no. 2 (Spring 1983): 75–92. Lavrin has written a good article that stresses the fact that Sor Juana was both typical and atypical of other women who entered convents in colonial Mexico at different times in her life.

Ludmer, Josefina. "Tricks of the Weak." In *Feminist Perspectives on Sor Juana Inés de la Cruz,* ed. Stephanie Merrim, 86–93. Detroit: Wayne State University Press, 1991. An in-depth analysis of Sor Juana's *Respuesta a Sor Filotea de la Cruz.*

Merrim, Stephanie. "Toward a Feminist Reading of Sor Juana Inés de la Cruz: Past, Present, and Future Directions in Sor Juana Criticism." In *Feminist Perspectives on Sor Juana Inés de la Cruz,* ed. Stephanie Merrim, 11–37. Detroit: Wayne State University Press, 1991. Merrim asks the question: Is Sor Juana a feminist?

Myers, Kathleen A. "The Addressee Determines the Discourse: The Role of the Confessor in the Spiritual Autobiography of Madre María de San Joseph (1656–1719)." *Bulletin of Hispanic Studies* 69 (1992): 39–47. Myers analyzes New World nuns' writings, especially those that were composed at the behest of a confessor. She mentions the work of Sor Juana as well as that of a contemporary, the Augustinian Recollect nun from Puebla, Madre María de San Joseph.

Paz, Octavio. *Sor Juana, or, The Traps of Faith.* Cambridge, MA: Belknap Press, Harvard University, 1988. This fat tome is the definitive biography of Sor Juana, written by an admiring modern Mexican poet. The depth of his knowledge and the acuity of his interpretation of his subject are unrivaled.

Schons, Dorothy. "Some Obscure Points in the Life of Sor Juana Inés de la Cruz." In *Feminist Perspectives on Sor Juana Inés de la Cruz,* ed. Stephanie Merrim, 38–60. Detroit: Wayne State University Press, 1991. Schons provides a short analysis of various points of Sor Juana's life, based on the nun's writings and other documents.

CHAPTER FIVE

The Mission and Historical Missions
Film and the Writing of History

JAMES SCHOFIELD SAEGER

The Mission *(1986); produced by Fernando Ghia and David Puttnam; directed by Roland Joffé; written by Robert Bolt; color; 126 minutes; Goldcrest. Father Gabriel (Jeremy Irons), a Jesuit missionary in colonial Paraguay, converts the pagan Guarani Indians to Christianity and saves slave trader Rodrigo Mendoza (Robert DeNiro) from despair. They all live together in peace until political considerations in Europe require that the Jesuits abandon their mission to the Portuguese, who threaten to re-enslave the natives.*

B ecause of the power of film, movies with historical themes affect public perceptions of the past more deeply than do scholarly reconstructions. Filmmakers and historians search for meaning in separate ways, but their quests can converge. Examples of different approaches to similar destinations are found in a newer film and older historical views of Catholic missions in South America. *The Mission*, directed by Roland Joffé with a screenplay by Robert Bolt, displays paternalistic attitudes like those of an earlier generation of North American academic historians.[1] The film's voice is a white European distortion of Native American reality. This essay will examine that voice, offer alternative explanations

From *The Americas* 51, no. 3 (January 1995): 393–415. Reprinted by permission.

of historical events, and suggest a research agenda for future study of the Guarani missions of Paraguay, often mentioned in surveys but seldom studied by North American historians.

Academic mission history pioneers in the United States, including Herbert Eugene Bolton and his students Peter Masten Dunne, S.J., and John Francis Bannon, S.J., would find comfort in *The Mission*.[2] English Jesuit Philip Caraman's *The Lost Paradise: The Jesuit Republic in South America*,[3] which informs the screenplay, is a bastard stepchild of scholarly histories. Claiming "The historical events represented in this story are true, and occurred around the Spanish borderlands of Argentina, Paraguay, and Brazil in the year 1750," the creators of *The Mission* invite historians to test their assertions. Bolt and Joffé in fact scorn accuracy and twist the truth, even though as artists they may legitimately reorder events, create new characters, and still retain historical integrity.[4]

In *The Mission*, as in the Boltonians' works, Native Americans appear throughout, but no Indian viewpoint emerges, even though creating three-dimensional Guaranis is as easy for filmmakers as it is difficult for historians. The ethnocentrism that treats Indians as mission furniture was an unpleasant part of the dominant culture of historians of Bolton's Berkeley seminar before World War II, and such a bias against Native Americans is even more objectionable for works like *Lost Paradise* (1976) and *The Mission*, which were created when decent men and women were expected to be sensitive to insulting stereotypes of colonized peoples.

Located in Jesuit Paraguay in the 1750s, the movie's climax is the Guarani War of 1754–1756, during which historical Guaranis defended their homes against Spanish-Portuguese forces implementing the Treaty of Madrid of 1750.[5] *The Mission* is partly narrated by "Altamirano" (Ray MacAnally), a cardinal and papal legate who "used to be a Jesuit." He corresponds to an Andalusian Jesuit, Father Luis Altamirano, who went to Paraguay in 1752 as Jesuit General Ignacio Visconti's appointee to transfer territory from Spain to Portugal. Visitor plenipotentiary with absolute authority over Platine Jesuits, Altamirano oversaw the attempted exchange from Spain to Portugal of seven missions[6] south and east of the Río Uruguay in return for other regions, according to the Treaty of Madrid. Reflecting in 1758 on the late Guarani War, the movie Altamirano says, "The Indians are once more free to be enslaved by the Spanish and Portuguese settlers," a misleading assertion initiating the ideological confusion to follow.

Joffé puts conversion efforts "above the falls," where Jesuits took religion to Indians "still in a natural state," presumably without religion, and received martyrdom in return. The movie location recalls missions founded on the Río Paranapanemá from 1610–1630 above Guairá Falls, from which Brazilian slave raids forced Guaranis and Jesuits to flee in 1631.[7] The moviemakers' site, far from the seven missions traded to Portugal, substitutes historical accuracy for the spectacular scenery of Iguasú Falls, a harmless trade-off.

In this wilderness, several nearly naked, painted Native American males (played by Onanís of Colombia) carry a priest lashed to a cross to the river, which sweeps him over the falls to his death. How did the priest offend the Guaranis? Because the movie never says, one inaccurately concludes that customarily killing whites was their nature. This initial "Indian problem" forecasts the ethnic and ethical confusion of Bolt and Joffé.[8] In the sixteenth century, historical Guaranis first accepted Catholic missions in the Río de la Plata because there they received protection from their Native American and European enemies and steady supplies of such iron tools as hatchets and knives, which revolutionized their lives. When Guaranis initially encountered Europeans in the early 1500s, they lived in the northern Río de la Plata and southern Brazil in fourteen *guarás*, regional-ethnic groups that included Carios of the Asunción area, Tobatines, Guarambarés, and also the Tapes, who eventually settled the missions west of the Río Uruguay.[9] At contact, Carios allied with Spaniards for help in struggles with Guaycuruan enemies to the west.

Guaranis gave Spaniards women, work, and food in exchange for military protection. The early amicable Spanish-Guarani relationship, based on reciprocity and linked by marriage and kinship, soon became exploitative. Guaranis realized that their presumed alliance of equals had become burdensome, and they unsuccessfully rebelled in 1539 and 1542. Formalized in 1556, the *encomienda mitaya* conditioned relations between Guaranis in central Paraguay and Spanish settlers, establishing regular labor service of Indians under Spanish masters for the rest of the colonial period. Owing to epidemic diseases of European origin and the loss of men and women to Spanish employment, Guarani settlements in touch with Asunción suffered.[10]

After 1580, Guaranis accepted missions from Franciscan friars, the first missionaries, whom they saw as more powerful magicians than their own shamans. Guaranis called Luis de Bolaños, O.F.M., *Pa'í*, their word for their own religious functionaries and the name of their culture hero Pa'í Sumé. At Altos, over a thousand Guaranis gathered to found a mission so that Bolaños and other Franciscans could protect their crops from the onslaughts of Spanish cattle.[11] Most early Guarani-Franciscan reductions,[12] including the surviving towns of Ypané, Guarambaré, Atyrá, Tobatí, and Yaguarón, were founded in the eastern part of the present republic of Paraguay; and, except for the towns of Caazapá and Yuty, secular clergy replaced Franciscans, as the monarchy intended.

A Paraguayan historian says, "Franciscan reductions were open, flexible and adapted to reality, as distinct from those of the Jesuits, where everything was ordered and preestablished." Many Franciscan missions survive today as Paraguayan communities, but few Jesuit-founded establishments do.[13] Despite the difference between open and closed policies toward Spanish officials, employers, and merchants, however, the early Franciscan and later Jesuit missions were fundamentally similar. In both instances, Spaniards concentrated Guaranis then living in dispersed settlements into towns laid out on European models and indoctrinated them into Christian ideology and European customs.[14]

Jesuits founded missions in Paraguay beginning in 1610. Guaranis in what is now northern and southern Paraguay, Paraná and Río Grande do Sul in Brazil, and the Misiones province of Argentina—who were then beyond the effective exploitation or protection of the Asunción government—gradually moved to missions. They welcomed Jesuit gifts of iron tools, which increased agricultural productivity by drastically reducing the time needed to cut trees and clear land for crops. Guarani missions staffed by Jesuits occupied five regions of the upper Plata. Soon-to-be-abandoned locations were Itatin in northern Paraguay and Guairá, east of the Alto Paraná, but the southern area came to form the heart of the Guarani reductions. This complex was divided into three clusters: between the Río Tebicuary and the Río Paraná, between the Paraná and the Río Uruguay, and east of the Uruguay. Guaranis and Jesuits erected thirty missions there by 1700, and in Taruma in east-central Paraguay, they settled two more by 1750. Allowed the use of firearms, Guaranis quickly learned European military tactics from Jesuits. Organized into as many as eight militia companies per mission, Guaranis repelled the less disciplined forces of slavers from

São Paulo.[15] Because *The Mission* martyr's goal was to convert his eventual killers, his duty falls to his superior, Father Gabriel (Jeremy Irons), the hero of the film. The Jesuit paddles upriver alone against the current,[16] ascends the falls,[17] and explores the dark Guarani land armed only with his oboe. His playing entices the simple movie Guaranis into choosing a mission. The bizarre suggestion that Guaranis accepted missions for European music echoes Caraman.[18] Although the screen people are seemingly hunters and fishermen, aboriginal Guaranis were horticulturalists who supplemented garden plots with hunting.[19] Agrarian peoples with an abundance of fertile land for crops if only they could clear the trees, Guaranis welcomed missions for the steady supply of iron implements supplied by Jesuits. Hatchets and machetes worked wonders. The Guaranis' agricultural traditions provided them with habits of cooperation and with technical skills essential to mission prosperity.

Father Gabriel uses music to charm the Guaranis. *Courtesy Museum of Modern Art*

The celluloid Indians, though, befriend Father Gabriel and accept the Jesuit mission for European music and for refuge from lay Paraguayan slavers. Captain Rodrigo Mendoza (Robert DeNiro), a "mercenary"[20] and Indian hunter,[21] who tours the new mission area for Indian slaves, typifies Spanish corruption and cruelty. He sells

Guaranis to the venal governor of Paraguay, Don Cabeza (Chuck Low), and executes Indians whom he could snare and sell for profit.

As in New Mexico, settlers in the greater Río de la Plata enslaved Indians, outright and under cover of the *encomienda originaria*.[22] Yet these were atypical ways of oppression, not characteristic regional labor institutions. When the film denounces Paraguayan employers' "slavery" of Native Americans, it seems to mean the traditional encomienda, in Paraguay called the *mitaria*. In this institution in the 1700s, adult males owed two months' annual labor to encomenderos, service on public works to the province, and community service to the village. Denouncing the labor practices of lay Paraguayans, the script recreates the language of colonial Jesuits, not disinterested observers but advocates. When describing encomienda, they aimed to persuade the crown to exempt "their" Guaranis from labor obligations to other Spanish employers.[23]

Rewriting history, the filmmakers introduce specific changes that nonetheless raise important issues. One is Jesuit "martyrdom," a complex problem. There were few Jesuits martyred by Guaranis in the 1700s, although many were earlier. The likeliest eighteenth-century candidate was Father Lucas Rodríguez, who, "after a long search of the fugitive Itatines, amid continual showers and thick woods, expired shortly on his return home."[24] From the Native American point of view, however, the "martyr" label is a pernicious European construct. Guaranis thought that they executed Jesuit transgressors for just cause. Another change is geography. Either San Joaquín or San Estanislao, in Taruma northeast of Asunción, is apparently a model for the film's new mission. Joffé simplified the Spanish-Portuguese deal of 1750 (seven towns east of the Rio Uruguay) for the story of the movie's San Carlos (actually shot at Santa Marta, Colombia) and San Miguel, the largest of the seven rebel missions,[25] whose movie representation resembles San Ignacio-guazú more than San Miguel. Simplification lets Joffé avoid material issues, including real estate and livestock that Jesuits wished to retain. Joffé thus ignores Jesuit and Guarani economic motives for resistance and presents the moral issue as Jesuit/good and Spaniard/bad. As compensation for the transfer, the crown promised each mission 4,000 pesos, or about 1 peso each for the 29,191 Guaranis of the seven missions. The lands, livestock, and buildings of these seven missions, however, were actually worth from 7 to 16 million pesos,[26] and Guaranis and Jesuits felt cheated.

Movie slave hunter Mendoza metamorphoses from violent villain to peaceful hero. After killing his brother, Mendoza withdraws from the world. Father Gabriel assuages Mendoza's guilt by letting him serve Guaranis. As penance, he drags a sack of armor until a Guarani severs him from his burden. Guarani witnesses to this act rejoice with words so trivial that Joffé thinks them unworthy of English translation. Movie Guaranis have such limited reason that gestures and Jesuits adequately represent their thoughts. The filmmakers assume Jesuit policies identical with Guarani interests, untrue historically and unconvincing on film.

Until now, Joffé's and Bolt's Indians have expressed nothing. Guaranis without English lines project a limited capacity. Unlike historians, who have few documents with authentic Guarani voices, the filmmaker's calling lets him fashion Guaranis with a full range of human responses.

The Mission, therefore, like the history of missions by American academics before 1960, is about priests, imperial administrators, and settlers. When movie missionaries help Guaranis build the mission of San Carlos,[27] they revolutionize a backward society. The film overlooks the fact that these activities were adaptations of aboriginal skills necessary for making tools and weapons, building homes, and raising crops. Explaining transitions from aboriginal to European-dominated ways should be an important part of the next histories of Guarani missions.

When the camera turns to women's work, it shows bare-breasted Guarani mothers bathing their children, as in an old *National Geographic*. Movie Jesuits, unlike real missionaries, are comfortable with public female nakedness. In the 1700s, though, Father Martin Dobrizhoffer, S.J., knew that breasts were "parts of the body . . . which modesty commands to be concealed." He also noted that the Guarani women of Taruma were "decently clad from the shoulders to the heels."[28] As these are the women who would have settled San Carlos, naked screen women alter history for prurient effect.

The San Carlos Guaranis embrace Mendoza, who now loves but remains superior to them. When they capture a pig, for example, Mendoza refuses to kill it. Guaranis who kill little pigs are brutal primitives. Mendoza's gentle tolerance lets him lose a "king of the canoe" game with an Indian boy. Rodrigo thanks Father Gabriel for receiving him in the missions, and the priest says, "You should thank the Guarani." Why he should thank them is unclear. The film

Guaranis were never consulted about Mendoza's refuge, just as real Guaranis would have had no say about European visitors to their mission.

Mendoza loves God and the Guaranis but does not love the Indians enough to learn about their ways. Film Jesuits imagine that Guaranis who joined missions immediately accepted Christianity, a historically inaccurate supposition. Most Guaranis rejected Christianity for decades, often generations.[29] In missions, Christian concepts clashed with aboriginal beliefs, and Guarani ideology failed to appreciate good and evil, sin, and other Christian doctrines. Thus, the conversion to Christianity by people without religion is ethnically demeaning, another image of "the white man's Indian."[30] Guaranis believed in capricious magical spirit powers, and native religious practitioners sought to persuade them to help and not to hurt their clients and themselves. Only shamans could influence these supernatural souls and only by magical means. From spiritual protectors, *tupichuás*, shamans derived their considerable authority. In the early years of the Jesuit enterprise, for example, a religious leader named Nezú convinced other Guaranis to desert the missions of Todos los Santos del Caaró.[31] Nevertheless, technical adviser Caraman thinks that, "From the forests, Indians came into the settlements drawn by the magnificence of divine worship and slowly penetrated the veil of drama to the truths of the Christian faith."[32] This assertion is wishful thinking, little related to the reality that Jesuit missionaries knew.

The Mission trades historical authenticity for a movie paradise. While the camera moves slowly over forest, village, and beautiful Guaranis, the lush score of Ennio Morricone romanticizes primitive life. Mendoza removes a splinter from a Guarani woman's foot, a task that only movie priests could perform better than other Guarani women. Suppressing the conflict that punctuated life in all missions, additional scenes show a paradise of interracial harmony, peace, mutual contentment, and the thriving economy of San Carlos. Guaranis and priests cultivate fields together, as they often did historically during the first years of a new mission.

In Asunción, Europeans gather to debate the fate of the missions and the legal and moral status of the Indian. Joffé here resurrects for the 1750s issues of Indian personhood that historical Spanish monarchs and theologians settled in the 1500s, a chronological rearrangement that blames Spanish lawmakers for the sin of neglecting Indian rights, of which they are innocent. Spanish concern included royal orders of 1503, the Laws of Burgos of 1512, and the New Laws and Ordinances of His Majesty for the Government of the Indies and Conservation of the Indians of 1542–43. The New Laws declared Indians free persons and vassals of the crown of Castile, outlawed future enslavement, prohibited branding, disapproved of Indians' rendering personal service to Spaniards, and set limits on tribute. In Paraguay, the Ordinances of Alfaro set high standards for Spanish conduct.[33] Laws in missions were the laws of Spain, and Jesuits and Guaranis usually obeyed them.[34] If these laws were too often ignored by others, their existence still shows a care for Indian well-being. Denying this concern confirms movie anti-Hispanicism. When Don Cabeza brands a San Carlos boy a "child of the jungle" to be subdued by force, Father Gabriel replies, "Guarani are not naturally animals. They're naturally spiritual";[35] but he gives no example of Guarani spirituality, obviously unworthy of explanation. He does, though, offer a gratuitous and culturally relativistic explanation of Indian infanticide. Guaranis kill children to escape Spanish slavers. They must execute infants whom they cannot carry as they flee. The Spanish menace dooms the rest. Guarani actions are only reactions to Spanish aggression. This logic would have horrified real Jesuits, who hated infanticide.[36]

Infanticide marked the culture of the Guaranis' nonsedentary Chaco enemies, constantly following game and ripening fruits and burdened by numerous infants, but it was of limited utility to Guaranis. Because they were an agrarian people, they mostly rejected infanticide.[37] They needed boys for agricultural labor. Girls the matrilocal Guaranis prized because they attracted husbands to the band and brought growth and stability. Defending a tradition foreign to Guaranis, Joffé denies their identity. In the same way, he has Paraguayans lie about owning Indian slaves so that Father Gabriel can insist that they do.[38] The priest asserts that colonists hate Jesuit missions because they draw Indians from Paraguayan oppressors, who, he later shows, beat their workers.

Historical Jesuits mixed coercion, persuasion, and material rewards to bring Guaranis to missions with the discipline that kept them there, and Guaranis in missions were unfree. Jesuits subjected them to a centralizing discipline and to economic conformity. Missions did not attract Guaranis from the civil province of Paraguay, whose ethnic origins were different and whose feelings for mission residents were hostile. In fact, some residents of missions fled north from ecclesiastical jurisdiction to the civil province of Paraguay, where the government allowed them to sell their labor services on the open market, a right forbidden by Jesuits. Moreover, in Jesuit missions, beatings were not unknown.[39]

Father Gabriel's movie Guaranis "come to us of their own free will" and stay because nine-tenths of their earnings return to their communities. Did mission Guaranis dispose of their harvests and herds as they wished? Only movie Guaranis have such choices. A priest of the great mission of San Miguel says that last year's income was shared equally among the people of the mission, implying that they controlled it. In fact, historical Jesuits supervised mission harvests, surpluses, and access to the market, and Guaranis yearned for more participation. Priests locked produce in mission warehouses and invested in other Jesuit enterprises.[40] Guaranis could not remove the fruits of their labor from mission repositories without permission. At times, Guaranis resisted; they broke the rules, broke the locks, and shared the surpluses. Caciques, whose status was hereditary, more often complained about the constraints than did Indian corregidores, appointed by Jesuits. In 1735, for example, the caciques of eight missions, led by Diego Chaupaí, demanded a greater voice in economic decision making and also insisted on a greater sexual freedom, which they thought proper for men of their rank.[41]

Nevertheless, the movie raises an issue that future histories of Guarani missions must include: a comparison of the daily lives of mission Guaranis and those of the civil province. The organizing principles of the civil province towns, which took lasting form in the late 1500s, and the towns of the Jesuit province, mostly founded in the 1600s, were the same. In both administrative regions, Europeans brought Guaranis together in towns, reeducated them in the norms of Christian civilization, and dominated their economic and social lives.[42]

Eighteenth-century Guaranis had three alternatives to Jesuit missions. One was living in such towns as Altos, Atyrá, Tobatí, Yagauarón, Guarambaré, and others, where they worked for their encomendero, their community, and the provincial government. Another was the wilderness beyond Spanish control, where a few Guaranis, the Monteses, still lived. A third alternative was to escape "Indian" status. Guaranis could merge into the general population while working for wages in Asunción, Corrientes, or Santa Fe. Earlier Guaranis became non-Indian Paraguayans, although they and their descendants continued to speak Guarani well into the twentieth century, by remaining permanently on the estate of their encomendero as dependent peons after performing their labor obligation. That colonial Guaranis elected to remain with encomenderos warns us against facile generalizations about labor systems.

The Indian towns of Paraguay were not havens. Guaranis fled them, leaving their families destitute. Controls in the civil province were less effective, and escape was easier. Thus, coercion, important to the daily lives of Guaranis, must be an issue of new mission histories; but examination of it will produce different versions explained from royal, Jesuit, Paraguayan, and Guarani perspectives. No one should be surprised to find that mission Guaranis disliked beatings as much as those to the north did. Similarly, historians must also compare the labor of people in the encomienda towns and missions,[43] where, as in the film, Indians performed for European directors.

To complete his assignment, Altamirano visits the "great mission of San Miguel." Although resigned to sacrificing missions to save the Society of Jesus, he is overwhelmed by "the beauty and the power" of the movie mission, reflecting historical achievements, which were in fact considerable. Jesuit prosperity was in part built on the profitable sale throughout South America of yerba maté, a tea made from the shrub *Ilex Paraguayensis* and drunk by the popular classes in the Río de la Plata, Chile, and Peru. Jesuit exploitation of the yerba market was more efficient and more profitable than that of their lay Paraguayan competitors, partly owing to low labor costs in missions. The missions also kept great herds of livestock for domestic consumption and sale. In 1768 the Guarani missions of the departed Jesuits had almost 700,000 cattle, over 240,000 sheep, 73,850 mares and horses, 15,235 mules, and 8,063 asses, about what they possessed in the 1750s. Guaranis slaughtered cattle for hides to sell at Buenos Aires and drove mounts and draft animals to sale in the Argentine northwest and Upper Peru.[44]

In the film, Altamirano marvels at Guarani educational success, a bounteous mission orchard, and Indian singing. Guaranis making violins fascinate him. These images proclaim Jesuit love, not Guarani capacity, and the movie's historical and Indian problems are revealed by the appearance of a Guarani priest at San

Miguel, because there were no Indian Jesuits in Paraguay. "Persons of Indian extraction were never adopted into the number of priests or brothers," Father Dobrizhoffer boasted.[45]

At San Miguel, Altamirano witnesses the scars on an Indian "slave" inflicted by a Paraguayan master; the man improbably fled from a civil province estate to the missions. When Indians deserted Paraguay, though, they headed not to missions, whose people they disliked, but to Corrientes, Santa Fe, and Buenos Aires, just as mission Guaranis did when the opportunity arose.[46] In these jurisdictions, they had the opportunity to escape the category "Indian" and could choose employers. When Altamirano visits San Carlos, he finds a "Garden of Eden," where Indians nevertheless lack personalities. At the mission, Joffé has them cheer, clap, whistle, dance, sing, wrestle, and reply to Jesuits in "Guarani."[47] These Guaranis have no myths, legends, or religious beliefs. They have no shamans. No leader challenges Jesuit authority, as did Tapé shamans Yaguarobí and Yeguacaporú in 1635 as they resisted Jesuit efforts to bring their people to missions.[48] Movie Guaranis are cultural ciphers.

Altamirano must order Indians from their homes. "Though I knew that everywhere in Europe states were tearing at the authority of the Church," he says, "and though I knew well that to preserve itself there, the Church must show its authority over the Jesuits here, I still couldn't help wondering whether these Indians would not have preferred that the sea and wind had not brought any of us to them."[49]

Guaranis finally resist. Joffé, however, conceals Indian decision making, recording only a missionary's paraphrase. In the 1750s the Guarani fight to retain the seven missions was a natural response to an ill-considered crown act. The Indians had contested Portuguese attacks for a century and hated them. In the 1630s, Paulistas had carried off thousands of Guaranis to Portuguese masters, until Jesuit-organized Guarani forces with firearms stopped them at the battle of Mbororé.[50] Living in missions west of the Uruguay for decades, Guaranis were rooted there by the 1750s. So strong an attachment to place as to lead to war is less comprehensible for movie Indians, newcomers to their mission. Through Father Gabriel, a movie cacique asks why God had them build a mission and changed his mind. This question lacks verisimilitude because Guarani deities reversed themselves whimsically, and such a turn would have seemed normal.

Condemned by Joffé to communicating through a priest, the nameless movie cacique declares that he will resist the royal order by force. To protect the Society of Jesus, Altamirano sends missionaries back to Asunción. Fathoming the intentions of the then king of Spain, Ferdinand VI, and of the next king, Charles III, who expelled the Jesuits in 1767, the legate prophesies the Order's fate.[51]

Unlike historical Guaranis, who resisted Catholic belief and cherished their own for decades,[52] San Carlos Guaranis have embraced European ideas and discarded their own, signifying little attachment to earlier ways. One example occurs as Fathers Gabriel and Altamirano approach a mission girl who says through Father Gabriel that she fears "the jungle" because "the Devil lives there," and that Guaranis "want to stay here." Had the filmmakers imagined that Native Americans had interior lives, this exchange could have shown how Europeans confused aboriginal deities with Christian devils. Eighteenth-century theologians denied "that any man in possession of his reason can . . . remain ignorant of God for any length of time." Living in Jesuit missions east of the Guarani settlements, Abipones called their shamans *Keebet*, after a spirit power on whom they often called for help. These religious functionaries were believed by Jesuits to be tools of "the devil" or were "devilish workers."[53]

Because they love the Guarani, Father Gabriel and Mendoza remain in the mission, violating their vows of obedience. English priests, Fathers Ralph and John, also disobey.[54] Because Mendoza prepares movie Guaranis for war, Father Gabriel warns him not to die with blood on his hands.

As Spaniards force Guaranis from missions,[55] the film's anti-Hispanicism intensifies. At San Miguel, Spanish soldiers abuse unresisting Indians, an unnecessary act that prejudices their interest in Guarani labor. Soldiers show how brutal are Spanish militiamen, whose sadism outweighs their economic interest. They strip the Indian priest of his clothes. Troops who humiliate a helpful cleric are stupid. When they make mothers put children in deep puddles of water, the film's confusion grows. Why would militiamen, whose superiors covet Guarani workers, irritate peaceful natives?

In San Carlos, Guaranis choose between Jesuit paths of resistance,[56] the nonviolence of Father Gabriel and the armed rebellion of Fathers Ralph, John, and Mendoza. While Gabriel and old Guaranis pray in church, the other three priests and most male

Guaranis prepare for war. Arranging for hostilities is more difficult in the movie than in historical missions, where an effective militia protected reductions beginning in the 1640s.[57] To recognize the missions' military potential and the Guaranis' century-long mastery of firearms, though, did not suit Joffé's purpose. Tutored by Europeans, his Guaranis fashion cannon from hollow logs, following his-

Rodrigo Mendoza prepares for war. *Courtesy Museum of Modern Art*

torical practice. Led by Mendoza, they raid the Spanish camp for weapons. Mendoza retrieves his rust-free sword from the stream where it reposed.[58]

The priest-led Indian resistance of the film was an all-Guarani affair historically. An early advocate of resistance was Cristóbal Paicá, originally from Mártires, who had returned from his Brazilian exile to rouse the people of San Nicolás. Of the forty-five caciques of this mission, forty-one opposed the move. The first overall military leader was Cacique José, or Sepé Tiarayo (Sape Tiaraju to the Portuguese), *alférez real* of the historical mission of San Miguel. In one of the early skirmishes of the war, Sepé fell victim to allied fire, and Nicolás Neenguirú, corregidor of Concepción, took his place as spokesman. Guarani troops in the 1750s addressed these leaders as *ñanderubicha*, meaning captain.[59]

San Carlos Guaranis of the movie resume aboriginal attire, paint themselves for war, and follow Jesuits into battle. From the church, Father Gabriel heads the passive resistance. In bewildering battle scenes, Father Fielding shoots at invaders and leads them over the falls to death while Mendoza fires on royal positions. Resisting Spanish authority, priests die with Guaranis. Why create a Jesuit-led resistance when Jesuits insisted credibly that they had no part of treason?[60]

Movie Indians need Jesuit help. Joffé's Guaranis are incapable of independent resistance. In historical fact, though, "This was a genuine and spontaneous revolt by the Guarani. The Jesuit authorities formally surrendered the . . . missions to the royal government. But no one could force the Indians themselves to comply." They even threatened Altamirano, for whom they had no respect. He fled the missions because he feared Guarani violence.[61]

Uniformed government killers in the film butcher surrendering Guaranis—as historical allied armies massacred them, though not Jesuits, at the battle of Caaibaté,[62] which broke Guarani resistance. The immediate cause of the slaughter was lack of unity of command within the Guarani forces. Captains of militia companies made crucial decisions without coordination. Early in the conflict, Guaranis fought successfully at the small-unit level. In a European-style battle like Caaibaté, however, where their sixteen hundred soldiers were outnumbered by about a thousand, lack of overall discipline was decisive. The movie soldiers and their Native American allies then set San Carlos ablaze.[63] European troops murder Father Gabriel and a procession of unarmed worshippers. This scene is another black-legend characterization because sending Indians to forced labor would be more rational and profitable. In the final scenes, Altamirano condemns the excessive slaughter, but the

Paraguayan governor defends the killings. As a counterpoint, beautiful young Guarani survivors retrieve a cross from the river. Still preferring European culture to their own, they paddle off treasuring a violin.

This confused yet beautifully filmed and scored movie[64] addresses important issues of mission history. The filmmakers' image of Native Americans resembles that of the academic pioneers of mission history, although the movie's spiteful anti-Hispanicism would be anathema to the Boltonians.

An example of the film's "Indian problem" is the origin of the Guarani War. Did Jesuits precipitate it? Did they favor armed resistance? How could Guaranis, often called docile puppets of priests, rebel without Jesuit encouragement? No scholar has yet shown priests culpable. Future ethnohistorians will likely conclude that Guaranis were never terribly docile or obedient,[65] because these able warriors rebelled against encomenderos in the 1500s and against Jesuits in the 1600s. In missions, they resisted Jesuit authority frequently, as in the case of residence choices. Many Guaranis moved to the missions' outskirts, rejecting cells built for them by Jesuits. Males departed missions for commerce and war, often disobeyed Jesuit instructions, mutinied, and rioted. Men who fled missions rejected Jesuit tutelage for greater autonomy in Hispanic communities, as the communally supported residences for female-headed families testify. In the late colonial period, Guaranis of Santa María de Fe, led by Crisanto Tapucú, rebelled against creole invasion of formerly protected lands.[66] Contradicting the movie picture of immediate conversion and acquisition of European ways, only slightly attenuated in some mission histories, aboriginal traditions persisted in the historical missions, as seen in the continuing desire of caciques for plural marriages in 1735.

The Mission's contempt for Native Americans grows from a Jesuit-centered point of view gone awry, echoing the academic founders of mission history. In his classic 1917 article, Bolton told historians to explain Spanish colonial policy, although he denounced propaganda that romanticized missionary heroics. In Bolton's history, Indians were on the peripheries because Bolton and his contemporaries were Eurocentric.[67] Bolton's own task was to explain how "Spain extended her rule, her language, her law, and her traditions." The customs of Native Americans were less important to him. Relegating "barbarian" peoples to an inferior position, he emphasized the "civilizing function of the typical Spanish mission."[68]

An even more passionate endorsement of missionary accomplishment than Bolton's is *Pioneer Jesuits in Northern Mexico*, by Peter Masten Dunne, S.J., whose treatment of Indians was more hostile and more racist than his mentor's. A history of missions of the 1950s is *The Mission Frontier in Sonora, 1620–1687* by John Francis Bannon, S.J., anti-Indian and Eurocentric but more moderate than Dunne. Nevertheless, David J. Weber criticizes Bannon for not acknowledging that "the Jesuits' 'success' might have represented another people's loss."[69]

Because Bolton, Bannon, and Dunne were the best of their generations, our criticism of them must be reasoned. Surely our own students will one day judge us for sins of which we are as yet unaware, and the strengths of the Boltonians were many. When Americans often heard that Hispanic peoples were inferior, lazy, and stupid, the Boltonians insisted that Spanish Americans had virtues. They wrote clear narratives carefully grounded in archival sources and set high scholarly standards.

The same cannot be said for *Lost Paradise*, the book most like *The Mission*. Caraman's racist attitude toward Native Americans and Spaniards is a parody of scholarly mission histories. Although *The Mission* strives to be politically progressive, it is compromised by its racism. One regrets that Father Daniel Berrigan,[70] supporting actor and technical adviser to the film, cares little about accuracy. Although he and Joffé oppose injustice and endorse humanitarian policies toward the oppressed, the film's demeaning of Guarani culture weakens their case.

The history of Guarani missions should be reinterpreted by placing the missionized at the center of the investigation. This will mean adopting an Indian point of view to the limited extent that the canons of our craft permit.[71] Obstacles to telling the story from an Indian viewpoint include an insufficiency of written sources[72] and the rules of our profession, a culture-bound endeavor. Standards of our guild deny us the opportunity to adopt wholly Native American attitudes and demand opinions that we derive from the scientific revolution.[73]

In the future, historians must begin with aboriginal Guarani society as a baseline and explain native adaptation to Hispanic domination in the sixteenth and seventeenth centuries. Scholars must investigate Guarani life in encomienda towns under Franciscan and secular priests and must explain their similarities to the Jesuit missions. They must probe the postexpulsion lives of Guaranis. A preview of this approach can be found in Paraguayan anthropologist Branislava Susnik's *El rol de los indígenas en la formación y en la vivencia del Paraguay* and her *Aborígenes del Paraguay*, suggestive works but no substitutes for multiarchival history.[74]

Creating a portrait of life in Guarani villages of the civil province is a part of the general history of colonial Paraguay. For Guaranis, one aspect of this was the encomienda, which lasted in Paraguay until the end of the colonial period. In the eighteenth century, for example, while most Guaranis lived in Jesuit missions, over 7,800 Guaranis lived in the civil province towns of Atyrá, Altos, Tobatí, Caazapá, Yuty, Yaguarón, Ytá, Guarambaré, and Ypané, where they were subject to the encomienda. The historian can thus reconstruct their lives from encomienda records available in the Archivo Nacional de Asunción (ANA). One useful source is the record of visits of the governor to these towns, a record originally collected for purposes of taxation and social control. These data can tell us the size of the Guarani villages of the civil province. They additionally give the names and families of females; the names, families, and ages of males; and the names of fugitives from these villages and how long they were gone. One can also reconstruct family groupings, retirements for men, and the names of refugees from the Jesuit and former missions who had come to live in the civil province. The Guarani complaints of ill-treatment by their encomenderos allow historians to investigate labor conditions. More formal sources can also reveal Guarani information. Encomienda titles, for example, contain information on Indian leaders, because caciques were present at the investiture of encomenderos.[75]

Even the most traditional kind of source, communications between Spanish bureaucrats, will often yield precious information on Guarani conditions. Letters in the Sección Historia of the ANA, normally considered the least innovative kind of document in the most traditional section of the Paraguayan archives, reveal that Guaranis from Guarambaré, Ytá, and Yaguarón were moving into the larger society of Paraguay as they worked in the shipyards of Asunción in the 1790s. There they received two reales a day and the meat, tobacco, corn or manioc, and yerba maté that they thought was the least that they needed to survive.[76] In the same way, traditional sources in the Audiencia de Charcas and Audiencia de Buenos Aires sections of the Archivo General de Indias in Seville contain countless nuggets of information of ethnohistorical value to the student of Guarani life in the civil province of Paraguay in the seventeenth century.

Future histories of Paraguayan missions that compare Guaranis of the civil and mission provinces from precontact to the Triple Alliance War should account for daily life, religion, economy, demography, politics, and warfare from about 1500 to 1850. They must not, however, neglect traditional themes: how priests treated their flocks, policies of imperial and local governments, changes in Spanish society, settler avarice, and labor practices. Crucial manuscript records are in archives in Rome, Seville, Asunción, Santiago de Chile, and Buenos Aires, and much material has been published. For the next students of Guarani-Jesuit missions, a recent article by Ernest J. A. Maeder gives a clear and comprehensive guide to the published sources, most of which are of Jesuit origin.[77]

Yet the secondary works and documents, to which the Boltonians also had access, are less important than sensibility. To advance beyond our academic parents, this generation must see the Guarani story as important. The major research tool, therefore, is the historical imagination that makes Spanish documents reveal Guarani truths. Historians must let archaeology, maps, oral traditions, and language study help shape the Guarani account of the mission experience.

For the Guarani past, the most important sources necessary for an ethnohistorical reinterpretation are also the most traditional ones—writings of Jesuit missionaries. Seen from a Native American angle, even familiar sources can yield new information. Jesuit Dobrizhoffer's *An Account of the Abipones: An Equestrian People of Paraguay* patronizes Native Americans in the manner of even altruistic European colonizers, but it contributes to an understanding of the nature of rebel leadership in the Guarani War. Nicolás Neengirú was the second leader of the insurgency, and enemies of the Jesuits called him the "King of Paraguay." Father Martin tells his story to refute contemporary charges that the Society sought to create an independent political entity in Paraguay. In his account, however, he includes data helpful to understanding Guarani relationships.[78] Ridiculing the idea of a Guarani king, Dobrizhoffer says, "At the very time when the feigned majesty of the King of Paraguay employed every mouth and press in Europe, I saw this Nicholas Neengirú, with naked feet, and garments after the Indian fashion, sometimes driving cattle before the shambles, sometimes chopping

wood in the market-place; and when I considered him and his occupation, could hardly refrain from laughter."

Dobrizhoffer further notes that Don Nicolás, as residents of his
own mission would have known him, was corregidor of Concepción,
located between the Río Uruguay and the Río Paraná. During the
war, Guarani followers referred to him as *ñanderubicha*, or captain, meaning a military leader. Significantly, they did not employ
the term *mburubicha*, meaning king or chief, a political designa-
tion. Father Martin then supplies valuable information about
Neengirú's life—what his fellow Guaranis thought of him; that he
held many offices in Concepción; that he had married there; that he
had suffered an affront to his dignity when Father Ignatius Zierheim
had him publicly whipped; that he was tall, good-looking, and grave;
that he went barefoot even though a respected Indian officeholder;
that he himself drove cattle and chopped wood despite his position; and that even after the Guarani War he continued as corregidor
with the approval of the governor of Buenos Aires. Readers closely
following Dobrizhoffer's argument, though, or those who read him
principally to understand Jesuit missionaries, could miss the meaning of this information.[79]

Another example of how missionary sources provide evidence
for conclusions distant from those of the authors comes from *Hacia
allá y para acá*, Father Florian Paucke's memoir of the Mocobi
mission of San Javier. Paucke described Mocobi cacique Cithaalin
as a "bad Indian" because he got drunk and was un-Christian and,
from the missionaries' point of view, untrustworthy. He was opposed by his brother-in-law and rival cacique Aletin, a "good Indian" in the eyes of missionaries. Aletin could please the priests
better than his rival. Paucke nevertheless shows the careful reader
the Native American meaning of the rivalry between the two Mocobi
leaders. Their differences arose from differing degrees of attachment to traditional ways. Paucke inadvertently tells how Aletin used
the priests' favor to gain high office and financial rewards. He became foreman of the mission estancia because of his ability to please
Europeans, but Mocobis recognized Cithaalin as socially superior,
the son of more illustrious parents. Paucke thus provides evidence
for the Mocobi view of Cithaalin even though he himself thinks of
him as a wayward child.[80]

A third example comes from the Mbayá mission of Belén, in
the north of Paraguay. There, Father José Sánchez Labrador thought,
Guaycuruan men were lazy because they rejected what he and other

Europeans deemed productive work for Indians. Seen from the Mbayá male's point of view, however, the very behavior that the priest condemned—reluctance to work in the fields, staying in shape for hunting and combat, making and repairing weapons while telling stories about the behavior of character animals shows that Mbayá men were industrious at tasks that *they* valued, such as training and tending horses, metalworking, or the obligations of war. The missionary assumption of Indian laziness really meant only that Native Americans rejected stoop labor in the fields. They turned their backs on missionary ideas of proper behavior for subject peoples, which the men of the mission associated with women's work.[81]

The challenge facing the next historians of Guarani-Jesuit missions, therefore, parallels that faced by the team that made *The Mission*: to create a Guarani humanity. These artists needed no documents. They had only to understand that Guaranis were culturally whole. Instead, they created Indians without culture. They did not imagine that Guaranis had inner lives apart from the Jesuits, as any group would. Future historians must correct their errors.

Suggested Readings

Becker, Felix. *Un mito jesuítico: Nicolás I, Rey del Paraguay: Aportación al estudio del ocaso del poderío de la Compañía de Jesús en el siglo XVIII*. Asunción: C. Schauman Editor, 1987. A study of the allegation that Jesuits intended to create an independent state in South America.

Berrigan, Daniel, S.J. *The Mission: A Film Journal*. San Francisco: Harper and Row, 1986. A memoir of the experience of moviemaking by a Jesuit who was both a technical adviser for the film and an actor.

Bolton, Herbert E. "The Mission as a Frontier Institution in the Spanish-American Colonies." *American Historical Review* 23 (October 1917): 42–61. The pioneering and influential study of mission policy by an important early authority.

Caraman, Philip, S.J. *The Lost Paradise: The Jesuit Republic in South America*. New York: Seabury Press, 1975; New York: Dorset Press, 1990. A popular, readable, and biased account of the Jesuit province of Paraguay that is unsympathetic to Native American culture.

Furlong [Cardiff], Guillermo. *Misiones y sus pueblos de guaraníes*. Buenos Aires: n.p., 1962; Posadas, Argentina: Lumicop, 1978. The still-standard encyclopedic work on the Guarani missions by an Argentine Jesuit.

Ganson, Barbara. "Like Children under Wise Parental Sway: Passive Portrayals of the Guaraní Indians in European Literature and *The Mission*."

Colonial Latin American Historical Review 3 (Fall 1994): 399–422. A recent analysis of how *The Mission* compares with European literary assessments by a well-informed and able younger scholar.

Hemming, John. *Red Gold: The Conquest of the Brazilian Indians*. Cambridge, MA: Harvard University Press, 1978. A comprehensive history sympathetic to the plight of the Native Americans includes Paraguay as well as Brazil.

Langer, Erick, and Robert H. Jackson. *The New Latin American Mission History*. Lincoln: University of Nebraska Press, 1995. A guide to mission history that represents the state of the art.

Mateos, Francisco, S.J. "La Guerra guaranítica y las misiones del Paraguay: Primera campaña (1753–1754)." *Missionalia Hispanica* 8, no. 22 (1951): 241–316; and 9, no. 25 (1952): 75–121. A factually reliable account of the Guarani War told from the Jesuit point of view.

Southey, Robert. *History of Brazil*. 3 vols. London: Longman, Hurst, Rees, and Orme, 1810–1819; reprint ed., New York: Greenwood, 1969. A classic work, parts of which remain useful today, by an English playwright and poet.

Susnik, Branislava. *El rol de los indígenas en la formación y en la vivencia del Paraguay*. 2 vols. Asunción: Instituto Paraguayo de Estudios Nacionales, 1982–83. The best survey in Spanish, written by a Paraguayan anthropologist with remarkable insight into Guarani culture.

CHAPTER SIX

Passion and Patriarchy in Nineteenth-Century Argentina
María Luisa Bemberg's *Camila*

DONALD F. STEVENS

Camila *(1984); produced by Lita Stantic; directed by María Luisa Bemberg; written by María Luisa Bemberg, Beda Docampo Feijoo, and Juan Batista Stagnaro; color; 105 minutes; GEA Cinematográfica. In nineteenth-century Argentina, Camila O'Gorman (Susu Pecoraro), the strong-willed and romantic daughter in a prominent and wealthy family, shocks her father (Hector Alterio), the Church, and the government by eloping with a priest (Imanol Arias).*

María Luisa Bemberg's feature film *Camila* is a vivid and provocative introduction to nineteenth-century Argentine history. Based on the true story of Camila O'Gorman, a young woman from a wealthy family who eloped with a Catholic priest named Ladislao Gutiérrez, the film is both a splendid evocation and a pointed criticism of Argentine culture during the Federalist dictatorship of Juan Manuel de Rosas (1829–1852). Intense internecine conflicts between Unitarians and Federalists provide the background for a brilliant illustration of the connections between patriarchal power in the family, the state, and the church. Bemberg's film is faithful to the style of the period in many of its details as it brings a feminist perspective to the struggle between patriarchy and passion.

Bemberg's denunciation of terrorism and patriarchal authority resonated strongly with an Argentine population just emerging from the brutal tyranny of a military dictatorship. *Camila* was a sensational success, attracting some of the largest audiences in the history of Argentine filmmaking.[1] It achieved international acclaim as well, including an Oscar nomination for best foreign film.

Unlike most newly acclaimed filmmakers, Bemberg was neither male nor relatively young; *Camila* was released when she was sixty-two. Born into a wealthy Argentine family descended from nineteenth-century German Catholic immigrants, young María Luisa was raised in material comfort but suffered the constraints of social propriety and intellectual stultification. Married at the age of twenty, she gave birth to four children before separating from her husband ten years later. Although divorce was not legal in Argentina at that time, Bemberg was able to reclaim her own name and raise her children with the cooperation of her husband. She found an understanding of her situation in feminist literature, particularly the works of Betty Friedan and Simone de Beauvoir. Although her efforts to form feminist groups were stifled by a series of military governments, after years of resentment and bitterness her creativity gradually emerged.[2]

Bemberg waited until she had finished raising her children before she turned her attention to making films. Then, she began with a clear vision. She knew that she must tell women's stories from their own point of view, "a bit like a promise to my own gender," in her words. The year she turned fifty, Bemberg directed her first film, a documentary entitled *El Mundo de Mujeres*, and wrote her first feature-length script. Having burst the bounds of traditional family roles, she continued to face the constraints of censorship by the military governments of the 1970s as she developed her craft with a series of scripts and films.[3]

Bemberg's feminism and her focus on Camila as the protagonist provide a distinct perspective. "If a man had directed 'Camila,' I'm sure it would have been a story of a gentle innocent seduced by a libertine priest. My story is about a passionate woman's intellectual and sexual seduction of a man she found morally desirable," she said. In Bemberg's version of the story, Camila is an assertive woman who knows what she wants: passionate love for a man she can be proud of, even if that means defying her father and social conventions. As Bemberg explained, "Camila was a transgressor, she broke the received pattern of Argentine, not to mention feminine, decorum. Not only did she enjoy a love affair with her priest, but her actions fought the paternalistic order—another triangle— of family, church and state."[4]

As it happened, Bemberg's own family opposed her plans to film Camila's story, but they could not stop her. In fact, it was her inheritance that made it possible for her to make movies. Bemberg began filming *Camila* (based on a script that she had cowritten) on the day after Raúl Alfonsín took power as Argentina's first democratically elected president in eight years. Fortunately for Bemberg, one of Alfonsín's first actions was to eliminate state censorship. Bemberg believed that the previous military regime would never have permitted her to make this film because of opposition from the Catholic Church. In 1912 a short film had been made about the affair of Camila and Ladislao, but every director since then had been forbidden to tell their story.[5]

In the absence of official censorship, the Church could create obstacles, such as preventing Bemberg from using a particular sanctuary she preferred, but ecclesiastical authority was no longer able to block the project. Bemberg's own internalized intellectual restraints had a larger effect on the film. Despite her feminism and the breakup of her marriage, Bemberg had not abandoned Roman Catholicism. She believed it helped her with the Church that, in her version of the story, the priest was the pure one, seduced by the romantic Camila. Before she began filming, she voluntarily showed her script to her confessor, who found it acceptable.[6]

Bemberg filmed *Camila* in what she acknowledged to be "a highly romantic style," the better to affect audiences emotionally and viscerally. "Melodrama is a very tricky genre, because at any minute it can turn into something sentimental, which I detest. So it had all those little tricks, such as the handkerchief, the gold coin, the priest who's sick with love, and the thunder when God gets angry. They're all like winks at the audience."[7] When Camila first touches Ladislao during a game of blindman's buff, three dowagers shake their heads in disapproval, a foreshadowing of the social condemnation that will confront their more intimate relationship later. The next time they touch, when Ladislao has succumbed to one of those Brontë-esque fevers that used to result from forbidden passions in romantic novels, even Camila is shocked at first by his carnality.

Vincent Canby described the film as "austere and unsentimental" and recognized that it used "the gestures and mannerisms of romantic fiction for distinctly unromantic ends." Some reviewers, particularly those from conservative perspectives in the *Chicago Tribune*, the *Washington Post*, and the *National Review*, did not

During a game of blindman's buff...

Camila O'Gorman first touches Father Ladislao Gutiérrez. *Courtesy Museum of Modern Art*

recognize her irony and took these allusions for clichés. John Simon, in his generally critical review, recognized that he was limited by his lack of historical perspective. How far did Bemberg's film go beyond what Simon called "mere factual reportage"?[8] What do we really know about the historical Camila?

The film begins with the arrival of Camila's lovesick and demented grandmother, who has been condemned to house arrest as the result of a scandalous, and treasonous, affair with the royalist interim viceroy, Santiago de Liniers. The grandmother, known as "La Perichona," is played by Mona Maris, an Argentine star of fifty-eight Latin American, European, and Hollywood films from the 1920s to the 1940s.[9] Ana María Perichón de Vandeuil married Camila's grandfather, Michael O'Gorman, who was a native of Ireland, born in county Clare. He was educated in France and arrived in Argentina as a physician in the entourage of Viceroy Juan José de Vértiz y Salcedo. A prominent figure in Enlightenment Argentina, Dr. O'Gorman introduced medical innovations such as smallpox vaccinations and opened insane asylums. He helped to found the Promedicato in 1780 and the Medical School in 1801. Dr. O'Gorman organized medical services for the military forces fighting for independence from Spain after May 25, 1810; he continued in that role until his death ten years later.

Adolfo O'Gorman y Perichón Vandeuil, Camila's father, was the second of their two sons. He married Joaquina Ximenes Pinto. Camila was the fifth of their six children, named (in order) Carlos, Carmen, Enrique, Clara, Camila, and Eduardo.[10] The older sons, Carlos and Enrique, do not appear and are never mentioned in Bemberg's film. The brothers' absence may be sensed by historians who will wonder why an elite family would apparently send its only male heir, Eduardo, into the priesthood. Who would inherit the wealth that had been so diligently accumulated? Although the film portrays the patriarchal structure of society and the family, it ignores the role of this same power in planning the family's future by shaping the lives of sons as well as daughters. Choice of career was not an individual decision. Fathers and extended family, rather than children alone, made the crucial decisions about access to the family's accumulated capital and whether or not to pursue specialized training for a career in the military, medicine, law, or the Church. Surplus sons who might only weaken the family's patrimony were frequently sent into the Church, but rarely would the perpetual celibacy demanded of priests have been an acceptable

option for a sole male heir. The patriarchal tradition required sons
to carry on the family name.

The same structure of patriarchal power would have shaped the
career path of Ladislao Gutiérrez, a nephew of the governor of
Tucumán, Celedonio Gutiérrez. As the son of one of that province's
wealthiest and most politically powerful families, Ladislao also
would have had limited options for a career. Older brothers would
inherit the family's land and wealth. Younger sons might make a
career of the military or the Church. Because the Gutiérrez family
was well connected politically, we may assume that the decision
was not Ladislao's alone. Might the preference for the Church over
a career in the military indicate a passive and pensive rather than
an active and aggressive nature, or even an ethical opposition to
killing, as Bemberg suggests? That question is hard to answer; because the focus of dramatic and historical attention has always been
on Camila, little has been published about Ladislao Gutiérrez and
his family.

Nevertheless, his uncle's political connections certainly led to
a speedy advance once the decision had been made. Ladislao arrived in Buenos Aires at the age of twenty-three with letters of introduction from his uncle to Governor Juan Manuel de Rosas, the
bishop, and to prominent families such as the O'Gormans. He was
sheltered for a time in the home of the secretary general of the
curate, Dr. Felipe Elortondo y Palacios (who later, after the scandal
broke, wrote a long, obsequious apology to Rosas explaining the
reasons for and exact extent of his aid to the young priest).[11]

Although Bemberg portrays Ladislao as a Jesuit, we know that
he was certainly not a member of that order. Governor Rosas always had enjoyed great support from both the clerical hierarchy
and the parish priests. Portraits of the governor adorned churches
all over the province and were typically placed on the altar itself.
Priests were outspoken in support of the "Holy Federal Cause" and
denounced Rosas's foes as liberal enemies of religion. When Rosas
invited the Society of Jesus to return to Argentina in 1836, some
seventy years after they were expelled by Spanish monarch
Charles III, he expected their support as well.

The Society of Jesus, however, had a different point of view.
After their expulsion from the Spanish empire, the Jesuits had
avoided political entanglements, but Rosas demanded that they
demonstrate their support of his regime. He was first disappointed,
then furious, to find that they insisted on remaining neutral. Al-

though there is no evidence to support his accusations that the Jesuits were subversive or organizing treason, Rosas accused them of being pro-Unitarian on the grounds that they would not submit to the use of their schools and churches for pro-Federal propaganda. He decreed their expulsion from the Province of Buenos Aires in 1843 (four years before Ladislao arrived in the city) and arranged with the governors of other provinces to expel them from all Argentine territory in the following years.[12] Although the cinematic Ladislao attracts the admiration of Bemberg's Camila with his courageous sermon attacking tyranny and asserting the love of God for all men, the situation is purely imaginary. Rosas would not have ignored an outspoken opponent of his regime. His hired assassins would have acted quickly on orders to silence such a person permanently.

The courtship of Camila and Ladislao probably took a more conventional course. Camila later described to Antonino Reyes, her jailer, how Ladislao had taken his priestly vows against his own will and that, in their view, these vows were invalid as a result. Given that society would not allow them to marry, Ladislao told her, he would take Camila for his partner before God. He visited her every day, gave her gifts, and accompanied her on horseback rides through the forest of Palermo, near Rosas's palace. Camila began spending all her time in the parish church to be near him. "If something was whispered about what the public or the neighbors presumed about this association, no one dared to denounce their relationship as a fact nor was an accusation of dishonor made."[13]

Although many authors have speculated on the timing, we do not know why Camila and Ladislao chose to flee on December 12, 1847, at the beginning of the Argentine summer. All of the documentation makes it clear that they fled at night and on horseback. Bemberg makes one of her few minor missteps when she has the pair flee in the middle of the afternoon siesta in a coach. Although the choice of that mode of transportation makes it possible for Bemberg to film the lovers passionately embracing during their flight, a black coach with the shades drawn on a summer afternoon would undoubtedly have been unbearably hot. More important, the young lovers could not have afforded to bribe into secrecy the driver, who would be a witness to their flight. Although the Unitarians accused Ladislao of stealing from the parish church and absconding with funds borrowed from the clergy, the lovers probably had little money to hire so luxurious a means of escape.

It is important to remember that Camila told this story to her jailer. Was she trying to reduce her responsibility and mitigate the circumstances? What do we know of her character? Bemberg portrays Camila as strong-willed and romantic, the instigator of the romance rather than Ladislao's pliable victim. Reyes tells us that when Camila and Ladislao were brought to the military prison at Santos Lugares, she appeared worn and disheveled but spoke with ease and simplicity. She announced immediately that she was ill and needed a doctor. Uncovering and distending her abdomen, she said, "Can't you see my condition?" She asked for food but not the meals that were prepared for prisoners. Reyes promised to give her the same food that was served to him. She asked what the governor would do and if he was very angry, and she mentioned her friendship with Rosas's daughter, Manuelita. Reyes advised her not to repeat to anyone else what she had told him about the course of the courtship. He recommended that, while maintaining this discreet silence, Camila rely on the reputation of her sex for weakness and beg Rosas for clemency. Clearly, Reyes believed during the course of his interview with Camila that she was not telling him a story or displaying the appropriate sort of feminine subordination that was likely to save her life.[14]

Camila's character showed in another way as well. Reyes was reluctant to carry out his orders to keep Camila and Ladislao shackled. He looked for the lightest leg irons in the prison and lined them with cloth before complying. Camila accepted her chains, indicating with assurance and affection tinged with a certain defiance that she would endure that punishment with pleasure, the more so since Ladislao was shackled, too.[15]

Camila does appear to have been willful and a true romantic in love with Ladislao. Does this mean that her father was vindictive? Bemberg portrays him as what one reviewer called the original "Pampas ass."[16] In one of the film's first scenes, Camila worries that her father will kill the litter of new kittens she has found, and he does. He keeps his own mother imprisoned in a tower and tries to prevent Camila from visiting her. When Camila and Ladislao flee, Eduardo finds him in the countryside in gaucho costume supervising the decapitation and evisceration of cattle. He reacts violently to the news, striking his son. On returning to Buenos Aires, he immediately writes to the governor, denouncing their flight as "the most atrocious act ever heard of in this country." This phrase is a direct quotation from a letter that Camila's father actually wrote to Rosas in the days after the lovers had fled from Buenos Aires.[17] (See text at end of chapter.)

Camila's father, dressed in traditional clothing, supervises the slaughter and evisceration of cattle.

When read carefully, though, a different Adolfo O'Gorman emerges from between the lines, a more appropriate paterfamilias who was less menacing and more sympathetic to Camila. His letter shows him to be a father attempting to salvage his daughter's and, if possible, his own reputation. He would not have regarded these objectives as separable. He could not uphold his family's honor without rescuing his daughter.

The letter is dated December 21, 1847, nine days after Camila and Ladislao disappeared. Even if he was not told that Camila was missing for the first four days (until December 16, as he says in the second paragraph) because he was away on his estancia, Adolfo still waited another five days before informing the authorities. No doubt, he hoped that his daughter would return or could be found, that the matter could be hushed up. In the absence of public scandal, his family's reputation would remain intact. Apparently it was not possible to maintain secrecy. Julio Llanos, who was among the first to publish many of the letters that the film quotes, suggests that Adolfo only wrote his letter after the governor had already learned of the scandal from his own daughter, Manuelita.[18] It is also possible that the news spread from the family's servants.

Bemberg portrays the household staff as stereotypically ignorant but affectionate and loyal flunkies. In contrast, the historian John Lynch reports that Rosas was popular among the large population of former slaves and that the governor encouraged them to spy on their masters for him.[19]

In his letter, Adolfo clearly denounced Ladislao as the perpetrator of a crime against his daughter and his family. He describes the priest's infraction as the seduction of his daughter "under the guise of religion." Ladislao "stole her away." All of his sentences accuse Ladislao alone, referring to "the preparations he has made," "he is heading inland," "he will cross into Bolivia," "he will not feel secure in the Argentine Republic." Adolfo portrays his daughter as a passive victim and fears that she will grow to accept her captivity. He asks Rosas to send out descriptions of the pair "in every direction to prevent that this poor wretch finds herself reduced to despair, and, understanding that she is lost, she may rush headlong into infamy."

Adolfo keeps Ladislao at a distance, referring to him as "the male individual." He describes his daughter as "the girl" and refers to her as "my youngest daughter," but it is significant that he never divulges her name. In writing about the fugitive lovers in this way, Adolfo was suggesting that his daughter's and his family's name could be kept from the public, that Camila could return home without public humiliation. He wrote, as one father to another, with the expectation that Rosas would be able to remedy the situation. Still hoping that the case might be kept from public knowledge, he describes his family as submerged in desolation and joined in begging Rosas to protect them. Adolfo O'Gorman was fulfilling his role as a familial patriarch. As the head of his family, O'Gorman has tried to protect his daughter from Ladislao. When he fails, O'Gorman appeals to the more powerful father figure, Governor Rosas, to protect both his daughter and his family. Camila's father describes her as a passive victim; he does not denounce and condemn her.

Bemberg also incorporates into her script phrases from a letter written a few days later by the bishop of Buenos Aires, although through juxtaposition and sequencing she implies that it was written prior to or simultaneously with Adolfo's letter. Unlike Adolfo O'Gorman, the bishop did condemn both Ladislao and Camila as "miserables, desgraciados, y infelices." The bishop also specifically named Ladislao Gutiérrez. Like Camila's father, he did not divulge her identity, referring to her only as "a young woman from a distinguished family."[20]

The bishop dictates his letter denouncing the fugitive lovers. Note one of the film's many portraits of Rosas in the central background.

If Adolfo had hoped to avoid a public scandal, he was severely disappointed. The descriptions that Rosas sent to all corners of the Argentine Republic contained not only physical descriptions of the fugitives but their real names as well. By deliberately publicizing their true identities, Rosas advertised the disgrace of the O'Gorman family. Adolfo must have felt the rejection of his private plea as the public repudiation that Rosas intended it to be. It was Rosas who ensured the dishonor of his family, not Camila and Ladislao's actions or Adolfo's letter alone.

It was not until after Rosas publicly divulged the scandal that his enemies used it to attack him. Valentín Alsina, an Argentine exiled in Montevideo, Uruguay, for his opposition to the Rosas dictatorship, published reports in his newspaper, *El Comercio de la Plata*, which brought the scandal international attention. His paper claimed that the Church was only distressed because Canonigo Palacios had loaned an ounce of gold to Ladislao, which he had used to finance their escape. *El Comercio* denounced Rosas for making light of the situation. At Rosas's home at Palermo, "they speak of all this as *something amusing*, since there they use a *free federal* language." Meanwhile, *El Comercio* reported that a nephew of Rosas had attempted to follow Ladislao's lead by kidnapping a young woman from another family, but was prevented in time. The lessons learned at Palermo could not be otherwise, *El Comercio* claimed, because "the examples seen there and the conversations heard there can bear no other fruits."[21] These examples demonstrate how the flight of Camila and Ladislao was interpreted as a scandal within the traditional patriarchal framework—that is, Alsina and the others did not assert the rights of children to pursue relationships based on their emotions. Rather, they castigated Rosas for his failure to control his subordinates, both in his own family and in the larger society.

As early as January 4, 1848, *El Comercio* denounced the crime of Ladislao in these words: "Is there on earth a sufficiently severe punishment for a man who behaves this way with a woman whose dishonor he cannot repair by marrying her?"[22] Clearly, if Ladislao were not a priest and were able to marry Camila, her family would suffer no disgrace. Ann Twinam has examined hundreds of cases where illicit sexual relations and even pregnancy out of wedlock could be prevented from damaging a family's honor, as long as the circumstances were kept from public knowledge.[23] In the understanding of the time, Camila and her family were both victims of a crime perpetrated by the degenerate priest, Ladislao Gutiérrez. Adolfo O'Gorman had failed to protect his daughter. The Church had failed to control its priest. Rosas had failed to prevent the breakdown of hierarchy and subordination. The patriarchal system was exposed as a failure. Within this system, Ladislao's crime is clear enough, but what about Camila? How did she come to be executed as well? Manuel Bilbao concludes, "For Rosas, the true crime of Gutiérrez and Camila was to have mocked his authority, and to have appeared to defy him in the eyes of society."[24]

In the Province of Buenos Aires, Rosas's word was law. There was no other authority, no balance of power, no source of appeal. In 1835 the provincial House of Representatives had voted to give Rosas unlimited power to make and enforce order for a term of five years. He preferred to maintain a pretense of constitutionalism and periodically offered his resignation, but it was only a charade. Woe to anyone who might consider accepting his offer to resign! His minions in the legislature repeatedly begged him to extend his term of unlimited power. Rosas was seriously challenged only during a brief period in 1839–40 when he used his control of the military and organized bands of assassins to murder anyone who appeared to question his authority. During the rest of his tenure as governor of the Province of Buenos Aires, Rosas used terror more sparingly. He manipulated the House of Representatives, controlled the bureaucracy, and dominated the judiciary. He took a personal interest in a variety of cases, personally examining the evidence and making judgments himself. Lynch describes Rosas as sitting alone at his desk "writing on the files 'shoot him', 'fine him', 'imprison him', 'to the army.' "[25]

The political justification for Rosas's power was classically Hobbesian. Anarchy was the only alternative; only a savage would oppose "The Restorer of Laws." Rosas used symbols and language to terrorize and control the population. It was not enough to accept his rule. Everyone had to be an enthusiastic supporter. Rosas demanded obvious and increasing displays of subordination. At first, he revived the use of the heading "Viva la federación" at the top of all official documents. In 1842 he ordered it to be changed to "¡Viva la Confederación Argentina!" and added the more bloodthirsty "Death to the Savage Unitarians!" The slogan was repeated constantly. Night watchmen called out "Death to the savage Unitarians!" before announcing the time each half hour. Supporters tried to outdo one another in their ferocious denunciations of their enemies. Lynch cites this example from a joint decree of a justice of the peace and a priest: "Stupid fools, . . . the angry people will hunt you through the streets, in your houses and in the fields; they will cut you down by the necks and [make] a deep pool of your blood for patriots to bathe in and cool their rage."[26]

Rosas restored the red emblem as "a sign of fidelity to the cause of order, tranquillity and well-being among the people of this land under the Federal system, as a proof and public acknowledgment of the triumph of this sacred cause in the whole republic and a mark of confraternity between Argentines." The governor initially demanded that persons in certain specific occupations and positions wear a red emblem bearing the words "Federation or Death" on the left side of their chests. Included among them were militia and army officers, everyone who received a salary from public funds whether government officials, laymen, or priests, professors and students as well as practitioners of law and medicine, and finally "all those who even though they do not receive a salary from the state are regarded as public servants." Eventually everyone was expected to conform, and the Federalist style was extended to other aspects of their appearance. Women as well began to pin the red emblem on their dresses and used only red ribbons in their hair. Men wore red hatbands, waistcoats and jackets, long sideburns, and mustaches. The wrong sort of facial hair was sufficient evidence of political unreliability. One wonders whether Adolfo O'Gorman's description of Ladislao Gutiérrez as having a full beard might bear this sort of symbolic weight. Houses, doors, and furnishings were red. Pale blue and green virtually disappeared from Buenos Aires. This chromatic conformity was not voluntary. It was enforced by gangs of thugs who broke into private homes to destroy property in the offending colors.[27]

Rosas permitted nothing less than complete deference and obedience. As Lynch put it, " 'Subordination' was his favorite word, authority his ideal, order his achievement."[28] Exemplary punishment could be meted out to those who defied him. When, in the film, the severed head of Mariano the bookseller appears on the fence outside the parish church, the fiancé of Camila's sister Clara repeats a saying attributed to Rosas that twenty drops of blood shed at the proper moment may prevent the need to spill twenty thousand more. These were Rosas's sentiments.[29] The executions of Camila and Ladislao were meant to warn others not to keep secrets from him, not to doubt patriarchal authority, and not to accept passion as an acceptable guide to choosing a mate. It was a struggle to control children that even in Rosas's own time was being lost, as Mark Szuchman has so ably demonstrated.[30]

Bemberg's film insinuates that all patriarchs were, like Rosas, monstrous. The governor remains in the shadows in the film, behind the omnipresent portraits, the universal red ribbons, and the pervasive atmosphere of menace and terror. His flesh may be absent, but his spirit inhabits the body of Camila's father. Later in the film, Adolfo is confronted by his wife and son, who beg him to intercede with Rosas to save his daughter's life. He refuses. He replies bitterly that a daughter who betrays her father does not deserve forgiveness. He is certain that she is not repentant. We have no way of knowing whether this conversation or another like it ever took place.[31] Many people were horrified by what they perceived as a grave injustice, and the execution of Camila played a role in undermining support for the Rosas dictatorship. Even loyal followers such as Antonino Reyes, the jailer who continued to support Rosas even after he was overthrown, regarded the executions as a terrible mistake.

The fact that Camila was a friend of Rosas's own daughter does not enter into Bemberg's film. Manuelita did in fact enjoy a reputation as the "last hope of the unfortunate," and documentation suggests that she did intercede with her father on Camila's behalf but to no avail. Rosas later claimed, "No one advised me to execute the priest Gutiérrez and Camila O'Gorman, nor did anyone speak to me on their behalf." This assertion was clearly not the case. Rosas contradicted himself in the next sentence, with the admission, "On the contrary, all the leading members of the clergy spoke or wrote to me about this insolent crime and the urgent necessity to make an exemplary punishment to prevent similar scandals in the future."[32] Reyes did write a last-minute letter to Manuelita trying to save Camila's life, but Rosas replied that the execution should be carried out the following morning. In addition, he demanded that the prison be surrounded by armed guards and that no one be allowed to enter or leave until the sentence had been carried out. These extraordinary orders indicate that Rosas expected some difficulty in ensuring that the executions would take place in a timely manner.[33]

The Unitarians and other enemies of the dictatorship had taken advantage of the scandal early in 1848, publicly attempting to humiliate Rosas while demanding exemplary punishment for Ladislao Gutiérrez. When later in that year the news came that both Camila and Ladislao had been executed, they continued to propagandize against Rosas, claiming that Camila was eight months pregnant and had nearly drowned after being forced to drink large amounts of water in a sadistic ritual that they called a "federalist baptism."[34] Accounts differ on whether the firing squad took one volley or more to kill Camila and Ladislao. Reyes, who could not bring himself to supervise their executions in person, recorded that he had the pair buried in a single coffin, with the enigmatic explanation that their relatives one day might wish to claim their bodies.[35]

The ending is not a happy one for modern audiences: traditional family values of patriarchal authority and dependent submission triumph over the romantic, utopian family based on mutual affection and individual choice. Bemberg's Camila is a courageous, romantic woman whose defiance of social conventions provokes the vicious retribution of patriarchal authorities, but the film is only one of many interpretations. The existing documentation and literary works based on their stories provide various and often disparate solutions to the multitude of endlessly fascinating questions provoked by the lives of Ladislao Gutiérrez and Camila O'Gorman.

LETTER FROM ADOLFO O'GORMAN
TO JUAN MANUEL DE ROSAS[36]

¡VIVA LA CONFEDERACIÓN ARGENTINA!
¡MUERAN LOS SALVAJES UNITARIOS!

Buenos Aires on 21 December 1847
Most Excellent Señor:

I take the liberty of addressing Your Excellency by means of this letter, to raise to your Superior understanding the most atrocious act ever heard of in this country; and convinced of Your Excellency's rectitude, I find a consolation in sharing with you the desolation in which all the family is submerged.

Most Excellent Señor, Monday the sixteenth of the current month I was advised at La Matanza (where I reside) that my youngest daughter had disappeared; I instantly returned and have learned that a clergyman from Tucumán named Ladislao Gutiérrez had seduced her under the guise of religion, and stole her away abandoning the parish on the twelfth of this month, letting it be understood that in the evening he needed to go to Quilmes.

Most Excellent Señor, the preparations he has made indicate that he is heading inland, and I have no doubt he will cross into Bolivia, if possible, since the wound that this act has caused is mortal for my unfortunate family, and the clergy in general; consequently he will not feel secure in the Argentine Republic. Thus, Señor, I beg Your Excellency to send orders in every direction to prevent that this poor wretch finds herself reduced to despair, and, understanding that she is lost, she may rush headlong into infamy.

Most Excellent Señor, that my presumptious letter may find you at Lujan, and the state of affliction in which I find myself, both compel me to bring to the attention of Your Excellency these descriptions of the fugitives. The male individual is of average height, thin of body, *moreno* in color, large brown eyes that bulge somewhat, curly black hair, a full but short beard of twelve to fifteen days; he has two woven ponchos, one black and the other dark with red stripes, he has used them to cover pistols in his saddlebags. The girl is very tall, black eyes, white skin, chestnut hair, thin of body, and has a front tooth that sticks out a bit.

Most Excellent Señor, deign to overlook the style of this letter. Your Excellency is a father and the only one capable of remediating a case of transcendental importance for all of my family, if this becomes public knowledge. All of them add their pleas to mine, to implore the protection of Your Excellency whose humble servant is Adolfo O'Gorman.

Suggested Readings

On Argentine Politics and Society

Lynch, John. *Argentine Dictator: Juan Manuel de Rosas, 1829–1852*. Oxford: Clarendon Press, 1981. The essential biography of Rosas by a distinguished historian.

Masiello, Francine. *Between Civilization and Barbarism: Women, Nation, and Literary Culture in Modern Argentina*. Lincoln: University of Nebraska Press, 1992. A contemporary scholar's gendered perspective.

Sarmiento, Domingo Faustino. *Life in the Argentine Republic in the Days of the Tyrants, or, Civilization and Barbarism*. New York: Gordon Press, 1976. English translation of the classic indictment of gaucho culture and Federalist caudillo Juan Facundo Quiroga and, by implication, of Rosas himself. Originally published in Spanish in 1845 as *Facundo*.

Shumway, Nicolas. *The Invention of Argentina*. Berkeley: University of California Press, 1991. Examines the intellectual development of the "guiding fictions" of Argentine nationalism with particular attention to the opposition to Rosas.

Szuchman, Mark D. "A Challenge to the Patriarchs: Love among the Youth in Nineteenth-Century Argentina." In *The Middle Period in Latin America: Values and Attitudes in the 18th–19th Centuries*, ed. Mark D. Szuchman, 141–65. Boulder, CO: Lynne Rienner Publishers, 1989. Lawsuits over choice of marriage partners demonstrate that parents were losing control over their children.

Historical, Literary, and Polemical Works on Camila O'Gorman

Ascasubi, Hilario. *Trobas y lamentos de Donato Jurao, soldado argentino, a la muerte de la infeliz Da. Camila Ogorman [sic] que en compañia del desgraciado Cura Gutiérrez fueron ferozmente asesinados en Buenos Aires por órden del famoso y cobarde carnicero Juan Manuel Rosas titulado Gefe Supremo*. Uruguay: Imprenta del Colejio, 1851(?).

Calvera, Leonor. *Camila O'Gorman, o, El amor y el poder*. Buenos Aires: Editorial Leviatan, 1986.

Espejo, Miguel. *Senderos en el viento*. Puebla, Pue., Mexico: Universidad Autónoma de Puebla, ICUAP, 1985.

Fajardo, Heraclio C. *Camila O'Gorman: Drama historico en seis cuadros y en verso*. Buenos Aires: Imprenta Americana, 1856.

Gorriti, Juana Manuela. "Camila O'Gorman." In *Obras completas*. 4 vols. Salta, Argentina: Fundación del Banco del Noroeste, 1992, 2:183–90. First published 1865.

Helguera, Luis Ignacio. *Camila y Uladislao: Tragedia en tres actos*. Buenos Aires: Ediciones Amaru, 1991.

Imbert, Julio. *Camila O'Gorman: Tragedia*. Buenos Aires: Talia, 1968.

Kisnerman, Natalio. *Camila O'Gorman: El hecho histórico y su proyección literaria*. Buenos Aires: Universidad de Buenos Aires, Instituto de Literatura Argentina "Ricardo Rojas," 1973.

Llanos, Julio. *Camila O'Gorman*. Buenos Aires: La Patria Argentina, 1883.

Mazzucchelli, Victor Hugo. *Se llamaba Camila y estaba encinta*. Buenos Aires: Ediciones "Mirtgradan," 1972.

Mendoza Ortiz, L. *Camila O'Gorman: Drama histórico, arreglado de la novela de Gutiérrez, del mismo titulo: En 5 actos y en verso*. Barracas al Sud (Avellaneda, Argentina): Imprenta El Censor, n.d.

Molina, Enrique. *Una sombra donde suena Camila O'Gorman*. Buenos Aires: Editorial Losada, 1973.

Olivera, Miguel Alfredo. *Camila O'Gorman, Una tragedia argentina*. Buenos Aires: Emece, 1959.

Pelissot, Felisberto. *Camila O'Gorman*. Buenos Aires: Las Artes, 1857.

Siri, Eros Nicola. *Rosas y el proceso de Camila O'Gorman (su responsibilidad de gobernante)*. Buenos Aires: n.p., 1939.

Vizoso Gorostiaga, Manuel de. *Camila O'Gorman y su época, La tragedia mas dolorosa ocurrida durante el gobierno del "Restaurador de las Leyes" estudiada a base de documentación y con opiniones de sus contemporaneos*. Santa Fe, Argentina: Talleres Gráficos Castellvi, 1943.

White, Anibal. *Camila O'Gorman: Drama histórico mas para ser leido, en tres actos y en verso, de la época de Juan Manuel de Rosas*. Buenos Aires: n.p., 1969.

CHAPTER SEVEN

Recasting Cuban Slavery
The Other Francisco and
The Last Supper

JOHN MRAZ*

El Otro Francisco *(1975), or* The Other Francisco; *produced by the Instituto Cubano de Arte e Industria Cinematográficos; directed by Sergio Giral; written by Sergio Giral from the novel* Francisco *(1880) by Anselmo Suárez y Romero; black & white; 100 minutes; Instituto Cubano de Arte e Industria Cinematográficos. The liberal, humanitarian, and romanticized version of slavery from the nineteenth-century novel on which the film is based is contrasted with modern historians' views of slavery. The film also demonstrates how the novelist's social position led him to adopt this particular stance.*

La Ultima Cena *(1976), or* The Last Supper; *produced by Santiago Llapur and Camilo Vives; directed by Tomás Gutiérrez Alea; written by Tomás González, María Eugenia Haya, and Tomás Gutiérrez Alea; color; 125 minutes; Instituto Cubano de Arte e Industria Cinematográficos. In 1790 a Cuban slaveowner decides to reenact the Last Supper and wash the feet of twelve of his slaves in an attempt to teach them the Christian values of obedience and endurance. His lesson fails; the slaves rebel and are brutally repressed.*

Filmic revisions of Cuba's history have been a major genre of ICAIC (Instituto Cubano de Arte e Industria Cinematográficos)

*I am grateful to Eli Bartra for her comments on this article, and to Julianne Burton, Janey Place, and David Sweet for their observations on a much earlier version.

since the institute was established shortly after the triumph of the revolution in 1959. Slavery is an integral part of that past and has been represented in several films. Sergio Giral is the cineaste who has demonstrated the most interest in this theme. One of the few black directors in ICAIC, Giral began to explore aspects of slavery in 1967 with a documentary short, *Cimarrón*, and then went on to make a trilogy: *El Otro Francisco* (*The Other Francisco*), *Rancheador* (1976), and *Maluala* (1979). At about the same time that Giral was directing *The Other Francisco*, Tomás Gutiérrez Alea, the dean of Cuban cineastes, was making *The Last Supper* (1976). Analyzing and comparing these two films will tell us much about the representation of slavery on screen.

The Other Francisco is the best of Giral's films on slavery, historically as well as cinematographically. It is set in the past but goes beyond being a simple period reconstruction by reflecting on how history is written: who writes it, from what perspective, and in light of which interests. *The Other Francisco* is a radical reworking of *Francisco, o, Las delicias del campo (Francisco, or The Pleasures of the Country)*, the first abolitionist novel of the Americas, which provided the starting point for the film. The movie begins as a cinematic reproduction of the idealized, romanticized, and individualized image of slavery found in the novel. But, in its course, the movie develops a critique of this portrayal by showing the "real" history of slavery.

The novel *Francisco* was written by Anselmo Suárez y Romero in 1839. This son of slaveholding sugar planters wrote his book, which was to remain unpublished for the better part of a century, for a literary salon composed of progressive colonial intellectuals. His conception of slavery was a product of their concrete historical situation, determined by their class interests and their avid embrace of European Romanticism. The first part of *The Other Francisco* presents us with a filmic re-creation of the novel's Arcadian vision. Francisco is an urban slave who lives in the house of Señora Mendizabal and works as her coachman. There, he falls deeply in love with Dorotea, the slave seamstress of the household. Unfortunately, Ricardo, the señora's depraved and sadistic son, is possessed by an "offensive lust" for the same young woman. Dorotea later becomes pregnant by Francisco, and they are punished. Refused the right to marry, Dorotea is sent to a French laundry, and Francisco is given to Ricardo to be used as a field laborer on the family's sugar plantation. There, he is viciously and wantonly abused by

Ricardo and ends by hanging himself because his "genuine and sensitive" love for Dorotea has been thwarted by Ricardo's evil designs.

The precredit sequence initiates the romantic vision of Suárez y Romero, but criticism of the slave society portrayed in the novel quickly gets under way, creating the juxtaposition of two alternating discourses. On the one hand, portions of the nineteenth-century novel are heard while the visual style and action reproduce that of classic Hollywood films such as *Gone with the Wind*. On the other hand, documentary form increasingly imposes itself as the film advances, with a voice-over narration that provides historical information. For example, shortly after the first romantic interlude of Francisco and Dorotea, the film cuts to a "documentary" rape by a river, while the "omniscient historian" talks about the reality of sexual relations under slavery in counterpoint to the novel's idealized version. The gross imbalance of power between men and women makes a romance such as that of Francisco and Dorotea highly improbable. The rape to which black women were constantly subjected casts serious doubts on Ricardo's obsession with Dorotea. The historical practice of self-induced abortion to keep from bringing more children into slavery indicates that the cherished child of the slave couple may never have seen the light of day.

   In general, the main criticisms offered of the novel are developed in the second part of the film. Here, we are told a truer or
more probable story of slavery—of the "other Francisco" and the
"other Ricardo." We see Ricardo's dispassionate rape of Dorotea
and his equally unemotional decision to have Francisco beaten to
death as an example for the other slaves when the new machine is
broken. We learn that even suicides were part of black resistance to
slavery and that its roots are part of an undying African heritage.
We discover the relationship between the moral concern of the British for ending slavery and their economic interest in reducing the
competition for West Indian cane growers employing free labor
while creating markets for new machines that can transform the
manufacture of sugar.
   The film's functioning on a broader, epistemological level is
an interesting example of dialectical materialism. The simultaneous
re-creation/critique that takes place in *The Other Francisco* is part
of a process characterized by an incessant critical reflection on what
we know and how we know it. The way in which people experience the world is seen to be a function of their concrete historical
situation; the forms in which they represent their experiences are
understood to be expressions of particular class interests.
   The Other Francisco most effectively conveys the dialectics of
perceptual/presentational categories through visual style—mainly

by filming those parts that represent the viewpoint of Suárez y Romero's novel in a form characteristic of classic Hollywood cinema. Long, smooth tracks, zooms, and pans sweep in on the protagonists. Focus extrapolates the actors from their background in close-ups, and lighting is carefully balanced to highlight the features of the attractive actors cast as Francisco and Dorotea. The romantic musical score composed by Leo Brouwer augments the sentimentalism of the imagery. The documentary technique utilized for the "other" view of Cuban slavery criticizes such romanticism through the use of realist aesthetics. The hand-held camera replicates the style of newsreel photography, as does the harsh and unbalanced lighting. Long takes of productive activities, such as cutting or grinding cane, replace close-ups of individuals. Further, the musical score becomes more African, and rhythm instruments provide the emotional force formerly offered through strings. At the same time, the language used by the slaves becomes less refined and reflects differences in their geographical origins.

Through the juxtaposition of the two cinematic forms, Giral points to the intimate relationship between consciousness and perception, a familiar procedure in Cuban cinema from 1965 through 1975. For example, Gutiérrez Alea employed this strategy to portray the different points of view embodied by the protagonist, Sergio, and the Cuban revolutionaries in *Memories of Underdevelopment* (1968). Humberto Solás used three different film styles to convey the distinct consciousnesses of the three historical periods (1895, 1932, 1960s) depicted in *Lucía* (1968). A year later, Manuel Octavio Gómez released *The First Charge of the Machete*, in which the modern television documentary form of cinema verité is juxtaposed with a high-contrast film that resembles primitive newsreel footage. *Girón* (1973) was the last of the historical films to utilize this particular formal structure; director Manuel Herrera contrasted footage from U.S. war movies with interviews and documentary recreation of events by participants in the Bay of Pigs battle. In *The Last Supper*, Gutiérrez Alea indicated that this particular form of experimentation had ended by making a film that was a completely closed narrative, offering a Hollywoodian window onto the world of the past.

In *The Other Francisco*, although the two film forms are different, they are not dramatically so. To render the two worldviews in drastically dissimilar styles would be too predictable in setting up the "subjectivity" of Suárez y Romero's portrayal (and that of

classical cinematic form) against the "objectivity" of contemporary reinterpretation. Instead, the subtlety of Giral's stylistic resonance insists at a formal level that, while no mode of presentation/
perception is fully objective, some provide for greater clarity than
others. Most important, it demonstrates that, though perception is
relative, the relativity exists in and is determined by a dialectical relationship with material reality. Thus, Giral's effective use
of subtle stylistic differences in the two parts conveys both the
context-bound nature of Suárez y Romero's portrayal of slavery in
particular and the more general notion that all perception occurs
within contexts that are being changed by the transformation of
material reality.

Critical reflection on classic historical portrayal in cinema also
takes place in relation to various elemental issues: the relative importance of individuals and classes, of the sexual and the economic,
of religion and law in specific historical circumstances. Thus, one
example of resonance between the film's two parts can be seen in
the analysis of the priority assigned to individuals as opposed to
groups. Those sections that represent Suárez y Romero's portrayal
emphasize the characters' individuality and their psychological
motivation. Here, the focus is on Francisco and Ricardo as persons: the slave whose humble nobility is equaled only by the vil-
lainy of his master. The system of slavery, in reality part of a
productive mode that conditioned the everyday lives of those caught
in it, is here reduced to a simple backdrop of historical trappings
against which to play out the timeless psychodrama of eternal human passion. Ricardo is as obsessed with Francisco as he is with
Dorotea, and his singling out of this individual for the wreaking of
a terrible vengeance is motivated entirely by unrequited love. This
familiar narrative structure is found, for example, in television dramas about high-minded policemen concerned only with the pursuit
of a single criminal, or about warm-hearted doctors whose practices seem to revolve around one patient.

The Other Francisco breaks with the classical narrative model,
in which action is impelled through individual crises, and replaces
it with historical analysis. Thus, we are never shown another "Francisco," for Giral's interest is in critiquing the book's ideology and
not in fomenting identification with a different fictional hero. The
director wants to create another *Francisco*, a new narrative, a film
to replace the book, rather than invent a "Superman stood on his
head." Certainly, we are confronted with individual slaves, such as

Crispín and Lucumí. However, we understand these characters not as the "exception" that Suárez y Romero explicitly portrays Francisco to be but as representatives of the slave class. Similarly, Ricardo is portrayed as acting within his general class interests rather than as a deranged individual. Thus, the martyrdom of Francisco is of no personal concern to Ricardo; the new sugar press had been broken, and Francisco served as a convenient scapegoat.

The same sort of critique is carried out in regard to the relative importance assigned the sexual and economic bases of human motivation in the two discourses. Sex is the motor force of human activity in the film's representation of the novel. This central position of sex is seen primarily in the "offensive lust" of Ricardo for Dorotea, a lasciviousness so strong that he offers to free her if she will consent to sexual relations: the 600 pesos she is worth are nothing compared to his desire for her. Francisco's fate is also determined by love: he feels compelled to commit suicide once his beloved has been "soiled." The determining power of sexual drive is emphasized at the visual level, particularly in the portrayal of Antonio, the *mayoral* (overseer). Phallic symbolism is apparent in Antonio's lighting of his cigar, as well as in his grabbing of his crotch while relating the punishments he has dealt out to various slaves. This imagery suggests that, in the novel, the humiliations of slavery are, above all, sexual.

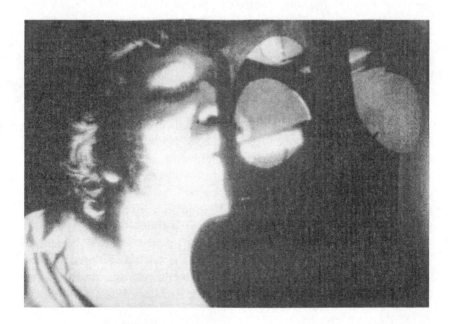

But we got him and I split his head open!

The documentary's critical revision of Suárez y Romero's narrative emphasizes economic, rather than sexual, relations as the central source of motivation for human activity. Ricardo unfeelingly rapes Dorotea in a way that suggests she is no more than an object to him. The absence of personal interest is reinforced by intercutting the rape scene with the slaves' destruction of the sugar press; as Ricardo forces himself onto Dorotea, the slaves jam a blade into the machine's rollers. The visual metaphor underlines Ricardo's perception of Dorotea as an element of the productive process rather than as a human being, as is made clear in his response to his mother's complaints about her: "Forget about the stupid slave, look at the account books!"

Giral's depiction of black resistance to the slave system is perhaps the most crucial area of resonance between the film's parts. Here the principal device is the presentation and re-presentation of a slave dance. The first time we are shown the dance, the slaves are photographed in a typically picturesque long shot. Antonio takes advantage of the occasion to humiliate Francisco by forcing him to kiss an old woman, who is portrayed as a stage prop and complacent accomplice in his debasement. In the critical revision, the dance is shot with close-ups that differentiate the various blacks, and the hand-held camera swirls among the dancers, reinforcing the flurry of their activity. The old woman, before a collaborator, is now presented as a figure whose importance is recognized by the others. The dance takes on a more African quality, with drums dominating the sound track, and it becomes an effort of resistance, for the slaves burn the bagasse shed at the sugar mill while several blacks make their escape into the mountains.

To Giral, the overlooking of slave resistance by Suárez y Romero is the novel's greatest shortcoming:

> At the same time that Suárez y Romero was writing the novel, there was a movement of slave conspiracies and uprisings throughout the island. It is extremely significant that Suárez y Romero at no time as much as alludes to these uprisings, though as a slaveholder himself he certainly must have been aware of them. . . . The simple fact that a wave of uprising and conspiracies existed which Suárez y Romero omits from his novel was what moved me to treat the novel as I did in the film.[1]

Giral not only portrays slave resistance in escape and vandalism, but he also ends the movie with a montage of a rebellion and the official reaction to it. Slaves are seen burning cane fields and killing the *mayoral* and *contramayoral* (assistant overseer), while the omniscient voice-over recounts the long tradition of slave revolt in nineteenth-century Cuba. For Giral, the history of this struggle contains the seeds of Cuban nationalism, and it is for that reason crucial that the Islanders become aware of the fact that such resistance was frequent in Cuban slave society, as well as of its systematic exclusion from much of Cuban historiography prior to the revolution.

In *The Other Francisco*, historical transformation is visually conveyed through the evolution of the slave-capitalist colonial mode of production and its effect on the slaves. In the beginning of the film, the sugar press is run by oxen. Later, we are introduced to a representative of Fawcett and Pearson, a British company that is producing and distributing cane-pressing machines run by steam. We come to understand in the course of the film that such mechanization not only increases productivity but also adds pressure on the slaves by making them work at machine time, thus reducing them even further than did the traditional system in their status as units of the productive mode. Mechanization, however, also sets into motion the very forces that will lead to the abolition of slavery and the institution of wage labor. This point is the core of an argument that takes place between a young progressive planter and an older and more conservative member of the sugar aristocracy, sardonically filmed at an elegantly appointed dinner table where the foreground is dominated by the carcass of a roast pig.

History is shown to be the determining context for the functioning of law and religion, in contradiction to the liberal notion that these are abstract and independently operating principles. The laws that ostensibly limit flogging and regulate work hours are nonfunctional in a situation in which the need for labor is great, as it was in the 1840s. A priest works assiduously for the ruling class, endeavoring to persuade the slaves that their lot is tolerable and just, while they stand formed beneath a cross.

Religion is a central element in *The Last Supper*. This film lacks the formal complexity of *The Other Francisco*, but it too uses a historical document as its catalyst. *The Last Supper* is based on an anecdote about a slaveholder who in 1790 decided to replicate Jesus' act of washing his disciples' feet. Gutiérrez Alea found the account in a work by one of Cuba's most eminent historians, Manuel Moreno Fraginals:

> His Excellency the Count de Casa Bayona decided in an act of deep Christian fervor to humble himself before the slaves. One Holy Thursday he washed twelve Negroes' feet, sat them at his table, and served them food in imitation of Christ. But their the-

ology was somewhat shallow and, instead of behaving like the Apostles, they took advantage of the prestige they thus acquired in their fellow-slaves' eyes to organize a mutiny and burn down the mill. The Christian performance ended with *rancheadores* [hunters of escaped slaves] hunting down the fugitives and sticking on twelve pikes the heads of the slaves before whom His Excellency had prostrated himself.[2]

This historical fragment was fleshed out by Gutiérrez Alea, who added several elements absent from the original description. For example, a slave is selected from each of the distinct African cultures found on the plantation, underlining the continuing influence of their origins. One of the twelve slaves chosen is the movie's "hero," Sebastian, a persistent fugitive whose ear is cut off in the very beginning of the film for having run away once again. The cultural variety among the slaves allows for much interaction between them and the count during the dinner scene. Another important aspect deals with the dilemma posed for the characters of the priest and the overseer. The priest's obligation to instruct the blacks in Christian doctrine is portrayed as being constantly in conflict with the overseer's duties to maximize production. Thus, in broad strokes, *The Last Supper* provides an insightful glance into the functioning of paternalism and religion in slave society.

Gutiérrez Alea has written of the historical analysis and reconstruction that went into the making of *The Last Supper*:

> The storyline was constructed beginning with a very simple paragraph that appears in *The Sugarmill* by Moreno Fraginals. Fortunately, the book offered a suggestive vision, rich in data, and superbly elaborated in relation to the moment which the anecdote recounts. We then had to engage in a more detailed investigation of the epoch, that is, provide ourselves with sufficient details and documentary information in order to arrive at a more concrete image of the reality we wished to depict. In this aspect we counted on the help of María Eugenia Haya, who also collaborated on the script. She efficiently researched documents and organized a file which was most useful not only in constructing the script, but in the later phases of production too (wardrobe, machinery and work tools, scenery, characters, working with the actors, etc.). Moreover, Moreno Fraginals provided us with much additional information and was always available for consultation. It was a collective work, undertaken with great rigor.
>
> The most difficult aspect to research was the world of the slaves since, obviously, there aren't many firsthand accounts. Nonetheless, we undertook an exhaustive and rigorous study here as well, so that our imaginations would be sufficiently motivated without overflowing. In this particular aspect we were aided by Rogelio Martínez Furé, whose research continually makes valuable contributions to understanding our culture's African component.[3]

Sergio Giral also has asserted that he carried out extensive historical research for his films on slavery. In preparing the ground for his adaptations, Giral studied chroniclers of the epoch, such as Suárez y Romero and Cirilo Villaverde, as well as a wide range of both pre- and postrevolutionary historians: José Antonio Saco, Fernando Ortiz, Emilio Roig de Leuchsenring, José Luciano Franco, Elías Entralgo, Grinan Peralta, Rogelio Martínez Furé, Manuel Moreno Fraginals, Rómulo Lachatanere, and others. He also relied on nineteenth-century engravings in order to re-create a rural village.

Robert Rosenstone has argued that, "to be considered 'historical,' rather than simply a costume drama that uses the past as an exotic setting for romance and adventure, a film must engage, directly or obliquely, the issues, ideas, data, and arguments of the ongoing discourse of history."[4] Given the apparent concern of Giral and Gutiérrez Alea with attempting to construct credible historical accounts, it is important to compare their films with some written histories of Cuban slavery.

It is very clear in both movies that the events presented occur in a period of transition. The "intimacy and patriarchy"[5] that were characteristic of earlier generations are here embodied as irrelevant vestiges in the count and in Suárez y Romero. These values are no longer appropriate; they are replaced, as can be seen in *The Other Francisco*, by "intensive exploitation of the Negro."[6] The films are particularly effective in presenting the technological transformations that will influence master-slave relations: the vertical sugar press is replaced by a new horizontal *trapiche* (sugar mill) in *The Last Supper*, the ox-driven machinery by steam power in *The Other Francisco*. In the latter, we see the effects of such transformations on the lives of the slaves: "The machines were a curse to the slave. . . . In their first stage they magnified slavery in an exploitation process that was progressively more bestial. . . . This partial mechanization increased the traditional barbarism of the mill by demanding synchronization of manual work with mechanical processes."[7]

Historical transformation is shown to be not only technological but environmental as well. Ducle, the French sugar master, is using bagasse as fuel to fire the sugar trains because of the tremendous deforestation.[8] The count marvels at his initiative and likes the idea in *The Last Supper*. The new order of slaveholders no longer subscribed to the religious obligations of yore. Pressured by the necessity to produce increasing amounts of sugar, as was Ricardo in *The Other Francisco*, and influenced by Enlightenment thought, "few of the slaveowners knew what those traditional relations were."[9] Ricardo's mother, as a representative of the older generation, attempts to convince her son to give the slaves a day off at Christmas, reminiscing about how things used to be easier. But Ricardo replies that the day makes little difference to the slaves, and all must continue to work in order to meet the demand. In the other film, although the count's behavior would seem to indicate the continued existence of religious belief, the reactions of those around him indicate that his attitudes are completely out of touch with the times. His retainers try to dissuade him from such a foolhardy act, and the slaves think he is crazy. Religion had become a handmaiden of the slave regime,[10] and the distrust of the priest manifested by the slaves in both films can be seen in the *desconfianza* they demonstrate in front of the cleric.[11]

In both of the films, law is conspicuous by its absence. For example, in *The Other Francisco*, although we are told that the law limits whipping to twenty-nine lashes, Francisco is whipped to

death; the count of *The Last Supper* encounters no legal obstacles to having his twelve "disciples" cruelly executed. In general, historians are in agreement with this image, Fernando Ortiz stating that "with great frequency, the slave laws were a dead letter among us, . . . , which were not complied with, but ridiculed."[12] As it is portrayed in these movies, local power was absolute, even to the extent that the *mayoral* in *The Last Supper* could ignore the count's freeing of a slave and force him to remain in bondage.[13] While some scholars, such as Herbert Klein, attempt to salvage the worth of law by arguing for the power of the Church in upholding it,[14] the great majority concur with Franklin Knight: "It was not the efficiency or laxity of the administrative bureaucracy (or, as some writers would have it, the Roman Catholic Church), which most weightily affected the conditions of the slaves. Rather, these conditions were determined by whether or not the slave found himself on the plantation or in the city, and by the unwritten laws of the individual, often very powerful, owner."[15]

The life of a city slave was eminently preferable, and that of a *calesero* (carriage driver), Francisco's position, was "the most desirable."[16] Thus, "the most dreadful threat" and the worst punishment was to send disobedient slaves to the countryside, Francisco's end.[17] There, "the most common punishment was flogging," in many cases with the slave tied to a ladder; called the *escalera*, the name came to describe the fierce repression that took place in the

1840s.[18] Runaways were hunted with dogs and forced to wear bells when captured, just as is Crispín in *The Other Francisco*, and his castration was not uncommon as a final solution to this problem.[19] In Giral's film, slaves sleep no more than four hours, which seems to have been the general rule.[20] It was particularly hard on children, such as "that little boy who fell asleep walking and died, trampled by the oxen."[21] As the exploitation of slave labor became increasingly intense, the *conucos* (small plots of land), which had served

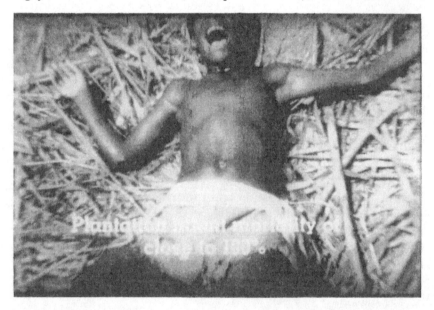

as the source of much nourishment, were eliminated.[22] For that reason, we hear slaves bemoan their absence in *The Other Francisco* while they wait in the dinner line.

The characterizations of the social roles of the rulers in these films are in accord with what is generally accepted in written history. The owners were usually absent, the *mayorales* were commonly white and sadistic, and the *contramayorales* were black. *The Last Supper* adds a nice historical detail in the French sugar master. Men such as Ducle had come to Cuba fleeing the Haitian revolt, which began in 1789.[23]

The portrayal of the slaves in these movies is also relatively accurate. One of the most important elements is the insistence on their varied origins, something rarely done in film or other forms of popular history. Dancing was not only one of the few recreational activities available, but slaves also were often forced to dance, as is Francisco by the *mayoral*, Antonio.[24] The presence of the *mayoral* at the dances was evidently common, perhaps to deter the drums from communicating conspiracies among the slaves.[25] The voice-over assertion in *The Other Francisco* that sexual relations among the slaves were unusual due to the "tremendous imbalance" and "great disequilibrium between the sexes" is undoubtedly correct.[26] Also, there appears to be no question that women very frequently aborted rather than bring children into slavery.[27] Orlando Patterson quoted a 1790 witness of Jamaican slavery as saying that he had often heard women "wish their own children dead, or that they had not bourne them, rather than be obliged to witness their daily punishment."[28]

Abortion, then, was one form of "passive" resistance against slavery; suicide was another. Ortiz recounts that, during the period portrayed in *The Other Francisco*, suicide—"the supreme recourse of the impotent oppressed"—reached epidemic figures, almost double that of homicides.[29] Runaways were a constant problem for Cuban slaveholders.[30] However, there is little doubt that the owners of slaves far preferred the less-active opposition of abortion, suicide, or flight to violent rebellion.

Both of the films end in lengthy montages celebrating slave uprisings. In *The Other Francisco*, we see the burning of the cane fields, the killing of the *contramayoral* with machetes, and the garroting of Antonio, while the omniscient voice recounts the list of nineteenth-century rebellions: 1802, 1824, 1830, 1835, 1837, 1842, and 1843. Then we see soldiers arrive to restore order, beheading and cutting off the hands of slaves, and hanging them with hooks thrust through their ribs, an image probably inspired by William Blake's well-known lithograph. At the end of the film, bands of blacks gather in the mountains overlooking the valleys below; the historical voice talks of the years that would pass before Máximo Gómez would gather blacks for the movement against the Spanish. In *The Last Supper*, the escaped slaves are hunted down and killed one by one; their heads are displayed on pikes. However, one head is missing: that of Sebastian. The film concludes with a montage of Sebastian running through the forest; cinematographically, we are given to understand that he has been transformed into other forms: a hawk, water, rocks, a horse. One intriguing possibility is that Sebastian represents the figure of Baldomero, a *santero* (witch doctor) who took to the hills with followers and avoided capture by changing "himself into a serpent, or a stone, or a tree."[31]

While the conclusions of these films extend the metaphor of rebellion to a degree that incorporates other struggles in Cuban history, it is nonetheless clear that such uprisings were a constant feature of slavery on the island. In some areas during the 1840s, cane fields were set on fire daily and machinery was often destroyed, probably much in the way presented in *The Other Francisco*.[32] Further, the *bagaceras*, the sheds where the bagasse was stored, were one of the "easiest targets for firebug saboteurs."[33] It is just such an arson that covers Crispín's escape. The Haitian revolution had left Cuban slaveholders trembling in fear, and the comments of the French sugar master in *The Last Supper* attest to this constant preoccupation.[34] By the period represented in *The Other Francisco*, "black rebellions had created a climate of terror."[35] Thus, while we might be tempted to argue that the filmmakers overstate their case for slave rebellion, in fact the list that Giral provides at the end of his film is a good deal shorter than that of Fernando Ortiz.[36]

In summary, it could be argued that both of these films meet many of our expectations about what history ought to be. There are, of course, minor objections: usually only second-generation slaves could occupy Francisco's post of *calesero*, although this job is attributable more to Suárez y Romero's interest in making him exceptional than to a decision on Giral's part.[37] And there is one or another absence: Where, for instance, are the backs bent from working in cane fields?[38] But, in general, the films are good history and very good cinema, and that is an irresistible combination.

In the end, however, it is *The Other Francisco* that makes the more important contribution to historical knowledge. *The Last Supper* follows the classic model of both written and filmed history in insisting on the reality of the world that it has in fact created, however much this universe has resulted from research. The major convention of such history is that it has opened a window onto the past rather than constructed a particular version of it. *The Other Francisco* is a different kind of history—a history filmed as a struggle against both much of prerevolutionary historiography as well as the codes of representation typical of Hollywood movies.

Film is an analogical language that can only say "no" by first showing what it wishes to criticize. Giral reproduces the classic style and the identification it creates with individual dramas, only to cut back against it with a critique at the level of both content and form. It could be argued with some justification that he then constructs another closed narrative, the dialectical materialist world of the omniscient historian's voice that excludes all but economic motivations. Nonetheless, in focusing on how history gets written, he has taught us not only about the past but also has explored different ways of re-creating it. *The Other Francisco* may not give all the correct answers, but it raises the right questions—questions as pertinent to historians who work with words as they are useful for those of us who prefer to depict history in visual images.

Suggested Readings

Cepero Bonilla, Raúl. *Azúcar y abolición*. Barcelona: Grijalbo, 1976. (1st ed., 1948.) Early study of the abolition of slavery in Cuba.

Klein, Herbert. *Slavery in the Americas: A Comparative Study of Virginia and Cuba*. Chicago: University of Chicago Press, 1967. Written by one of the first historians to compare conditions in Cuba to those in another country.

Knight, Franklin. *Slave Society in Cuba during the Nineteenth Century*. Madison: University of Wisconsin Press, 1970. Overall analysis of Cuban slave society in the nineteenth century.

Mintz, Sidney W. *Sweetness and Power: The Place of Sugar in Modern History*. New York: Viking, 1985. Focuses on cultural history and the commercialization of sugar.

Montejo, Esteban. *The Autobiography of a Runaway Slave*. Ed. Miguel Barnet. New York: World Publishing Co., 1969. An extraordinary account of life under slavery.

Moreno Fraginals, Manuel. *The Sugarmill: The Socioeconomic Complex of Sugar in Cuba, 1760–1860.* Trans. Cedric Belfrage. New York: Monthly Review Press, 1976. (Spanish publication, 1964.) A superb analysis by Cuba's leading historian.

Mraz, John. "Absolved by History: On the Aesthetics and Ideology of History in the Cuban Film Institute," *Film-Historia* (Barcelona) 3, no. 3 (1993): 385–410. A study of the ways in which Cuban cineastes have incorporated history into their films and thought.

Ortiz, Fernando. *Los negros esclavos.* Havana: Editorial de Ciencias Sociales, 1975. (First published, 1916.) A seminal study of Cuban slavery.

Paquette, Robert L. *Sugar Is Made with Blood: The Conspiracy of La Escalera and the Conflict between Empires over Slavery in Cuba.* Middletown, CT: Wesleyan University Press, 1988. Puts domestic conspiracies to end slavery in Cuba in an international context.

Patterson, Orlando. *The Sociology of Slavery: An Analysis of the Origins, Development, and Structure of Negro Slave Society in Jamaica.* Rutherford, NJ: Fairleigh Dickinson University Press, 1967. An important analysis of slavery in the Caribbean.

Pérez de la Riva, J. *El barracón y otros ensayos.* Havana: Editorial de Ciencias Sociales, 1975. A study of life in the slave quarters.

Rosenstone, Robert A. "The Historical Film as Real History," *Film-Historia* 5, no. 1 (1995): 5–23. An important article that opens up the question of how we think about film and history.

Scott, Rebecca J. *Slave Emancipation in Cuba: The Transition to Free Labor, 1860–1899.* Princeton, NJ: Princeton University Press, 1985. Reveals the resiliency of plantation labor and the role played by the slaves themselves in ending slavery in Cuba.

Suárez y Romero, Anselmo. *Francisco el ingenio, o, Las delicias del campo.* Havana: Publicaciones del Ministerio de Educación, Dirección de Cultura, 1947. The Cuban *Uncle Tom's Cabin*, written in the midnineteenth century and finally published almost one hundred years later.

Thomas, Hugh. *Cuba: The Pursuit of Freedom.* New York: Harper and Row, 1971. A fundamental overview of Cuban history.

CHAPTER EIGHT

Lucía
Inventing Women's History on Film

BARBARA WEINSTEIN

Lucía (1968); produced by Raúl Canosa; directed by
Humberto Solas; written by Humberto Solas, Julio García
Espinosa, and Nelson Rodríguez; black & white; 160 minutes; Instituto Cubano de Arte e Industria Cinematográficos.
In each of three segments (set during key moments in Cuban history in 1895, 1932, and the 1960s), a different woman
named Lucía confronts personal and political crises.

The year 1968—a time of student rebellion, global antiwar protests, and tragic assassinations—was also the moment when
Cuban revolutionary cinema came of age. The two most important
Cuban films of the sixties are Tomás Gutiérrez Alea's Memories of
Underdevelopment and Humberto Solas's Lucía.[1] Each debuted in
1968 and quickly gained the acclaim of critics and the attention of
international audiences. Lucía was particularly appealing to a public, in Cuba and abroad, attracted to its vivid portrayal of Cuban
history, made even more intriguing by the novelty of the film's focus on three Cuban women, each named Lucía.

The format of Solas's film was not, in and of itself, particularly
unusual; many previous European and North American films had
adopted this convention in which three separate stories are knit together by a common theme, object, or person.[2] But Solas's use of
the triptych was especially ambitious because each of the three stories took place at a formative moment in Cuban history—the War
for Independence (1895), the "failed" revolution of 1932–33, and

123

the socialist revolution's Literacy Campaign ("196?"). Each segment was made with a different cinematic technique: exaggerated melodrama for the 1895 one, grim realism for the second one, and situation comedy for the contemporary story. Yet, what earned the greatest attention for the film was the significant presence of women in its stories. Indeed, *Lucía* is often described as a history of Cuban women, or of Cuban women's emancipation.[3] As such, it is unique among Latin American films of that era and is especially appealing to history instructors sensitive to the need to incorporate women's history into their courses. Yet, how accurate is the historical depiction in the film? Can it be reasonably characterized as chronicling the history of Cuban women? If so, what are its limitations as a work of "women's history"?

I ask these questions not to determine whether *Lucía* is a historically sound or sufficiently feminist film for Latin American history courses. Whatever its shortcomings, it is a remarkable film that is still worth viewing. Rather, I am interested in exploring the relationship between *Lucía*'s portrayal of women in history and the embryonic state of women's history, as a subdiscipline, at the time that the film was made. There has been such an explosion of historical studies on women and gender over the last two decades that it is easy to forget that in 1968 there were very few serious works on women's history in Cuba or anywhere else. Not only has there been a massive increase in research on women in the last two decades, but recent years also have witnessed intense debates about the way in which attention to women or gender roles challenges traditional or official historical narratives. Such conversations were either incipient or uninitiated at the moment that Solas made *Lucía*. I am assuming, therefore, that Solas's film will reflect this vacuum in the historiography and will be limited by the absence of both serious historical research on women and an autonomous women's movement in Cuba. Even so, I would argue that the film contains images of women's experience that easily lend themselves to feminist interpretation and provide an excellent basis for discussing the challenges involved in portraying women in history.

Before analyzing the film itself, we need to consider the context in which it was made. Humberto Solas, the film's director and author, joined the revolutionary struggle against Fulgencio Batista at the age of fourteen and then became deeply involved in the emergence of film as a crucial medium for politicization in revolutionary Cuba. It thus seems reasonable to assume that his desire to make this film was partly a response to a particular phase of Cuban revolutionary politics. Moreover, to make such a long, ambitious, and expensive film, he needed the enthusiastic approval of the official film institute (ICAIC, or Instituto Cubano de Arte e Industria Cinematográficos). Two separate factors probably served to prepare the ground for this project. First, 1968 was the one-hundredth anniversary of the outbreak of Cuba's Ten Years' War (1868–1878), a failed anticolonial insurrection portrayed in the official revolutionary history as the initial step toward the eventual emancipation of the island from foreign political and economic domination. This anniversary created an auspicious moment for a film that would provide a revolutionary interpretation of Cuban history.

Less predictably, it also offered an excellent opportunity to emphasize the role of women in earlier political struggles. Throughout 1968 the women's magazine *Mujeres* published a series of short biographies of heroic women who had participated in the campaign for independence. The Federation of Cuban Women (FMC, or Federación de Mujeres Cubanas), a government-sponsored "feminine" (not feminist) organization, resurrected such historical figures as Ana Betancourt de Mora, who spoke on behalf of women's rights before the insurrectionary congress in 1869, and collections of articles on "exemplary Cuban women" began to circulate.[4]

All of this attention to heroic women was unprecedented for a revolutionary culture whose symbols, up to that point, had been resolutely masculine. There were very few women within the inner circles of the revolutionary leadership, and their participation in the paid work force actually declined during the first five years of the revolutionary era.[5] As for the prerevolutionary Cuban women's movement, which could be considered the most successful "first-wave" feminist movement in Latin America, it had been dismissed by the revolutionary regime as hopelessly bourgeois due to its emphasis on suffrage and legal reforms.[6]

The disengagement of women from certain aspects of the socialist project became unacceptable to the revolutionary leadership as Cuba entered the phase known as Communist Construction. From 1966 to 1970 the Havana government embarked on a program that emphasized capital accumulation through increased production for export (mainly sugar) and reduced levels of consumption. The intense demand for workers in the export sector caused labor shortages and made volunteer work the foremost badge of revolutionary ardor. The strategy also led to severe shortages of even some basic consumer goods, making "moral" rather than "material" incentives the order of the day.[7] Under these circumstances, a large pool of unemployed women, whose lives were more closely linked to the process of consumption than production, was a luxury that the revolution could ill afford. Moreover, the government sought not only to mobilize women's labor but also their political enthusiasm for this period of revolutionary self-sacrifice.[8] The year 1968, then, was the perfect time to release a film that not only chronicled the historical struggles of the Cuban people but also highlighted the role of women in those struggles and demonstrated the benefits gained by women as a result of the revolution.

Solas may have been responding to political exigencies in making this film, but he eschewed the most politically didactic approach, which would have been to depict a trio of "great women" in Cuban history. This strategy might have been the easiest—a series of portraits that showed notable women being as brave and heroic as Cuba's great men—and it would have been consistent with existing feminist historiographical traditions. But for Solas, the committed socialist, it would have been incompatible with the desire to portray "ordinary" women in extraordinary circumstances. And a film about great women would have been a poor vehicle for demonstrating how much women's status in Cuba had improved with the triumph of the revolution.

From the perspective of a women's historian, Solas's rejection of the portraits-of-great-women approach is hardly lamentable. When women's history first emerged as a major enterprise in the 1970s, there was a wave of criticism directed against precisely this tendency in feminist scholarship, with the new women historians arguing that an exclusive emphasis on great women tended to marginalize the experiences of the vast majority of women, who had been barred from formal participation in public life. Indeed, in emphasizing the as-good-as-men qualities of great women, such portrayals even ran the risk of denigrating the struggles and achievements of "unknown" women and of ignoring the entire issue of gender and difference and the processes by which female identities are constructed.[9]

However, once Solas resolved to organize his film around the experiences and struggles of three ordinary women, he was effectively navigating without a map. There were few or no studies of the alternative forms adopted by women to participate in political life or of the changing configurations of gender roles and symbols in response to political change. There had been no significant scholarly effort to valorize the informal networks and solidarities of women's everyday lives, to document their particular experiences during periods of political turmoil, and even less to rethink sexuality and traditional family structures.

Furthermore, Solas's strategy of portraying three "epic" moments in Cuban history was not necessarily compatible with the goal of highlighting women's roles in that nation's history. One of the crucial tenets of women's history has been, precisely, that once historians concern themselves primarily with women's experience, they may have to rethink the master narratives and conventional periodizations of "men's history." A particular epoch may have a very different impact on men and women, and crucial moments for women's emancipation may not coincide with especially important moments in the more conventional accounts.[10] Solas, therefore, was operating with two handicaps when viewed through contemporary eyes: the absence of sophisticated historical interpretations of women's political activity, and his conceptualization of the film around three standard "great moments" in Cuban history.

～

Lacking alternative guideposts for his film, Solas had to resort to more traditional images of women and women's sexuality in his construction of the three Lucías. Perhaps the clearest example is Lucía number one, a sexually frustrated "spinster," a female figure straight out of the melodramatic tradition. Her characterization seems the most at odds with any sort of feminist or emancipatory project, but *all* three women appear politically passive despite being surrounded by intense political activity; each is the victim or the beneficiary of historical events, but not one has an active hand in making that history, except inadvertently.

Lucía number one is an upper-class white woman already consigned to "old maid" status. She appears to be living a normal life amid the chaos and catastrophe of Cuba's bloody war for independence, but gradually the facade of normalcy cracks. An innocuous-looking sewing circle in Lucía's home is revealed to be part of the effort to supply the rebel troops, and we soon learn that Lucía's brother, Felipe, is a rebel leader whose troops are camped on the family's remote coffee plantation. Even more disturbing is the ongoing presence of Fernandina, a madwoman who roams the streets of this provincial town raving and moaning. During the sewing

Solas's first Lucía is a " 'spinster'... straight out of the melodramatic tradition." *Courtesy Museum of Modern Art*

circle, another "old maid" titillates these proper young women (and visibly upsets Lucía) with the story of the event that drove Fernandina to madness—a gang-rape of nuns (including Fernandina) by Spanish soldiers. The storyteller's delight in recounting this tale raises some doubt about its veracity, but we do not doubt that Fernandina's condition is somehow connected to the horrors of war.

Despite her concern for her brother and dutiful sewing of clothing for the rebels, Lucía's involvement in the conflict seems, at best, superficial. A sensitive and romantic soul, she is easily and eagerly distracted by the attentions of a handsome stranger, Rafael. But the scenes of her "girlish" ecstasy at finally falling in love are extremely painful for the viewer because we are almost instantly aware that she is being deceived. Yet, in the classic "love-is-blind" mode, she does not even become suspicious when Rafael repeatedly interrogates her as to the location of the family's coffee plantation.

Lucía's romantic reverie is briefly interrupted by the "revelation" that Rafael has a wife and child in Spain. But her desperate desire for love—both romantic and carnal—makes her vulnerable to his entreaties despite all the evidence of deception (and despite a frantic warning from Fernandina). Eventually succumbing to Rafael's powers of seduction in an especially tawdry scene, Lucía at last agrees to run away with him to the mysterious coffee plantation. As they approach their destination, Rafael shoves Lucía off his horse to the ground, and from this humiliating position she witnesses the disaster provoked by her uncontrollable passion. The Spanish troops that she has unintentionally led to the estate surprise the rebel soldiers; a complete slaughter would have ensued were it not for the dramatic arrival of African rebel soldiers who, completely naked and fearless, rout the Spanish. (The representation of Afro-Cubans in this scene as "noble primitives" indicates that women were not the only group that Solas portrayed with generic images.) Nonetheless, when the smoke of battle clears, the field is littered with dead bodies, including that of Lucía's beloved brother, Felipe.

Lucía is then transformed into another stock figure of melodrama—the woman scorned. Somehow managing to find her way back to her hometown, she comes upon Rafael in the main square and stabs him to death. Now completely mad, she is about to be dragged off by Spanish officials when Fernandina (with the special authority that madwomen have in this type of situation) stops them and takes Lucía's tormented face in her hands. The segment ends with this moment of communion between the two victims of war's horrors.

As a work of women's history, this segment is problematic in many respects. Some are obvious without additional historical context: this Lucía is only a marginal participant in the great event of her time, except when she inadvertently causes a terrible disaster, including the death of her own brother, through her "feminine" weakness. Indeed, this weakness is made even starker by contrast with Felipe, who shows up for a brief visit looking like a nineteenth-century version of Che Guevara, and who effortlessly resists the comforts of home, despite the pleas of the women in the household, to return to the battlefield. Lucía and Felipe can be viewed as representing (Solas's view of) factions of the Cuban bourgeoisie in this period. If Felipe is the virile, elite figure who embraces the cause of independence and allies with the popular classes, then Lucía represents the weak upper-class Cuban who is seduced by foreign promises and pleasures and betrays her or his own people as a result. (To be sure, Lucía does avenge herself and her people

by killing Rafael, but only after hundreds of lives have been lost.)
This representation of the Cuban upper class's role in the War for
Independence is intriguing, but it hardly illuminates the role of
women in that conflict.

It should be emphasized that this role was not inconsiderable.
Aside from the participation of the famous "women warriors," the
mambisas who fought side by side with men or nursed the wounded
on the battlefield, many "ordinary" Cuban women had their lives
transformed by a war in which the line between civilian and com-
batant was blurred. The Spanish troops employed a scorched-earth
strategy and foreshadowed twentieth-century warfare techniques
by relocating large portions of the rural population, male and female, in what we now call concentration camps. Thus, many of the
war's victims, like Fernandina and Lucía, were women. But many
of them, far from becoming pathetic madwomen, routinely fled from
the Spanish authorities into rebel-held areas where they played a
crucial role in clothing and feeding the Cuban soldiers and running
the field hospitals. These women also played an essential role in
the struggle by forming proindependence clubs that raised funds
and gathered support for the movement. The sewing circle portrayed
in the film is only a faint shadow of the serious efforts made by
Cuban women away from the battlefield to advance the cause of
independence. Lucía herself gently chastizes her sewing companions by reminding them that "if anyone will win the war, it will be
our troops" (the latter being figured as entirely male in the film).
Typically, heroism in war is associated with men and serves to legitimate women's subordinate position, but in the War for Independence, it was often women who were directly in harm's way.
The unusually prominent role played by women was actually used
as a major moral justification for the postindependence campaign
for women's rights. But there is no hint of this in Solas's film.[11]

Lucía number two is the least memorable of the three heroines; and
the second segment, set in 1932, with its grim realism and melancholy mood, recedes into the background whenever critics discuss
the film.[12] The story opens with a pregnant Lucía working in a
cigar factory, but we quickly flash back to her earlier life as a pam-
pered daughter in an urban middle-class family. Despite her comfortable material circumstances, this Lucía is vaguely dissatisfied

with her existence. This discontent manifests itself in her disdain for her vain and frivolous mother and in her attraction to the serious and committed Aldo, who is in the thick of the struggle against the dictator, Gerardo Machado.

Abruptly, and with no apparent hesitation, Lucía decides to defy bourgeois convention and go live with Aldo. She becomes his devoted helpmate; and, through him, she too becomes involved in the struggle against Machado. At first, her role mainly takes the form of anxiously awaiting the return of Aldo and his mates from intermittent gun battles with Machado's police and tending to their wounds and bruises. But in order to be of more help to Aldo, she seeks a job in a cigar factory. In the workplace, she and Flora, whose husband is Aldo's friend and associate, begin stirring up the other women workers against the dictatorship, eventually organizing a walkout and protest.

These scenes are followed by a brief period of euphoria as Machado falls and a new "revolutionary" government takes power. However, disillusionment soon sets in as Aldo, the true believer, witnesses the easy corruption of his former comrades, who discard their (ill-defined) revolutionary ideals for cushy jobs and orgies with prostitutes. Unlike Flora, who seems to be encouraging her husband to sell out, the now-pregnant Lucía supports Aldo, morally and financially, as he resists the temptation to trade in his principles for a comfortable government post. Indeed, he resolves to resume the armed struggle, now against the fraudulent revolutionary regime, and in the next scene we witness his (inevitable) death at the hands of the new security forces. Without Aldo, Lucía is alone, pregnant and grieving. Although not driven to madness like Lucía number one (which would have been inappropriate to the realistic, melancholy tone of this segment), Lucía ends up abandoned and dejected, wandering with suitcase in hand and with nowhere to go.

Again, the crucial question that faced Solas in making this segment was how to put a woman into this political episode. As with the first segment, a man is the vehicle for Lucía's entrance into political life. Furthermore, all of her political activity is portrayed as help for Aldo and as support for *his* struggle. To be sure, we sense her dissatisfaction with middle-class life in Cuba, which explains her attraction to the sweet but serious Aldo, but her ideas and motives are inchoate, and she never goes beyond her role as the loyal and dedicated wife who provides her husband with the moral support he needs to fulfill his revolutionary destiny. Even her heroic role in the tobacco workers' protest against Machado appears as an effort to help Aldo.

It is undeniable that women often become involved in politics precisely through their roles as wives and mothers of politically active men. But the events of the 1930s certainly offered other options for portraying women in politics or public life. However, the way in which Solas conceptualizes the "revolution" of 1932–33 and, indeed, this entire period of Cuban history makes it unlikely that he will resort to these alternative portrayals.

The movement against Machado is depicted as having been led by small bands of (male) armed fighters; only in the final moments before his fall do we witness mass mobilization and protest against his dictatorship. As such, the movement seems to be a foreshadowing of the guerrilla struggle that will topple the Batista dictatorship in 1959 (which helps to explain why the director never feels compelled to defend the use of armed force against the Machado regime).[13] But this depiction leaves little space for women's participation, except through their traditional roles as loyal wives and lovers who comfort the wounded and mourn the dead.

While armed bands of university students did play a significant role in the anti-Machado struggle, the movement was much more protracted and complicated than one might conclude from watching this film. By 1930 a broad spectrum of political groups had begun organizing and openly protesting against the regime, and prominent among them were the left-wing and reformist factions of the feminist movement. Women played an active role in the anti-Machado struggle, and many were beaten up—and a few killed—by his security police.[14]

The early 1930s was also a period of extraordinary economic hardship for the Cuban people as the bottom fell out of the sugar market and as political turbulence left the nation with an only partially functioning government. Not only were the poor unable to find work, but also even middle-class civil servants received their salaries on an irregular basis, and hunger was a widespread phenomenon. Because women were almost always responsible for the purchase and preparation of food, this crisis would have affected them even more directly than their husbands and would have meant that very few of them could have remained aloof from the political events of that time.[15]

Then there is the issue of periodization. Of the three segments of the film, the second is most illustrative of the way in which women's history becomes distorted or marginalized by a periodization that emphasizes "great events." There is no indication whatsoever in this depiction of Cuba during the 1930s that it was the home of Latin America's most active and successful feminist movement. Due to their pre-1933 political activism, leaders of women's groups were able to push through female suffrage in 1934 and to promote a series of social reforms—maternity leave, equal pay for equal work—that were among the most progressive in the world in the late 1930s. This accomplishment is all the more remarkable considering that, until 1930, it was perfectly legal in Cuba for a husband to murder his wife if he suspected her of infidelity. But the story of these campaigns for women's rights would hardly be compatible with the official image of the 1933 revolution as an utter, if noble, failure. And this story would hardly be regarded as instructive for a revolutionary society that had dismissed pre-1959 Cuban feminism as a bourgeois movement whose emphasis on suffrage and constitutional rights made it irrelevant to lower-class Cuban women. The 1933 revolution, represented as a complete failure, was more inspiring to the post-1959 revolutionary regime than the partial successes of the feminist movement during the 1930s.

~

The mood alters radically, along with Cuban society, in the story of Lucía number three. Set in "196?", this segment seems to blend the concerns of the Communist Construction era (1966–1970) with the Literacy Campaign of 1961. The very vagueness of the date reflects the official view of the revolution as an ongoing process, confronting obstacles that will not disappear overnight. With this segment we also continue our journey down the traditional Cuban social hierarchy; Lucía number three is a rural worker, the figure often cited as the leading beneficiary of the Cuban Revolution. And she is a woman of color—a beautiful *mulata* who embodies the nationalist image of the naturally sensual woman of the Cuban countryside.

The final Lucía follows the conventions of slapstick and situation comedy, a welcome relief from the heavy melodrama and melancholy of the first two segments. A running narration, set to the tune of "Guantanamera" and punctuated by the gossip of older women in the community, accompanies the story of Lucía and Tomás. The segment opens with the other women workers teasing Lucía as she emerges from a "rough night" in her boyfriend's house,

The third Lucía is a "beautiful *mulata* who embodies the nationalist image of the naturally sensual woman of the Cuban countryside." *Courtesy Museum of Modern Art*

but the viewer can sense trouble brewing from this very first en-counter. On her way to work in the fields, Lucía informs one of her companions that Tomás has forbidden her to work outside the home once they are married. While in prerevolutionary Cuba such a pro-hibition might have been regarded as a benefit, here it is portrayed as a deprivation for Lucía and as strictly opposed to the interests of the revolution.

We next see the newlyweds on their weeklong honeymoon, which they spend shut up in their home in a prolonged sexual frolic. This idyll ends when Lucía and Tomás emerge to attend a birthday party for a relative at the community center. Tomás is instantly iden-tifiable as the classic jealous husband; predictably, when another man tries to teach Lucía a new dance introduced by some rather decadent-looking foreigners, Tomás physically attacks him. Fur-thermore, when Tomás has to return to work the next day, leaving him unable to check on Lucía's whereabouts, he decides to lock her up in the house and nail the windows shut, forbidding her even to have female visitors.

Despite her boredom and loneliness, Lucía obeys Tomás and makes only half-hearted attempts to alter the terms of her impris-

onment. But the other members of the community are less ame-
nable. Led by Flavio and Angelina, an older couple who head the
local Committee for the Defense of the Revolution, the neighbors
informally denounce Tomás for treating Lucía as his slave and for
"falling behind" in Cuba's march toward a socialist society, and
they urge him to let her go back to work. Ignoring this considerable
pressure, Tomás declares that "the revolution stops at my door,"
and he refuses to loosen his grip.

Relief soon arrives in the form of a literacy teacher from Havana, a young man designated to live and work in Lucía and Tomás's
home because she is illiterate. Tomás predictably refuses to have
the young man in his house, but the teacher has the moral force of
the revolution on his side, and Lucía clinches the argument by asking Tomás, if they throw the teacher out, "What will the counterrevolutionaries think?" By this point, Lucía is starting to chafe at
her confinement. And, needless to say, the teacher plays precisely
the subversive role that Tomás feared; horrified by Lucía's subservience and "enslavement," the young man asks her how she can
put up with such conditions. She responds, as always, that she loves
Tomás, but when jealousy prompts her husband to assault the
teacher, she finally snaps. Fleeing to Angelina's home, she declares
her intention to leave Tomás, and the next day she returns to work.

Determined to force his wife to come back to him, Tomás seeks
her out at the salt marsh where she is working, only to be set upon
and driven off by her female workmates. Dejected and humiliated,
Tomás collapses on a beach but is soon joined by Lucía, who announces that she still loves him and wants to come back to him, but
it must be on different terms, and she must be allowed to work. He
refuses to accept her terms, but the scene ends with a playful, slapstick chase, suggesting that they will eventually work out their
difficulties. Meanwhile, a young girl—representing the new generation—observes their antics and bursts into laughter.

Compared to the other two segments, the story of Lucía number three is more successful at raising the central issues facing
Cuban women at that particular point in time. And given the
director's class sympathies for his characters in the final segment,
the portrayal of women's social life is much more positive and
less demeaning than in the previous stories. The story of Lucía number three also seems undeniably critical of traditional macho attitudes and constraints on women's lives. At the same time, it bears
some similarities to the first two segments. This Lucía, despite her

considerable charm and personality, is mainly a passive spectator, not an active historical figure, or even someone who directly shapes her immediate circumstances. As for the other women in her community, they try to intervene in her situation, but their efforts amount to little until a man arrives. Only under the influence of the male teacher is Lucía finally able to take decisive action to resolve her predicament.

It is also important to consider how the immediate political context for this segment affected the choice of cinematic techniques and to reflect on the inclusions and omissions dictated by its political objectives. The decision to make the final segment of the film a comedy was by no means incidental to the director's political project. While the Cuban government was eager for women to enter the labor force, this campaign was not envisioned as disrupting traditional family structures or challenging established gender roles. On the contrary, the official rhetoric of the revolution extolled the nuclear family as the basic building block of the Cuban nation. Furthermore, the government could hardly afford to alienate the affections of the male population by aggressively promoting a feminist agenda or by intruding too heavily into domestic life.[16]

Given the delicate balance the government was trying to strike on the "woman question," the choice of a comic motif for the final segment made perfect sense. Rather than a harsh denunciation of male chauvinism, we have the film making gentle fun of men's foibles. *Lucía* also avoids presenting the issue as a broad or societal problem by focusing on one couple and on an extreme case of masculine possessiveness. Contrasted with all the other men in the community, who seem to be complying with their wives' desire to work, Tomás is presented as a caricature of the jealous husband. The explanation for his behavior (implicit and explicit) is similarly peculiar to him. According to the local gossip, his father was also a domestic tyrant and never let his mother leave the home. Moreover, his relationship with Lucía reproduces some of the hierarchical characteristics of prerevolutionary society. He looks white, while she is clearly a *mulata*, a "racial" difference heightened by the frequent references to Tomás treating his wife like a slave. Despite the new Cuba being a "classless" society, we can also perceive lingering differences in social status: Tomás is literate and a truck driver, while Lucía is illiterate and a field hand. And we witness another one of Tomás's prerevolutionary defects when he exploits the labor of the visiting literacy teacher. In short, Tomás is a neanderthal, a pathetic remnant of the presocialist era, rather than someone whose behavior is symptomatic of gender tensions in Cuban society as a whole.[17]

What is omitted as a result of the comic strategy that Solas employs in this segment? There is no reference to the thorniest issue for feminist discussions of women and work: the problems of mothers with young children. All of Lucía's workmates seem to be older women with grown children, and Lucía herself manages to avoid pregnancy despite frequent sex and the absence of any evident birth control methods. There is also no reference to the less dramatic but certainly widespread struggles over the division of household tasks; given that Tomás will not even let Lucía leave the house, we cannot imagine that he is going to agree to do the cooking. It is also interesting to consider how the story would have changed if the literacy teacher were a woman (as the majority were). While this switch would have eliminated any possibility of sexual innuendo between Lucía and her teacher (at least in the homophobic Cuba of the 1960s), it would have created a different type of tension by having Lucía living in the same house with a woman who had been willing to leave home and family for the revolution.

There is yet another issue that this segment of the film simultaneously raises and skirts: the question of domestic violence.[18] Lucía, forcibly confined to her home, is surely by current standards an abused wife, but Solas stops short of portraying her as a victim of physical aggression. There are several scenes that show Tomás restraining her, where the balance threatens to tip away from slapstick comedy toward overt violence, but the director is careful never to cross that line. Thus, when Lucía flees to Angelina's home, she looks "messed up"; her hair is disheveled, and her eyes are swollen with tears. But her face reveals no shiner, no bruises, no bloody lip, all of which would have been incompatible with the comic tone of the segment. She is both abused and not abused. The director once again treads this fine line in the final scene, which shows Lucía and the still unreconciled Tomás struggling with each other on the beach. Film critics always call attention to the laughter of the little girl who is watching them (and who embodies the "new socialist Cuban" free from the taint of prerevolutionary culture).[19] What they usually do not mention is that just before she laughs, when she first catches sight of the warring couple, we see a look of concern on her face—as one might expect from a child witnessing a potentially violent encounter. But the notes of an upbeat musical refrain

signal to the audience that this moment is a comical one, reinforced
by the girl's rapid change in mood. It was, in the late 1960s, a cheer-
ful and reassuring end to the film; even if Lucía and Tomás *could*
not work things out, surely the next generation would. With the
passage of time, and the fading of the film's utopian promise, the
comic antics and the little girl's laughter seem less effective at ef-
facing the underlying violence.

~

Despite the constant presence of women in this film, the three Lucías
seem more illustrative of the relationship between class and nation
than of the role of women in Cuban history. Indeed, one way in
which this film can be read is as allegory, with each Lucía representing, not Cuban women, or even a particular Cuban woman, but
the evolution of the Cuban nation toward a socialist society through
the progression of social classes. The Lucía of the 1895 struggle
for independence represents the declining colonial aristocracy, finally forced to face the tyranny of Spanish colonial rule. The Lucía
of 1932–33 represents an urban middle class that, despite some
progressive impulses, lacked a well-defined ideology that would
allow it to resist the decadence and corruption of Cuban society
during the period of U.S. domination. The Lucía of "196?", meanwhile, is a rural worker and a woman of color, and thus represents
the backbone of the new socialist society.

This allegorical function may help explain Solas's omission of
motherhood as an important female identity. Lucía number two,
the least sensual of the three women, does become pregnant, but
otherwise motherhood is virtually absent as a theme. This omission may be a consequence of the film's structure, with each Lucía
intensely focused on her (sexual) relationship with a particular male.
Such intensity would have been severely complicated by the presence of children, who would inevitably share the mother's attention and detract from her sexual identity. It is also possible that
Solas *did* see the three Lucías as mothers—whose collective offspring is the Cuban nation.

By current standards, Solas's film may be unsatisfying as a
portrayal of women in history, but by no means should it be dismissed for being insufficiently feminist. As one reviewer pointed
out, "The film makes an important contribution to the image of
women in film by the very length of time given to female activities." Viewing *Lucía* with our now (presumably) heightened sensi-

bilities regarding women's history allows us not only to critique its deficiencies but also to appreciate and explore issues that the film raises but fails to develop. For example, if we view Lucía number one in terms of her limited options for personal expression and sexual satisfaction, her vulnerability to her seducer becomes the result of social circumstances, not personal weakness. A more critical view of romantic love, and a more positive evaluation of female collective activities (portrayed in the film as frivolous or infantile), would also complicate the whole question of pleasure and personal satisfaction. But perhaps the most compelling and potentially feminist moment is the final scene, the instant of profound solidarity between the degraded Fernandina and the outraged Lucía, which is a result of their shared sexual vulnerability and which raises a host of issues about gender as a social and political bond that can transcend class.[20]

When viewed from this perspective, the second segment also contains many issues of relevance to discussions of women's history. An obvious one is the solidarity among the women of different generations and backgrounds who work in the cigar factory. There is also a minor, but recurring, theme that deserves greater attention. Lucía's despised mother repeatedly refers to the rumors that her husband has taken a mistress, and nervously asserts her own charms as well as her disdain for the "other woman," who is reputedly a woman of color. Lucía dismisses her mother's anxieties as foolish prattle, but the audience presumes that the mother's fears are well grounded. Later on, Flora voices the same concerns about her husband, Antonio, who has taken a government post in Havana, and once again Lucía dismisses the concern as nothing but foolishness. This time the audience *knows* that Flora's fears are not baseless because we actually see Antonio enthusiastically participating in a drunken orgy. Solas never develops this theme; indeed, it is Lucía's lack of empathy for these betrayed middle-class women (and her automatic defense of men's honor) that makes her untenable as a protofeminist figure. But these instances offer an excellent opportunity to discuss women's sexuality, the sexual double standard, and the precariousness of their class position in bourgeois Cuban society.

The third segment, despite its omissions and evasions, is a veritable banquet of issues for discussion and inquiry from a feminist perspective. Work is portrayed in the film as being both a revolutionary duty and as a source of pleasure and accomplishment. The women clearly enjoy each other's company in the workplace, and the network of friendships they develop through their work routines are central to their lives in the community. While this portrayal may have reflected the government's desire to make work outside the home more attractive to women, it also shows a female culture that is vibrant, supportive, and energizing. And it implies that if labor conditions are decent, even women from modest backgrounds may want to work for reasons other than material survival.[21]

The film also raises the very vexing and crucial issue of how a feminist agenda can be implemented in the presumably private space of the home. Even if the Cuban government had limited objectives in persuading women to enter the work force (and in convincing their husbands to cooperate), the campaign entailed some "interference" in existing domestic arrangements as well as a challenge to aspects of traditional patriarchal authority. The women in this segment of the film repeatedly resort to this countervailing state authority in claiming their right to work. Thus, while the viewer knows that Lucía wants to go back to work because she is going stir crazy, she and all her workmates use the language of revolutionary duty to dispute Tomás's authority over her person. And when Tomás wants to send the literacy teacher away, Lucía stops him, not by telling him how much she wants to learn to read but by asking, "What will the counterrevolutionaries think?" The comic setting, of course, blunts the implied threat of state coercion in this comment, but it is nonetheless the decisive factor in the installation of the "subversive" literacy teacher in their home. Furthermore, it implies that the boundaries between public and private space (so jealously guarded by Tomás) have been virtually erased by the revolution and that this erasure is to women's advantage.

As a strategy for women's resistance and emancipation, this recourse to the state is a delicate and ambiguous one, for it counters male authority by accepting the potentially even more constraining authority of the state. In a farcical setting, Lucía can casually use the threat that Tomás will be seen as giving aid and comfort to counterrevolutionaries, but I suspect that many Cuban women (and quite a few public officials) would have felt uncomfortable regularly asserting state authority to ensure more equitable domestic arrangements.[22] Yet women's emancipation, almost alone among movements for social change, heavily depends upon the transformation of the domestic sphere.

Finally, it is tempting to contemplate what a fourth Lucía, set in the Cuba of 1995 (exactly one hundred years from the initial segment), would be like. Over the last three decades, the position of women in Cuba has changed radically, with divorce, political activity, and paid employment becoming routine aspects of their lives. To complicate matters further, recent years also have seen profound economic hardship, serious ideological challenges to the socialist project, and the return of such prerevolutionary "cancers" as prostitution. Indeed, it seems unlikely that Solas's film could absorb this fourth Lucía, whose story would be difficult to reduce to a male-centered relationship. And there could be little doubt that her tale would undermine the director's vision of history as a steady progression toward national liberation.

Suggested Readings

Carroll, Berenice A., ed. *Liberating Women's History*. Urbana: University of Illinois Press, 1976. A pioneering anthology that examines the issues involved in making women visible in history, with particular attention paid to the relationship between gender and class.

Miller, Francesca. *Latin American Women and the Search for Social Justice*. Hanover, NH: University Press of New England, 1991. An excellent survey of the roles women have played in a variety of social movements, both reformist and revolutionary, in Latin America.

Nazzari, Muriel. "The 'Woman Question' in Cuba: An Analysis of Material Constraints on Its Solution." *Signs* 2 (1983): 246–63. Written well before the current crisis in the Cuban economy, this article offers an intriguing discussion of the low priority assigned to services crucial to the transformation of gender roles in society.

Padula, Alfred, and Lois Smith. "Women in Socialist Cuba, 1959–84." In *Cuba: Twenty-five Years of Revolution*, ed. Sandor Halebsky and John M. Kirk, 79–92. New York: Praeger, 1985. A brief but stimulating account of women's gains in socialist Cuba, which the authors show to be considerable despite male resistance and government ambivalence.

Pérez-Stable, Marifeli. *The Cuban Revolution: Origins, Course, and Legacy*. New York: Oxford University Press, 1993. A comprehensive study of the transformations and limitations of Cuban socialism. The author devotes substantial space to changes in family law and gender roles.

Stoner, K. Lynn. *From the House to the Streets: The Cuban Women's Movement for Legal Reform, 1898–1940*. Durham, NC: Duke University Press, 1993. By far the best account of pre-1959 Cuban feminism.

A thoroughly researched and carefully argued study of women's political participation and social activism from the independence period to 1940.

CHAPTER NINE

Gabriela
An Evocation of Elite Culture in Early Twentieth-Century Latin America

JAMES D. HENDERSON

Gabriela *(1983); produced by Ibrahim Moussa and Harold Nebenzal; directed by Bruno Barreto; written by Bruno Barreto and Leopoldo Serran based on the novel* Gabriela, cravo e canela *(1958) by Jorge Amado; color; 99 minutes; Sultana. In a Brazilian port city in 1925, sensual and free-spirited Gabriela (Sonia Braga) marries old-fashioned bar owner Nacib (Marcello Mastroianni), but their passion for each other is tested by their contrasting ideas of proper behavior.*

In spite of its steamy sex scenes, and notwithstanding the miscasting of portly, middle-aged Marcello Mastroianni as the lover of sultry Sonia Braga, *Gabriela* stands as the best feature-length film depicting elite culture and mentality in early twentieth-century Latin America. Set in the Brazilian port town of Ilhéus in 1925, the film is at a glance the love story of a thirty-year-old Syrian immigrant and bar owner named Nacib and the orphan Gabriela, a refugee from Brazil's drought-ravaged Northeast. Yet the film is much more than that. Thanks to the fact that *Gabriela* closely follows the novel upon which it is based, Jorge Amado's celebrated *Gabriela, cravo e canela* (1958; translated as *Gabriela, Clove and Cinnamon*, 1962), it splendidly conveys the excitement with which

Latin American leaders bent to the task of modernizing their nations during the first decades of the twentieth century. By the 1920s, Brazilian cacao growers and exporters (like the protagonists of *Gabriela*), Argentine cattlemen, Colombian coffee exporters, and businessmen elsewhere in the region were filled with a confidence fired by the extraordinary earnings of commodity exports to the global market. Men of a positivist temperament, they shared a belief in the idea of progress. They were confident that their newfound wealth would help them to close the gap between their backward nations and the admired advanced civilizations of Europe.

This essay endeavors to help viewers of *Gabriela* get behind its distracting carnality in order to see the film as the exploration of a significant though little-studied moment in Latin American history.[1] First, *Gabriela* is related to the novel upon which it is based and to the novel's author. Second, the film's three principal themes—elite mentality in early twentieth-century Latin America, economic and political change produced by the bonanza in commodity and raw material exports, and criticism of bourgeois attitudes dominating society during that historical moment—are discussed. Finally, the issues of sex and nudity as portrayed both in *Gabriela* and in Latin American popular culture at large are addressed.

Brazil's best-known contemporary novelist, Jorge Amado, gained international recognition during the 1960s, first through the publication of *Gabriela, Clove and Cinnamon* and, subsequently, of *Dona Flor and Her Two Husbands* (1969). Each of the novels inspired both a popular television series in Brazil and a feature-length film. *Gabriela* and *Dona Flor and Her Two Husbands* are novels of Amado's maturity. They stand as loving evocations of his home state, Bahia, and its culture, cuisine, and people.

Amado emerged as one of Brazil's leading writers in 1942 when he published *The Violent Land*, a novel set in the time when armed men fought for possession of land in the rich frontier zone of Ilhéus.[2] *The Violent Land* and three earlier novels published during the 1930s were written in Marxist didactic style, depicting abuse of the humble people by brutal, greedy landowners. Radicalized during his student years in the 1930s, Amado joined Brazil's Communist Party, going on to serve as its representative to the national Chamber of Deputies during the 1940s. In 1942 he published a biography of Communist leader Luis Carlos Prestes, suffering exile for his trouble, and in 1951 won the Stalin International Peace Prize. During the 1950s, Amado withdrew from politics and concentrated on

writing. His work became more earthy and good-humored, yet social criticism remained a principal feature.

Gabriela, Clove and Cinnamon is his recollection of the Ilhéus
of his youth.[3] Amado was born in 1912, not far from Ilhéus, on his
father's cacao plantation. There he worked side by side with the
plantation's laborers, becoming familiar with their ways and sensi-
tized to their plight as Brazil's least-favored citizens.

In a very real sense Amado lived the history he wrote about in
his novel. A boy of thirteen in the year of *Gabriela*'s setting, he
perceived Ilhéus as a bustling, exciting place. Money earned through
cacao exports convinced local leaders, Amado's father among them,
that their future was as golden as their fields of ripening cacao. The
enthusiasm of all those profiting from the cacao bonanza is conveyed to us throughout Amado's novel.

The nostalgia suffusing *Gabriela, Clove and Cinnamon* per-
vades its film adaptation. Director Bruno Barreto achieves that effect through his use of colorful pastels softened by filters, through
the stagy period look that he gives the film, and through his use of
a melodious musical accompaniment composed by Antonio Carlos
Jobim and Gal Costa.[4] By setting his film in the historically preserved town of Parati, located on Brazil's cacao coast, Barreto conveys the look of the Ilhéus of the 1920s. After its initial panning
shot of the town and its harbor and as the credits roll, the action
moves to its principal locus, Nacib's bar. From that point we follow both the love story of Nacib and Gabriela and the theme of
Ilhéus's economic progress through the export of cacao.

Progress was uppermost in the minds of Latin American elites
during the late nineteenth and early twentieth centuries. Western
Europe's extraordinary advance in material culture was the envy of
leaders across the region who wanted Latin America to experience
similar development. But economic progress eluded them owing to
their inability to agree on a range of crucial public policy issues.
Their disagreements condemned most nations of the region to ongoing political turmoil and civil war.

Toward the end of the nineteenth century, Latin America's leaders reconciled their differences, thanks in large measure to their
acceptance of two related sets of ideas. The first was Comtean positivism, which argued that material progress was inevitable when
strong leaders applied scientific principles to the resolution of national problems. The second was the notion of comparative economic advantage, which stood at the core of classical economics.

The comparative advantage doctrine held that national economies should be geared toward providing the world market with whatever goods they could produce most cheaply and sell at the highest cost. The profits earned through international trade could then be used to make the long-delayed dream of development a reality. By the early twentieth century it was clear that even backwaters such as Ilhéus were capable of lifting themselves from poverty and backwardness by supplying the global market with a much sought-after commodity.

It is not surprising that the Brazilian film *Gabriela* should so clearly suggest this elite preoccupation with progress. While other Latin American nations drank deeply of Auguste Comte's philosophy, notably Mexico with its *científicos* of the Porfirio Díaz era (1876–1910), none of them carried their infatuation with the Frenchman's ideas to Brazil's extreme. Brazilians were the only people in the region to establish a positivist church. And in 1889, when the Brazilian Republic was proclaimed, national leaders went so far as to place the Comtean slogan, "Order and Progress," upon their national flag.

The important place that positivism held in the thought of Brazilian and other Latin American elites is suggested early in *Gabriela*. Seated in Nacib's bar, the town's leaders remark on Ilhéus's remarkable physical progress and discuss ways of enhancing it. Of overriding concern is the sandbar blocking the harbor and barring the way to the ship that they hope will soon transport their cacao to Sweden. The town's leading light, dynamic cacao exporter Mundinho Falção, newspaper editor and founder of the exclusive Progress Club, has hired an engineer from Rio de Janeiro to supervise the dredging of the harbor. The engineer's imminent arrival excites Nacib's customers, who see their future assured once they are no longer forced to ship their cacao to Europe via the port of Salvador de Bahia, some three hundred kilometers up the coast.

The possibility of political reform also animates the bar's patrons. Local elections approach, and there is excitement over the chance that Falçao's faction will win the mayoralty, thereby ending the old guard's monopoly on political power. The entrenched faction is made up of the cacao "colonels," who decades earlier tamed the frontier with the help of hired gunmen. The insurgent political faction, representing export interests, avidly supports Falçao. Plantation owners support the aged but vigorous Colonel Ramiro Bastos, longtime arbiter of life in and around Ilhéus. Will the progressive faction be thwarted through violence? Will the terrible "cacao wars" again ravage the region? Or will the election be a clean one, bearing Falçao and his supporters to power? These are the political questions raised by Nacib's clients. If violence can be averted, as everyone hopes will be the case, and if the progressive faction wins, as they anticipate, their triumph will stand as indisputable proof that Ilhéus has achieved political maturity.

The final issue discussed by the men in the Vesuvius Bar, by far the most immediate and titillating, is the double murder that has just been committed in a nearby dentist's office. There, as we learn through a provocative flashback, Colonel Jesuíno Mendonça has shot his wife, Dona Sinhàzinha, and her lover, Dr. Osmundo Pimentel, having caught them in flagrante delicto. In earlier times such action was seen as the absolute right of a husband whose honor had been besmirched. But the passage of time had rendered such an act illegal and punishable by a lengthy prison term.

Ilhéus's leading citizens debate the crime of passion at great length. While most of them, Nacib included, vow that it is a man's right to slay an unfaithful spouse, they also accept the fact that greater society has deemed such behavior a crime. As they talk about issues of conjugal fidelity, they ponder the fate of the powerful Colonel Mendonça. In an ideal world, prison would be his destination. But in the cacao zone, where planters traditionally obeyed no law but their own, statutes drawn up in Rio—even in the state capital of Salvador de Bahia—are easily ignored. Still, progress implies an increasing level of civilization. And respect for law is one of the crowning achievements of civilization. Thus, the tragic murder of Dona Sinhàzinha and Dr. Pimentel takes on an importance for Nacib's clients that transcends its fleeting, prurient interest. It looms as a sort of acid test of positivist faith. If, in spite of the fact that his peers, the other cacao colonels, have rallied around him, Colonel Mendonça is sent to prison, then Ilhéus will have definitively entered history's positivist era, the culminating stage of human evolution.

As these transcendent issues are discussed, Nacib meets and falls in love with Gabriela. Brazil's social problems form a backdrop to their love story. Gabriela is first seen on the road, heading south through the barren *sertão* (back country) with a small group of refugees from the drought in the country's impoverished Northeast region. They are ragged and filthy and pause only long enough to bury those who die along the way. Both the *sertão* and the drought-plagued Northeast form vast themes in both the history and the literature of Brazil. Eventually the survivors reach verdant Ilhéus, their destination. They make their way to the town's old slave market where they docilely await their fate. Much as it was prior to 1888, when Brazil abolished slavery, society's most wretched members remain at the disposal of those having the means to command their service.

Gabriela arrives in Ilhéus as a refugee from the drought in Brazil's Northeast.

Nacib needs a cook, old Filomena having abruptly left his employ to go live with her son in a nearby town. As his clients demand snacks to nibble on as they drink, gossip, and ogle women, it is crucial that he replace old Filomena as quickly as possible. Finding the dirty, bedraggled Gabriela at the slave market, Nacib hires her against his better judgment. "I once cooked for rich folks," she assures him as he grudgingly takes her home and installs her behind his house in old Filomena's former quarters. "Take a bath," Nacib tells her as he hurries back to the bar. Late that same night he returns to find a sleeping, ravishing young woman waiting for him. Within twenty-four hours they are lovers. To make Nacib's delight complete, Gabriela is a wonderful cook!

Nacib's contentment is short-lived. He falls in love with Gabriela and becomes jealous when his lascivious clients undress her with their eyes and give her affectionate pats on her posterior as she passes bearing trays of delectable pastries. His friend Tónico Bastos, the town's notary and its foremost womanizer, advises Nacib that if he wants to protect Gabriela he must marry her. Aghast at the thought of marrying a woman who is neither of good family nor a virgin, Nacib protests, but to no avail. Love and jealousy triumph. His friend forges an identity for Gabriela—"What difference will one more forged document make?" he asks Nacib; "Ilhéus is built on forged documents"—thus clearing the way for marriage. The wedding soon follows. Nacib and Gabriela begin a life of bourgeois respectability.

Gabriela serves treats that she has baked to eager clients in Nacib's bar.

At this point all progress-related issues are quickly and satisfactorily resolved. The engineer arrives, to the great excitement of all Ilhéus, and sets dredges to work clearing the harbor. The election draws near, and old-style violence threatens to engulf the town. Mundinho Falção's newspaper is burned, and Gabriela's friend from the *sertão*, the gunman Negro Fagundes, who has been hired by one of the planter faction, mistakenly wounds a colonel who has joined the progressive faction. Only timely intervention by Gabriela saves the day. Falçao wins the contest to the joy of most. Not long afterward old Colonel Bastos expires peacefully, while sitting on his favorite park bench. During the celebration of the arrival of the Swedish ship, a former Bastos supporter confides in Falçao: "I had planned to have you killed, but now I support you. Let's go shoot a game of pool."

As for the double murder, its resolution is suggested indirectly. Across the street from Nacib's bar is the house of Gloria, mistress of grizzled, gun-toting Colonel Coriolano. But the colonel spends most of his time tending his plantations, leaving the voluptuous young woman to gaze wistfully from her window, displaying her charms to Nacib's admiring clients. At length, Professor Josué, the town poet, becomes infatuated with her and is soon seen sneaking into her house every evening. Nacib and his clients view this with amusement mixed with envy and fear. Their friend is taking a great chance. All know that Colonel Coriolano is a jealous man; and, should he find the two together, gunplay will inevitably result.

Late one evening, while Professor Josué is enjoying Gloria's charms, the colonel rides into town and bursts into his concubine's house. A hush falls over the bar; all look on aghast. Seconds pass. Nothing happens. Seconds stretch into minutes, many minutes. At length the door opens and Colonel Coriolano and Professor Josué emerge, shake hands, and depart in different directions. It is obvious that a very modern ménage à trois has been arranged.

Among the spectators is Colonel Jesuíno Mendonça, who watches the scene unfold with mounting dismay. He and everyone in the bar suddenly understand that his goose is cooked, that murder in the defense of manly honor has ceased to be the unwritten law of Brazil's cacao zone. Colonel Mendonça's fate is told in the epilogue of *Gabriela, Clove and Cinnamon*:

> Some time afterwards, Colonel Jesuíno Mendonça stood before a jury, accused of having shot to death his wife, Sinhàzinha Guedes Mendonça, and the dental surgeon, Osmundo Pimentel, for reasons of jealousy. The lawyers talked, all in all, for twenty-eight hours. Dr. Maurício Caires quoted the Bible and referred to scandalous black stockings, morality, and depravity. Dr. Ezequiel Prado said that Ilhéus was no longer a land of bandits, a paradise of assassins; his theme was civilization and progress. With a sob he pointed to Osmundo's father and mother, in mourning and tears. For the first time in the history of Ilhéus, a cacao colonel

found himself sentenced to prison for having murdered his adulterous wife and her lover.[5]

Progress, of course, has many consequences, not all of them to the liking of those who reap the lion's share of its rewards. Growing wealth, marked by the extraordinary expansion of material culture, has the effect of increasing individual freedom. Enhanced personal freedom works to weaken the social institutions that anchored traditional society. The pivotal, freedom-enhancing consequence of economic growth in early twentieth-century Latin America is suggested in *Gabriela* through scenes centering upon the beautiful Malvina, nubile daughter of the wealthiest of the cacao planters, Melk Tavares. Colonel Tavares is the quintessential patriarch, harsh and unyielding, given to carrying a horsewhip as he strides through the streets of Ilhéus.

Malvina is a romantic, headstrong girl who hates the pettiness and cruelty that are so much a part of bourgeois small-town life. Only she and the good-hearted Nacib attend the wake for the disgraced Dona Sinhàzinha. That unfortunate woman's former friends have callously refused to remember her even in death. Malvina similarly rejects the attentions of Professor Josué (thereby driving him into the arms of Gloria). She is waiting for someone better, and she finds him in the person of the handsome young engineer from Rio. She meets him and the two become lovers.

Colonel Tavares is furious when he learns of his daughter's indiscretion. Confronting the couple, he threatens the engineer and orders him out of town on the next boat. The engineer complies, but Malvina leaves with him. In the novel, she deepens her father's humiliation by living openly with her paramour once they are ensconced in Rio. Patriarchy is thus brought low. Even so formidable a character as Colonel Tavares is impotent before the acid of modernity that eats away at traditional authority.

Gabriela herself is the person who most effectively, albeit unknowingly, strikes at middle-class pretensions. Nacib and Gabriela represent polar opposites. He is determined to ape his social superiors, while she is blissfully ignorant in the ways of the elite. The Gabriela of film and novel is the feminine epitome of the "noble savage." Beautiful, passionate, and oblivious to artifice, she does not hesitate to reject stodgy convention. When she and Nacib become engaged, he banishes her from his house because suddenly it is not proper for the two to be alone together. Gabriela dutifully moves next door to Dona Arminda's house but refuses to abide by her fiancé's absurd notions of propriety. She simply waits until nightfall, slips across Nacib's garden wall, and returns to his bed. And when, after marriage, Nacib forces her to play the role of a proper housewife, she can scarcely tolerate it. Gabriela does not understand why she must attend boring poetry readings, wear uncomfortable high-heeled shoes, and refrain from cavorting in the street with the children of the town. Nor does she understand why marriage has stolen the passion from her lovemaking with Nacib.

Bored and confined as a bourgeois housewife, Gabriela falls asleep at a poetry reading.

At length, Gabriela defies propriety by taking a lover, none other than the roué Tónico Bastos, erstwhile friend of Nacib and best man at their wedding. Inevitably, Nacib catches the two in his bed and confronts them, pistol in hand. But he cannot pull the trigger. His love for Gabriela is too strong. And, too, the murder of an unfaithful spouse runs counter to his kindly nature, is clearly illegal, and stands as the distasteful vestige of an earlier time, before civilization came to Ilhéus.

Brokenhearted, Nacib banishes Gabriela from his life. Tónico Bastos is forced to prepare a new fraudulent document, this time one annulling the marriage. He does so under threat that if he fails to comply, disgrace and prison await him for his earlier forgery. Thus, Nacib and Gabriela part, though both are miserable for they still love one another. Social convention demands, after all, that while an aggrieved husband may not now kill his wife, he cannot simply take her back.

Is there no way to resolve the problem? Gabriela again provides the answer. Sometime later a mournful Nacib returns home late from the bar. Weeks of drinking and womanizing with his friends have not erased the memory of Gabriela. Suddenly he hears a sound and turns to find her standing there in the moonlight, looking just as she had their first night together. All is forgotten in a moment of blind passion, just as it was on that first memorable night in each other's arms. It was only marriage, and the demands that meaningless social forms placed upon them, that had ruined their romantic idyll.

It scarcely need be added that Gabriela and Nacib live happily ever after as man and cook. Their love story lives on to form a small chapter in the bustling life of orderly, progressive Ilhéus, Brazil's new deepwater gateway to the world's cacao markets.

~

A concluding note is in order concerning Latin American attitudes toward sex and nudity as treated in the popular media and on the portrayal of female characters in the works of Amado. Both these subjects might well be discussed prior to classroom showings of either Gabriela or *Dona Flor and Her Two Husbands.*

Latin Americans are given to depicting portions of the human anatomy in film and print media unabashedly, in ways that are taboo in Anglo America. One innocent example of this cultural difference involves a 1995 photograph of First Lady Hillary Rodham Clinton, sitting in such a way that her underwear was visible. A Brazilian lingerie maker saw nothing wrong with using the photo in a humorous advertisement promoting its product. The U.S. government, and many U.S. citizens, found the ad to be offensive and pressured the Brazilians to withdraw it from circulation. Other, similar, examples abound.[6]

It is not surprising that U.S. audiences are taken aback by the joyous celebration of Sonia Braga's nude body in *Gabriela.*[7] Hollywood films, it is true, are full of nudity and simulated sex. But such scenes possess a voyeuristic quality that in turn suffuses the viewer with a vague sense of guilt. Not so in Brazilian films, at least not in those directed by men.[8]

A final point must be made in reference to the sex and nudity in *Gabriela*. It should not be forgotten that the film and its predecessor, *Dona Flor and Her Two Husbands*, closely follow the plots of the Amado novels that inspired them. In both films, director Barreto is at pains to convey the novelist's enduring themes of bourgeois hypocrisy and social cruelty. The fictional Gabriela is an impoverished young woman who assumes that her employer will use her sexually. Dona Flor is a housewife who finds herself enjoying bourgeois respectability with her stodgy second husband while, incredibly, continuing to enjoy great sex with her deceased first mate. Other Amado female protagonists, Tereza Batista and Tieta the Goat Girl, are also abused women who are scorned by the cruel and shallow members of "polite society" but eventually triumph over social injustice. It is upon this recurring theme of brave, admirable, often saintly female characters rising above adversity that Amado's reputation as a feminist rests. "They say that I am a novelist of whores and vagabonds," said Amado, "and there is truth in that. My characters are increasingly anti-heroes. I believe that only the people struggle selflessly, decently, without hidden motives."[9]

Still, feminists are made uncomfortable by Amado's obvious novelistic fondness for sex and beautiful women. Let those who use *Gabriela* in the classroom be forewarned that sensitive viewers may react to this film in the same way.

Suggested Readings

Charles A. Hale, "Political and Social Ideas in Latin America, 1870–1930," in *The Cambridge History of Latin America*, vol. 4, *c. 1870 to 1930*, ed. Leslie Bethell (New York: Cambridge University Press, 1986), 367–441, is a good introduction to the subject of elite attitudes in early twentieth-century Latin America and includes abundant references for further reading. Those interested in pursuing late nineteenth- and early twentieth-century elite mentality through film should view *Sugar Cane Alley* (1984), *Lucía* (1968), *The Ballad of Gregorio Cortés* (1983), *Viva Zapata* (1952), *Like Water for Chocolate* (1993), and *House of the Spirits* (1994).

English sources on Brazilian filmmaking are Randal Johnson and Robert Stam, *Brazilian Cinema* (Rutherford, NJ: Fairleigh Dickinson University Press; Associated University Presses, 1982); Randal Johnson, *Cinema Novo x 5: Masters of Contemporary Brazilian Film* (Austin: University of Texas Press, 1984); and *The Film Industry in Brazil: Culture and the State* (Pittsburgh, PA: University of Pittsburgh Press, 1987).

A comprehensive single-volume guide to Brazilian cinema, containing an extensive bibliography on the subject, is Paulo Antonio Paranagua, ed., *Le Cinéma brésilien* (Paris: Centre Georges Pompidou, 1987). John King, "Latin American Cinema," in *The Cambridge History of Latin America*, vol. 10, *Latin America since 1930: Ideas, Culture, and Society*, ed. Leslie Bethell (New York: Cambridge University Press, 1995), 455–518, is a good recent survey of the subject.

Three splendid evocations of the *sertão*, the first nonfiction and the latter two fictional, are Euclides da Cunha, *Rebellion in the Backlands* (Chicago: University of Chicago Press, 1944); João Guimaraes Rosa, *The Devil to Pay in the Backlands* (New York: Alfred A. Knopf, 1963); and Mario Vargas Llosa, *The War of the End of the World* (New York: Farrar, Straus, and Giroux, 1984). Da Cunha's treatment of the important rebellion of the religious mystic Antonio the Counselor during the 1890s, first published in 1902, is itself an expression of elite mentality of that time and is suffused with positivist attitudes. Guimaraes Rosa's *The Devil to Pay*, one of Brazil's most celebrated novels of the twentieth century, treats bandit life in the *sertão*. Vargas Llosa recounts the uprising of Antonio the Counselor and his followers.

There is an extensive body of historical writing on slavery and race relations in Brazil. Gilberto Freyre, *The Masters and the Slaves* (New York: Alfred A. Knopf, 1946), is an ideal starting point for the exploration of that topic. Robert Conrad, *The Destruction of Brazilian Slavery, 1850–1889* (Berkeley: University of California Press, 1971); and Robert Brent Toplin, *The Abolition of Slavery in Brazil* (New York: Atheneum, 1972), are among the better studies of the abolition movement.

Novels by Jorge Amado in English translation mentioned in the text include: *Dona Flor and Her Two Husbands: A Moral and Amorous Tale* (New York: Alfred A. Knopf, 1969); *Gabriela, Clove and Cinnamon* (New York: Alfred A. Knopf, 1962); *Tereza Batista, Home from the Wars* (New York: Alfred A. Knopf, 1975); *Tieta, the Goat Girl; or, the Return of the Prodigal Daughter: Melodramatic Serial Novel in Five Sensational Episodes, with a Touching Epilogue, Thrills and Suspense!* (New York: Alfred A. Knopf, 1979); and *The Violent Land* (New York: Alfred A. Knopf, 1945).

CHAPTER TEN

Why Tita Didn't Marry the Doctor,
or Mexican History in
Like Water for Chocolate

BARBARA A. TENENBAUM

Como Agua para Chocolate (1992), or Like Water for Chocolate; produced by Alfonso Arau, Emilia Arau, and Oscar Castillo; directed by Alfonso Arau; written by Laura Esquivel based on her novel of the same name; color; 123 minutes; Arau Films Internacional/Cinevista/Fonatur/ Fondo de Fomento a la Calidad Cinematográfica/Insti- tuto Mexicano de Cinematográfica (IMCINE). In early twentieth-century Mexico, a young woman named Tita (Lumi Cavazos), who is forced to remain unmarried to care for her aging mother, puts all her repressed energy and sen- suality into her cooking.

M y mother has only seen one Mexican movie—*Like Water for Chocolate*. It is understandable that she should have seen that particular picture because the film was both a commercial and a critical success. In the seven months following its February 1993 release, it had already grossed $6.1 million, the most ever by a Latin American film.[1] Janet Maslin, film critic of the *New York Times*, suggests a reason for its popularity: "It relies so enchantingly upon fate, magic, and a taste for the supernatural that it suggests Gabriel García Márquez in a cookbook-writing mode."[2] Such praise and success at the U.S. box office does not necessarily mean, however, that audiences in the United States fully understood the action presented. In fact, many among the subtitle readers proclaimed themselves perplexed. Like my mother, they asked, "Why didn't the girl marry that nice doctor?" Aside from my Jewish mother's fascination with doctors as the sine qua non of husband material, the general question underscores not only the important ways in which Mexico developed differently from many other nations in the Western Hemisphere but also how Laura Esquivel was able to adjust the screenplay of her novel of the same title to fit a crossover audience in the United States without alienating its Mexican public.

There is much in the movie that remains unexplained to the uninitiated. Take its title, for instance. Nowhere does the movie inform the audience what "like water for chocolate" means. According to the book, Tita was "literally 'like water for chocolate'— she was on the verge of boiling over. . . . She felt her head about to burst, like a kernel of popcorn."[3] In addition, in Mexican slang, the phrase often implies the height of as-yet-unfulfilled sexual longing, particularly in women. Despite the fact that the movie is about passion repressed by societal constraints, the movie could just as easily have stolen its title from the Chilean author Isabel Allende and called itself *The House of the Spirits*, for its raison d'être and plot revolve around the power of superstition and unseen voices. And that is particularly appropriate for Mexico, whose conquest by a white man with blond hair had been foretold to the Aztec emperor Motecuhzoma II (Montezuma) by his soothsayers. The movie brims with pronouncements or curses that come true or do not, wreaking havoc on the lives of the characters. The dead speak, and even food takes on an unearthly power to unsettle the unwary. No one escapes his or her preordained fate, except the revolutionary Gertrudis, who, after all, has mulatto blood and rhythm, in a particularly unsubtle exemplar of racism that Esquivel chose to retain from her original text.

There are countless examples of spiritual restlessness throughout the movie, and, even when offered a "calm, secure, and peaceful" life through marriage to the American doctor who adores her, Tita, our heroine, eschews probable happiness or at least contentment in favor of maintaining her forbidden passion for the Pedro she fell in love with as a child. This decision generally confused viewers in the United States, yet it nevertheless embodies a traditional Mexican worldview and reflects Mexico's distinctive lack of massive European immigration.

In the period during which most of the movie takes place, 1880–1914, immigrants from Europe flooded many countries of the Western Hemisphere. Indeed, it was during that time that my mother's parents left Russia and Poland to settle in Philadelphia. While we think of the United States, Canada, Brazil, Uruguay, and Argentina as immigrant societies, we have not thought about what it meant to their counterparts—Mexico, Ecuador, Bolivia, and, to a lesser degree, Peru—not to have undergone that immigrant experience.

Of course, we well know that Mexico is not simply an indigenous society; it was conquered and colonized and mestizoized by those living in the area currently known as Spain, who came there in hopes of winning for themselves a better life. However, unlike nineteenth-century immigrants, these Spaniards came to the New World as representatives of their government and could count on its support, in most cases. They did what they did in the name of the crown or the church, which in this particular case was the same thing. They imposed, or tried to impose, their culture and way of life on the indigenous empires and tribes they found in the land that they conquered. And, over time, they blended more or less openly, and not so openly, with that population, creating something that Mexican author and statesman José Vasconcelos called "the cosmic race."

Immigrants, like conquerors, risk their lives in a new society for the sake of bettering themselves, but many who left home in the period under discussion felt that they had few choices—their native lands had little or nothing to offer them except starvation or persecution and possible death. These pioneers undertook risky journeys in their personal, individual efforts to outwit fate. They decided that life held something better for them than what they had been given at birth, and they went after it, literally and figuratively. The preordained held no sway over their imagination, or, if it did, they firmly brushed it aside and followed another star on another continent, a long and uncomfortable voyage away.

They injected into the societies they entered their lively optimism about the future. If life in their adopted home would not necessarily be better for them, surely it would grant its riches to their children and grandchildren. There are countless examples in immigrant lore of marriages in which passion played little part and financial security held sway. When my mother's mother was slightly older than Tita, her father married her to a much older man who owned a business. By the time my mother was ready to marry, however, she exchanged vows with the suitor of her own choice, much to my grandmother's chagrin. Nevertheless, my grandmother never denied her daughter the right that had been denied her, reinforcing the axiomatic belief that life would be better for the next generation.

That optimism also affected life in the new homeland on a more abstract level as well. With the influx of so many immigrants, the native-born assumed an automatically higher status and profited from the expanding economy as so many of the lower-paying difficult jobs went to immigrants (or to former slaves in the case of the United States and Brazil). In those countries that had little or no immigration, the pressures of industrialization coupled with new egalitarian ideologies led to revolutions (Mexico in 1910, Bolivia in 1954, and, to a much lesser extent, Peru in 1968) rather than to the formation of labor unions and pro-proletarian political parties as they had in Europe, the United States, Brazil, Uruguay, and Argentina.

It is no accident that Mexico never became a sought-after destination for these adventurous immigrants. Beginning with their burgeoning rationale for independence from a Spain whose control had become too burdensome, Mexicans looked to the indigenous culture of their past for answers and alternatives rather than to European interpretations. For example, as early as 1794, Fray Servando Teresa de Mier proclaimed that Quetzalcoatl, the feathered serpent god of Teotihuacán, the Toltecs, and the Aztecs, was really an indigenous response to the arrival of Saint Thomas, who had brought the word of Christ to Mexico centuries before the arrival of the Spaniards. When Father Miguel Hidalgo y Costilla led the armies of independence into battle in 1810, he used the image of the Virgin of Guadalupe (about whom more later), the patron saint of indigenous Mexico, as his banner. Although that struggle was not successful, Mexicans could never fully embrace the victor of the Independence Wars, the creole and former royalist soldier Agustín de Iturbide, as their hero. The statue ("the Angel") erected to commemorate the Independence on its centenary in 1910 by the supposedly reactionary Porfirio Díaz filled its spaces with heroes, the majority of whom were already dead by 1821 when Mexico achieved its independence; it had no room left for Iturbide.

Yet, following Iturbide's abortive monarchy in 1823, the Mexicans could still have developed a pro-European or, at least, a more neutral stance toward the indigenous past had it not been for a se-

ries of disasters sponsored by the Conservatives—who also champi-
oned Iturbide—concluding with the French invasion in 1862 and
the pitiful empire of Maximiliano and Carlota. With Benito Juárez's
victory over the French in 1867, Mexico had no choice but to base
its nationalism on an indigenous past in which "minor" sins such
as Aztec human sacrifice and terrorism over its tributary states (that
is, the rest of the country outside of Mexico City) were conveniently
forgotten when placed in the context of the saga of the vile Spanish
conquest.[4]

That embrace of the indigenous past virtually closed the door
to European immigration at a time when the native inhabitants of
the Western Hemisphere were seen as threatening subhumans in
both the United States and the Southern Cone. Mexico did attempt
to attract immigrants; it offered land and other enticements but to
little avail. Although European intellectuals and some members of
the elite perhaps were charmed by the idea of noble savages across
the sea, they were not about to leave home and settle among them.
As for the real potential immigrants like my grandparents, imagine
their reactions to the supposed temple of Montezuma and the full-
size statue of Cuauhtemoc, the last Aztec emperor, that they would
have seen at the Mexican pavilion at the 1889 Paris Exposition!
How could they not have preferred the European buildings and progressive machinery found at the exhibitions from the United States
or Argentina close by? Suffice it to say that Argentina did not even
bother to exhibit in the 1900 Exposition; it already had more immigrants than it could ever have thought possible.

To further complicate an already complex scenario, *Like Water
for Chocolate* presumably concerns itself with an area far away
from the core of Mexico, where yet a very different culture evolved
on what would become after 1848 the border between the Mexican
world and Anglo-Saxon territory. The movie quickly introduces us
to the landscape of the border state of Coahuila and the relationship between the towns of Piedras Negras and Eagle Pass in the
Rio Grande Valley in 1895. In addition, it alerts us to the fact that
the movie will be what used to be called a tearjerker, but a tearjerker
with a twist, for tears overtly play an important part in the plot. The
film begins with the contemporary narrator's putting an onion on
her head to prevent tears flowing while she cuts onions. She introduces us to her tale by relating the birth of her great-aunt and our
heroine, Tita, who supposedly cried so much in the womb that her
dried birthwater yielded a forty-pound sack of salt (only ten pounds

in the book). According to Celsa, a peasant woman from whom we will hear more later, "Crying is a good way to purge your soul of evil. It's just as good a medicine as the herbal teas."[5] Welcome to magical realism, Mexican style.

A few days later, the family holds a party to celebrate the birth of the new baby. When one of the guests chides the father for producing three girls, another notes that not all of those girls are his, that his daughter Gertrudis was fathered by "the mulatto"— whereupon the host promptly has a heart attack and dies, leaving his wife Elena and "his" three daughters to fend for themselves. A few years later, Nacha, the family cook and Tita's mother in the kitchen, remarks that Tita's beauty is such that the first man who sees her will want to marry her. Elena, her real mother, responds with the operating premise of the story, "Tita can never marry! As my youngest daughter, her responsibility is to take care of me." If *Like Water for Chocolate* had been a silent film, music filled with dread would have followed.

U.S. audiences watching this movie in 1993 were unable to empathize with Doña Elena, even though they could well believe that she could have demanded such daughterly devotion. What mother sitting in the audience could imagine herself uttering such a pronouncement without fear of prompting uncontrollable laughter from her offspring? Further, the beliefs in individual will and romantic love are so firmly embedded in the mythology of the United States that any cinematic parent who would try to control a child's destiny in such a way would evoke great resentment in viewers, as it is meant to do. The audience is not supposed to like Doña Elena; it is meant to side with the victimized Tita.

When we next join the family, it is 1910, the year in which the Mexican Revolution begins. We are preparing for Tita's fifteenth birthday, her *quincenera*, when she would officially become a woman and thus marriageable. A neighbor's son, Pedro Múzquiz, sees her and, true to Nacha's prediction, falls in love with her. She returns his feelings. As Tita says, "Now I know how raw dough feels when it hits boiling oil; I expected to break out all over my body." The lovers acknowledge their passion verbally, and Pedro promises to marry Tita. But when he with his father asks for Tita's hand, Elena forbids the match and offers her eldest daughter Rosaura instead.

This move, curiously, is a slight but significant departure from the book. In the book version, Gertrudis is Elena's eldest daughter

Forbidden by her mother to marry, Tita puts her energy and emotions into her cooking.

and was fathered by the mulatto José Treviño before Elena's family married her off to Juan de la Garza, the father of Rosaura and Tita, who did not know she was already pregnant by someone else. That explanation is much more logical and makes understandable why Elena would want Pedro to marry Rosaura rather than Gertrudis. After all, Gertrudis might very well have dark-skinned children, as indeed the book tells us she did, much to the horror of her revolutionary husband, who thought she was cheating on him, until Tita explained everything.[6] In order to omit the racist implications of this plot line, Rosaura was made the eldest daughter with Gertrudis the product of an affair that occurred during Elena's marriage to Tita's father.

In a move shocking to both his father and to Tita's household at large, Pedro accepts, even though, as the servant Chencha notes, "You just can't substitute tacos for enchiladas" (that is, the plain for something fancier). At this point the audience who understands Mexican history begins to shake its collective head. As historian William French has noted for the neighboring state of Chihuahua, it was common during that period for prospective but forbidden grooms to "kidnap" their brides and marry without parental consent.[7] Tita herself screams this to Pedro later in the movie. In this case, despite the probable approval of his father for such an action, in service to a tragic plot, Pedro agrees to marry a woman he does not love in order to be near the one he does. Yet there is precedent in central Mexico for this behavior. For example, Celsa, the protagonist of *Celsa's World: Conversations with a Mexican Peasant Woman*, suggests that Elena's laying down the law is quite reasonable if not likable. According to Celsa, a peasant woman who lives in San Antonio, a village near Cuernavaca, whose comments were gathered in 1979–80, "People have respect for you if you can manage a house or farm well *and* control your children. If the head of a family cannot control the children, that person loses the respect of the people. . . . A woman can do as good a job as a man if the children listen to her and do as she says."[8] Elena, living alone and having three girls to raise, had to maintain the respect of her neighbors in order to survive independently. The use of this pattern of parental control common in central Mexico, rather than the bride kidnapping found on the northern border, is only one suggestion among many that Esquivel took a plot valid in the center and imposed it on the northern frontier. That explains why she did not make more of the typical aspects of the frontier, including its cuisine.

To reinforce her authority, Elena forces Tita to prepare the wedding banquet when the man she loves will marry her sister. While making the wedding cake, which requires 170 eggs (eggs being Mexican slang for male genitalia), Tita's and the servant Nacha's tears fall into the batter, creating a cake that "intoxicates" the guests. They all start crying from melancholy and frustration over "the love of their lives," and even Elena is moved to unlock her box of secrets and stare at the hidden picture of a well-dressed mulatto, presumably the father of Gertrudis. Then the collective vomiting begins.

The incident of the wedding cake parallels that of a typical Mexican party, as presented by noted journalist and observer of the Mexican scene Alma Guillermoprieto:

> Mexicans know that a party has been outstandingly successful if at the end of it there are at least a couple of clusters of longtime or first-time acquaintances leaning on each other against a wall, sobbing helplessly. The activities one normally associates with a party—flirting and conversation, and even the kind of dancing that leads to an amnesiac dawn in a strange bed—are considered

here mere preludes to or distractions from the ultimate goal, which
is weeping and the free, luxurious expression of pain.[9]

Presumably they too, intoxicated, are shedding tears over what might
have been, and the vomiting will commence shortly thereafter. In
fact, the movie gives us that explicit scene somewhat later as a
male-bonding ritual between Pedro and the revolutionary husband
of Gertrudis, Juan Alejandrez, who drunkenly sing together with
bottles in hand.

The last dish presented, the glorious *chiles en nogada* (chiles
in walnut sauce), has a special significance for Mexicans and for
Puebla in particular. In no way, throughout the movie, does the cuisine ever reflect the place of the action—that is, none of the special
dishes from Coahuila listed in *Comida familiar en el Estado de
Coahuila* appear here.[10] The *chiles en nogada* comes from Puebla
in central Mexico. It was created for the Liberator, Agustín de
Iturbide, as he passed through Puebla on his nameday on his way
to Mexico City to take the reins of the newly independent republic.
It even looks patriotic: the colors of the dish—green (chiles), white
(sauce), and red (pomegranate seeds) reflect the national flag. The
dish is an enchantment in itself under the most prosaic circumstances, but in the hands of the miraculous Tita, it becomes the
repository of sensuality. A generation later, upon eating the chiles
(in Mexico the word is slang for the male organ), the wedding guests
all rush away to satisfy a hunger of a different sort.

Another miraculous dish prepared by Tita is quail in rose petal
sauce, which she concocts from a bouquet of roses that Pedro gives
her in honor of her first year as the chief cook of the ranch. Upon
tasting the dish, Pedro, a man of few words, exclaims, "This is the
nectar of the gods!"—a poetic statement meant, of course, to remind those in the know of another instance in which Mexico's history is intimately linked to rose petals—the revelation of the Virgin
of Guadalupe, its patron saint. (As legend has it, an Indian named
Juan Diego had a vision of the Virgin Mary, an Indian virgin, at a
particular spot that used to be the holy place of the Aztec goddess
Tonantzin. She commands him to gather the flowers from a nearby
rosebush into his cloak to take to Bishop Juan de Zumarraga as
proof of his vision. When Diego arrives at the bishop's residence
and opens his cloak, there are no roses but simply the image of the
Virgin, another example of the transformation of rose petals into a
manifestation of the divine.[11]) Indeed, as Tita concocts the dish,

While enjoying the perfume of one of Pedro's forbidden roses, Tita decides . . .

to make the quail in rose petal sauce that will have unsettling effects on her family.

her hands and breasts begin to bleed in symbolic union with the suffering Christ.

In the film, the narrator explains how, with each bite, Tita enters Pedro's body, with her sister Gertrudis acting as a kind of go-between, yet another reference to the Madonna and the miraculous conception of Christ. Gertrudis is so carried away with the passion she is feeling that she runs to take a shower and cool down. Instead, the shower stall bursts into flames, and she runs naked out into the desert only to be swept up into the arms of a Villista on horseback, lured there by the aroma of the roses. Mama Elena later is told that Gertrudis has become a prostitute in a brothel on the border. In retaliation for this disobedience and breach of morals, Elena is forced to disinherit her favorite, her beloved love child, and ban her from the family. The movie tends to gloss over Gertrudis's becoming a whore, but the book explains that the dish prepared by Tita had so inflamed her that no one man could satisfy her lust, and she went to the brothel until she was "healed," so to speak. If Tita represents the Madonna in this passion play, then Gertrudis surely has been given the role of Mary Magdalene. In one beautiful scene, Elena sits on a bed, mourning Gertrudis and literally flattening Tita, who is hiding underneath it, a perfect metaphor for Elena's insistence on taking out the transgressions that produced Gertrudis on her innocent and legitimate youngest daughter.

It is surprising that the revolution, the most important phenomenon in twentieth-century Mexican history, plays such a small part in the action. If the drama had been set in central Mexico, that would have been much more understandable. It appears that residents of Mexico City, like Edith O'Shaughnessy, did not really know a revolution was taking place until 1913![12] Here is yet another clue that makes us realize that the book and movie only adopt the northern frontier as a backdrop, a not-so-artful disguise for the all-powerful central valley of Mexico. The food comes from there as do the customs and behavior, which seem much more Indian than is customary along *la frontera*, which even then had been strongly influenced by the United States—a typical case, then, of the center dominating the periphery as it has since 1433, when the Aztec Triple Alliance took control of the central valley.

In a sense, Esquivel had little choice. Although, as Lesley Byrd Simpson astutely noted, there are "many Mexicos," the vast majority of the population is basically comfortable with the culture of the central valley. Even those who grew up in Piedras Negras did not seem to mind that the cuisine and other cultural markers came from elsewhere; they still felt right at home in the landscape of the movie. Had the Mexico City-born Esquivel presented a more *norteño* way of life, she would have lost the central premise—that prior to the revolution, the weight of culture, tradition, and even the spirit world made people conform to ways of behavior inimical to their best interests.

This mixture of the spiritual, the sensual, and the emotional gives the film its poignancy and its resonance with Mexicans. It is a celebration of the female sphere—the kitchen with its smells, its wonders, its sacrifices, dangers, and pleasures, a world that for many Mexicans still exists, if in part due to the affordability of servants. For if Mexico is not an immigrant country, it is a nation that can proclaim "thirty centuries of splendor," as the 1992 exhibit at New York's Metropolitan Museum of Art called itself in hopes of winning recognition of Mexican greatness on the other side of the border. Such tradition, as Tita's plight reminds us, is not easily dismissed.

There are few nations in the world as culturally rich as Mexico, where the past so intrudes on the present that it hardly seems past. In a recent talk in Washington at the Library of Congress, Dr. María Carmen Serra Puche, director of the National Museum of Anthropology in Mexico City, spoke of her awareness of hidden spirits as she began directing the excavation of a pre-Columbian site in central Mexico in 1993, the same year that the film was released. Finally, she decided that crew members would sacrifice a turkey to the gods before they began their labors.

In that regard, Mexico is unlike any other nation in the Western Hemisphere. Although countries such as Guatemala and Bolivia have a vibrant Indian past and present, the first choses to turn its back on its Indian heritage (as shown quite beautifully in the film *El Norte*), and the second merely tolerates it. However, Mexico has built its history as an independent nation on its Indian past. It is no accident that one of its major presidential candidates in 1988 and 1994 bore the name of the last Aztec emperor, Cuauhtemoc.

There are other ways of life in central Mexico that Tita continues to act out. As Celsa relates:

> I wanted to go to normal school in Morelia and become a teacher, but my mother wouldn't let me even though my *padrino* [godfather] was going to give me a scholarship. . . . But my mother said

I couldn't go, and I didn't. One time when I was angry with her over something, I said to her, "I am nothing because you didn't let me go away to school." She said that it was the only decision she could make because she could not accept a gift from don Emilio . . . and I would have become too selfish for the good of the family. . . . I could have gone if I had abandoned my mother. But I didn't want to be on my own. When you disobey your parents, it means you abandon them as well. It's so much easier for a man. . . . For me it was different; I had to take what was given to me by life; I didn't control my own destiny.[13]

So we return to my mother's question: Why didn't Tita marry the nice Dr. Brown, who loved her? Quite apart from the fate that Tita felt bound her to Pedro, there are several other reasons in a book and a film meant, at least in part, for Mexicans. The nice Dr. Brown was not brown at all; he was a *güero*—tall, blond, and Anglo even to his heavily accented fluent Spanish. Would it not have been a repetition of the conquest for the Mexican Tita to surrender her virtue to the blond from across the border? Mexico even has a special word for women who give themselves to the enemy (and those who love foreigners too much): they are known as *malinchistas* in "honor" of Doña Marina, the hated mistress of the blond Cortés, who betrayed her people only to be cast aside herself and given to another conquistador when the mission had been completed. In one of the first silent films made in Mexico by a company based in the United States, an American soldier says to the Mexican girl he is embracing, "And soon you'll be Mrs. Shorty." Obviously, in a film made in Mexico, the heroine cannot become Mrs. Brown, regardless of the reason.

Of course, U.S. audiences perceive no such impediment and look at the doctor as a prize catch—he loves Tita, he is a doctor, he has a fine sense of humor, he seems to have a good character, and, most important, he is an American. The book and script cheat a little; in order to make Mexican audiences more sympathetic to the gringo, the author gives him a grandmother from the Kickapoo, a tribe that voluntarily chose to abandon the United States and live in Mexico. Partly, American audiences' resonance with this character can be blamed on the appealing actor who plays the forsaken sawbones; his sweetness and gentle humor make him much more attractive than he ought to be, particularly to happily married women of a certain age. The actor who plays Pedro, by contrast, displays none of the smoldering fire that the role demands.

The book, however, leaves no doubts as to the rightness of Tita's choices. In the United States, there are many kinds of love, and a marriage based solely on passion is seen as quite a risky enterprise. In Mexico, however, love is defined by passion; whether it lasts an hour or a lifetime is of little consequence. The book revolves around the central premise that women experience love promised and not fulfilled, making them forever "like water for chocolate." Given this construct, going after the one you love, regardless of the consequences, becomes in itself a revolutionary act. All throughout the story, women think about the men whom they have loved and who loved them, and whom they have not been permitted to marry. From the servant Nacha to Mama Elena, unfulfilled passion knows no class distinctions. When the naked Gertrudis vanishes in a cloud of passion, swooped up by the Villista captain, she excites both Tita and Pedro into thinking momentarily that another course is possible for them, until Mama Elena appears to break their spell. Perhaps another meaning of the revolution is that Gertrudis, Tita, Esperanza, and Chencha will all eventually have the opportunity to be with their true loves, regardless of the cost.

Another thing that my mother did not understand about this movie was its ending. The book clearly informs the reader that, following Mama Elena's death, Tita and Pedro become lovers with Rosaura's knowledge. Their love continues a secret, even after Rosaura's death, until the day of the wedding of Pedro's daughter Esperanza and John Brown's son Alex, when Pedro asks Tita to marry him. The passion cooked with the *chiles en nogada* burns even more fiercely in the hidden lovers, who, at the first opportunity, go to their favorite room to indulge in the finally unguarded manifestation of their feelings. Horribly, at the triumphant moment of their union, Pedro suffers a heart attack and dies. Tita quickly decides that life without him, without someone to light the fire within her, would be torture, so she lights a fire within herself and joins Pedro as she burns to death, taking the ranch with her. Her cookbook, alone, survives.

How Mexican an ending! What other culture so teases death that it spends a whole day each year, November 2, to celebrate it? As Frances Toor, the chronicler of Mexican folkways, notes, "For days before and after, death is everywhere present. He leers invitingly from bakery windows, where there are special . . . breads of the dead in animal and human forms; from candy shops, in skulls with bright tinsel eyes." Families get together for a trip to the cemetery, there to clean gravestones, plant flowers, sing songs, play games, make chalk designs, and eat meals with their beloved ancestors. Whereas, across the border, the highest medical expenses are incurred in the last year of life using heroic measures to keep a person breathing, in Mexico death is not so feared. Toor notes that a typical attitude is found in "Valentina," the marching song of those who followed Carranza and Obregón in the revolution. As the soldier sings to his Valentina, "If I must be killed tomorrow/Let them kill me today."[14] What the Mexican fears, rather, is the abandonment of the family and its inevitable alienation and loneliness. That unendurable situation is to be avoided at all costs, even to the extent of the restraint of individual desire. Tita's resolute determination to surrender to her first love, regardless of its consequences, keeps her tied to her mothers—her birth mother Elena and her kitchen mother Nacha—and to her family. After all, it is her grandniece who tells her story and cooks her recipes, a more positive equivalent to cleaning her gravestone.

And it is this feeling that ultimately has my mother and U.S. audiences stumped. What the movie evokes in them is a baffled nostalgia for a time when mothers really mattered and women's work was defined differently than it is today, when dinner all too often for all too many comes from a box and satisfies only the most elemental hunger. There is something alluring for them about a solid family tradition, according to which children live at home until marriage and do not move so far away that they cannot come back for Sunday dinner every week. Although these audiences recognize that in the real world that way of life stifled individual will and led to spiritual, if not physical, death, particularly for women, it seems sensuous and exotic while on screen. Then, as the audience emerges from the theater, it starts to tinker with the movie, trying to meld American individualism uneasily onto Mexican tradition, so that Tita too will have a happy ending. Good food and a blond doctor—what could possibly be wrong with that?

Suggested Readings

Esquivel, Laura. *Like Water for Chocolate: A Novel in Monthly Installments, with Recipes, Romances, and Home Remedies*. Trans. Carol and Thomas Christensen. New York: Doubleday, 1992. By reading the book, the filmwatcher gets a better idea of how Esquivel's spirit world was transformed into the wondrous universe on screen.

French, William E. "Rapto and Estupro in Porfirian and Revolutionary Chihuahua." In *Reconstructing Criminality in Latin America*, ed. Robert Buffington and Carlos Aguirre. Wilmington, DE: Scholarly Resources, forthcoming. A historian's view of courtship on the Mexican-American frontier that contrasts with the film.

Guillermoprieto, Alma. *The Heart That Bleeds: Latin America Now*. New York: Alfred A. Knopf, 1994. Guillermoprieto's insights on Latin America today are an open window on the region's culture. They are beautifully written and often profound.

Pilcher, Jeffrey. "Tamales or Timbales: Cuisine and the Negotiation of Mexican National Identity, 1821–1911." *The Americas* 53, no. 2 (October 1996): 193–216. One of the first essays on the relationship between food and thought in Mexican culture.

Poole, Stafford. *Our Lady of Guadalupe: The Origins and Sources of a Mexican National Symbol, 1531–1797*. Tucson: University of Arizona Press, 1995. The most recent look at the patron saint of Mexico and the Americas.

Tenenbaum, Barbara A. "Streetwise History: The Paseo de la Reforma and the Porfirian State, 1876–1910." In *Rituals of Rule, Rituals of Resistance: Public Celebrations and Popular Culture in Mexico*, ed. William H. Beezley, Cheryl English Martin, and William E. French, 127–50. Wilmington, DE: Scholarly Resources, 1994. A brief survey of how Mexicans created their history through the selection of subjects for highly visible statuary.

Tirado, Thomas C. *Celsa's World: Conversations with a Mexican Peasant Woman*. Tempe, AZ: Center for Latin American Studies, Arizona State University at Tempe, 1991. A lovely look into how Mexican rural women understand their reality.

Toor, Frances. *A Treasury of Mexican Folkways: The Customs, Myths, Folklore, Traditions, Beliefs, Fiestas, Dances, and Songs of the Mexican People*. New York: Crown Publishers, 1947. The best collection in English on Mexican life before cable television and satellite dishes. Filled with illustrations.

Zamudio-Taylor, Victor, and Inma Guiu. "Criss-Crossing Texts: Reading Images in *Like Water for Chocolate*." In *The Mexican Cinema Project*, ed. Chon A. Noriega and Steven Ricci, 45–51. Los Angeles: UCLA Film and Television Archive, Research and Study Center, 1994. Presents helpful insights into the transformations of the linear into the visual art form.

CHAPTER ELEVEN

Depicting the Past in Argentine Films
Family Drama and Historical Debate in *Miss Mary* and *The Official Story*

MARK D. SZUCHMAN

Miss Mary *(1986); produced by Lita Stantic; directed by María Luisa Bemberg; written by Jorge Goldenberg and María Luisa Bemberg based on an original story by María Luisa Bemberg, Beda Docampo Feijoo, and Juan Batista Stagnaro; color; 100 minutes; GEA Cinematográfica, New World Pictures. In a series of flashbacks, Miss Mary Mulligan (Julie Christie), an English immigrant in midtwentieth-century Argentina, looks back on her experiences as governess in the wealthy and conservative Martínez-Bordagain family as General Juan Domingo Perón rises to power.*

La Historia Oficial *(1985), or* The Official Story, *also known as* The Official Version; *produced by Marcelo Pineyro; directed by Luis Puenzo; written by Aida Bortnik and Luis Puenzo; color; 112 minutes; Virgin/Almi/Historias Cinematográficas/ Progress Communications. In Argentina during the early 1980s, Alicia (Norma Aleandro), a history teacher with a comfortable life, tries to instruct her obstreperous students, coax information from her increasingly worried and irritated husband (Hector Alterio), investigate the circumstances of her adopted daughter's birth, and understand the truth of what has been happening around her as the military government collapses.*

Argentina's popular culture is filled with images of a people who, since the early nineteenth century, have struggled to create a sense of nation through a series of contests, often violent, seldom decisive. These images include the nineteenth-century gaucho and his *facón* (knife), combining skills related to cattle ranching with survival, equally efficient for slaughtering cattle in the fields as for cutting an opponent's face in a saloon brawl. Other icons of Argentine culture include the intellectual guiding lights in areas of social criticism and literature: writers such as Domingo F. Sarmiento and Esteban Echeverría, who blended their nineteenth-century experiences with liberal ideological tenets to present probing analyses of the colonial past and bemoan its injurious effects on the political stability of the independent nation-states.

Finally, any student of Latin American popular culture will recognize Argentina as one of the largest producers of films in Latin America. Cinema has loomed large as a medium for the transmission of values and lore both within the country and as a cultural export to other regions of Latin America and Spain. Moreover, Argentine cinema became such an important medium for entertainment and the presention of cultural norms that it provided actors with the medium of recognition that proved essential for subsequent careers as important political leaders. Arguably the most famous of these cinematic icons, who went on to become a political idol, was Evita Perón, who, with her husband, Juan Domingo Perón, dominated the political culture of Argentina for decades beyond her death in 1953. Evita Perón had started her artistic career in radio and continued on in film, though she never starred in a major or highly respected production. Still, moviegoers saw a familiar face as Evita made her political rounds on behalf of her husband's presidential bid in the 1946 elections. Following their victory, many Peronists of the popular classes saw in the First Lady a kind of Cinderella story: humble young woman, discovered by the studios, becomes the darling and protector of the nation.

This essay discusses the connections between history and its popular rendition in the form of films designed for the consumption of audiences in Argentina. It explores briefly some of the history of Argentine cinema, especially as it pertains to the portrayal of folkloric tales and historical icons, some of which had originally appeared as novels and plays written during the nineteenth century. In this regard, film in Argentina can be said to appear as an extension of the traditional literary medium of historical presentation, preserving, extending, and altering the past in flexible ways. Films that treated historical themes were linked to the political debates taking place at the time of production. The cinematic medium, therefore, was integral to prevailing ideological currents, and in this way remained dynamic and current; historical tales were not presented in a detached manner.

Two Argentine films will be closely explored, *Miss Mary* and *The Official Story*. Both were released after the redemocratization process and restoration of civilian rule that began in 1983, following seven years of brutal military governments. These films, which address issues deeply embedded in Argentine political culture, will be contrasted in both content and approach with their predecessors. Finally, some conclusions will be drawn and the essay will present an analysis of the role that cinema has played in clarifying the social and economic tenets that have characterized the Argentine historiography and the way that Argentines themselves have reflected on their historical experiences.

The Nature of Historical Truth in Argentina

The depiction of past times in Argentina reflects a pattern of historical representation consistent with the experiences of peoples throughout the world. Every nation constructs its past in accordance with the needs of both the popular sectors and the governing elites. The ease with which we can find multiple versions of the biographies of national heroes and endless material representations of a nation's most dramatic historical experiences speaks to the need of all peoples to construct their past in the most widely understandable ways. Thus, we find the cult of national heroes, the celebration of patriotic landscapes, and the iconography of the victors of wars as vital components of the cultural elements of virtually every nation. The similarity of portrayals tells us a great deal about the need of every people—literate and preliterate, Western and non-Western, across boundaries of time and space—to construct intelligible and accessible frames of historical reference. In Latin America, we have indications of this natural tendency from as early as the seventeenth century, for example, in the works of the writer and artist Carlos Sigüenza y Góngora, who designed iconography depicting the achievements of the twelve Aztec emperors.[1]

Because of the peripheral standing of Indians in the Argentine formative experiences, they do not figure prominently; indeed, Indians appear largely as obstacles along the frontier until their elimination as a population tied to their own territorial domains. But in many other ways the construction of the Argentine past follows familiar patterns. As is true of other countries in Latin America, Argentine history has long been represented through its hagiography, heroic figures whose efforts and personal sacrifices made the nation possible or maintained its independence.[2] Presenting the past required the depiction of its actors in the best possible light, which sometimes meant that characteristics of important historical actors that might be considered inappropriate or inconsistent with the image of unblemished heroism and purity would be excised from the record, lest such a patriotic figure suffer from appearing unseemly. One of the better-known writers who engaged in manipulating the historical record was Bartolomé Mitre, the nineteenth-century political leader and military hero who was also a dedicated historian. Mitre wrote a multivolume history of José de San Martín, the renowned liberator of the southern half of Spanish South America. His *Historia de San Martín* presents a warrior and liberator pure of heart, a loving husband, and a political thinker fully dedicated to the highest ideals of republican virtues. However, his frustrations and his strong and sometimes offensive language, directed at the governing revolutionary junta of Buenos Aires for its inadequate response to his army's needs in Chile, are not visible in the book. Moreover, Mitre made sure that the historical records were purged of all such references.[3] This action is an example of the manner in which political leaders or influential people could appropriate historical personalities and shape them in the light deemed best by such observers.

In other, perhaps less subtle, ways the evidence from historical representations in the realm of popular culture demonstrates the blurring of the historical record with the propagandistic nature of the creators' political objectives. Thus, Doris Sommer reminds us that the heroes and heroines in the works of the Argentine writer José Mármol, a leading literary figure of the first half of the nineteenth century and a political enemy of General Juan Manuel de Rosas, Argentina's strongman from 1829 until 1852, "are flawlessly white," in contradistinction to the presentation of the dictator's popular supporters as a dark-skinned rabble.[4]

Rendering the Argentine Past and Society in Film, 1930–1984

The medium of film has shown producers, writers, and directors to be similarly concerned with portraying the Argentine past and social conditions in special ways. In movies we have the opportunity to observe new forms of representations and new mechanisms for portrayals strategically designed for their impact and for a reach incomparably greater than any literary medium or oral tradition of the past. This essay will concentrate on two Argentine films, *Miss Mary* and *The Official Story*, that have had a significant impact on our views of the Argentine experience and that have achieved an international level of success. These two films share several important characteristics: 1) they challenge the Argentine collective consciousness at a moment of violent awakening from a traditionally complacent disposition toward the institutional representation of truths; 2) they treat and contest some of the political and cultural tenets long held sacred in Argentina; and 3) they depict the tensions between followers and individualists and the price paid by each.

Argentine film production dates to the early 1930s. During the first years, films failed to attract the attention of the upper classes, who considered the efforts too simple and crass, closer to the low-brow tastes of the masses. They were right in this assessment insofar as film transferred tango, folkloric, and gauchesque cultural elements to celluloid. Furthermore, the characters tended to be exalted in their apparent country brusqueness, which hid their ingenuous poking of fun at the social and political powers.[5] The first generation of Argentine films shied away from references to social problems. Whatever tensions or distances existed between the common folk and the dominant classes were presented in the form of picaresque oppositions between the Chaplinesque countryside creole and those whom he successfully exploited for his own benefit. In Manuel Romero's films, the characters are *pícaros* without permanent jobs but not out to destroy their social system. The 1930s also witnessed the production of *costumbrista* films exalting the regional themes and the social-folkloric tragedy. These were maud-lin renditions of traditional literature, portrayed especially through films produced by Mario Soffici. The rate of film production rose astronomically: Argentina released approximately fifty films an-nually between 1938 and 1942, far ahead of any other country ex-cept the United States.[6]

By the early 1940s other producers, such as Francisco Mújica and Lucas Demar, had joined the trend toward social realism. In 1942, Demar's *La Guerra Gaucha* (*The Gaucho War*) aroused the greatest public response in the history of film in Argentina. The film, based on stories by the nationalist thinker and historian Leopoldo Lugones, drew from the nationalism increasingly in vogue by depicting the heroic struggles of creoles fighting under the lead-ership of Martín Güemes in the northern provinces during the war for independence. The movie served as a medium to evoke a flow-ery gaucho language, weaving heroic scenes with a script written by Homero Manzi, a poet, tango composer, and political activist. The nationalist overtones of *La Guerra Gaucha* would be echoed in the period of leftist nationalism that swept the country during the 1970s.

Argentine cinema fell sharply both in quality and volume by 1943, when a military coup overthrew a government notoriously riddled with political corruption. Moreover, the military men who now ruled tended to have pro-Fascist leanings, were intolerant of dissidence, and looked to eradicate voices of contention. The origi-nal cinematic themes that had given a critical edge to the depiction of the social and cultural condition of Argentina virtually disap-peared. Movies were rendered, instead, in repetitive, stereotyped, and standard fare. American cinema had begun its domination of the international film market, and Hollywood also had begun to invest in the nascent Mexican film industry, which would grow and displace the Argentine production from the Central and South American market. Finally, the cultural precepts of the first Peronist administration, which began in 1946 and was heavily imbued with the nationalist leitmotif, served to temper the critical edge toward which Argentine cinema had been moving. In its appropriation of the nationalist sentiment and in its intolerance of criticism, the Peronist state witnessed the abandonment by independent produc-ers of their incipient condemnations of the existing social system.[7]

By the early 1960s, average cinematic production value was raised. Typically, movie plot lines dealt with broken hearts and broken homes, or with *policiales*—movies depicting crime and the police. Women figured prominently, and not always as victims of men's ways. The actresses Libertad Lamarque and Mirtha Legrand portrayed women struggling with the social difficulties created by a system of unfair income distribution in which the poor stood little chance to improve their conditions. Yet the bases of the socioeconomic system remained unquestioned; indeed, they were habitually accepted through the vehicle of the lower classes' pious fatalism.

By the start of the 1970s, Argentine filmmaking took on a newly radical social and political consciousness. Argentine cinema in the 1970s provided some titles with very high impact, designed to act as political statements and social criticism. *La Hora de los Hornos* (*The Hour of the Furnaces*), a ten-hour production, depicted the wide-ranging crisis of Argentina's society, culture, and labor movement, and an intelligentsia wearing the slippery fabric of social dismemberment. The scenes were shot with a brusquely challenging and iconoclastic quality. By the film's end, no Argentine institution remained intact and the whole nation was depicted as doomed.

La Hora de los Hornos and other 1970s-vintage films that questioned the precarious nature of Argentine bourgeois society owe their existence to another heritage, an equally complex and more iconoclastic rendition of the phenomenon of self-criticism, the famed *autocrítica argentina. Autocrítica* (self-criticism) has long formed part of the Argentine genre of letters and cultural self-depiction. This tradition dates to the first third of the nineteenth century, when the efficiently authoritarian regime of General Rosas demonstrated to the younger generation of educated Argentines that the original revolutionaries may have achieved independence in the 1810s but had failed to establish consensus or lasting liberalism. Beginning with the "Generation of '37," the collective term for the country's thinkers and essayists who wrote starting in the 1830s and 1840s, the Argentine intelligentsia has long been preoccupied with explaining failure. What gives a special quality to this concern is the unusually deep level of introspection that characterizes the treatises. Writers of the Generation of '37 created "what has become an unfortunate genre in Argentine letters: the explanation of failure." The literary device employs a mechanism of "mercilessness that borders on self-defeating negativism."[8]

The Argentine cinematic medium has not escaped this cultural tradition, which is felt especially strongly among creative artists.

One of the most successful productions to question the status quo was *La Fiaca*, a work written for the stage by Ricardo Talesnik in 1967. Subsequently made into a film of the same title, it achieved an unexpectedly high level of success and popularity within an Argentine public mired in the early stages of acute self-doubt. The material success of Argentine industry, the recruitment of hundreds of thousands into the ranks of the middle class, and the growing anonymity found at the base of a consumer society are thrown together into a dark comedy of one man's effort at regaining his status as an independent agent of his actions. Nestor, the principal character, is the prototype member of the Buenos Aires middle class. Happily married, a midlevel manager in a large corporation where he has been working for several years, Nestor wakes up early on a Monday morning with an overwhelming desire to stay home from the office just this once. The rules of the social order, however, forbid the articulation of his sentiments: ennui is not an acceptable reason for neglecting obligations. Emergency conditions, such as illness or death, are another matter. Thus, in conformity with the rules, Nestor adopts a conformist approach to his dilemma by constructing his illness: *fiaca* (a loose adaptation of the Italian *fiacco*, or laziness). It cannot be clearly defined, it cannot be precisely located, it cannot be found in the medical literature. *Fiaca* can, however, be sensed but only after a concerted effort at understanding the very personal nature of its origins.

By the middle of Nestor's saga, the contagion of *fiaca* threatens other workers, including the company's medical doctor who is sent to Nestor's apartment to check on the patient and provide the diagnosis needed prior to approval of the health insurance coverage. The press reports this outbreak of a new virus. In the end, however, the invisible hand of capitalism wins. Nestor faces strains in his marriage, his family is under pressure to convince him to give up his sickness, and company management is presenting an ultimatum. Painfully acknowledging that much more than his own needs are at stake, Nestor is forced to submit. The sense of humiliation is almost more than he can bear as he shuffles to his office, with a glazed look, while humming the national anthem.[9] Talesnik's *La Fiaca* grafted itself onto the Argentine psyche, its invented word forming part of the national language and popular culture. Suffering from occasional *fiaca* came to signify the national malaise. Thus, films that depicted the state of Argentine society in the

1960s implicitly critiqued the paths followed by the nation on its way to a state of high anxiety.

A film that questions the established order by its protagonist's futile attempt at personal redemption is one thing, but redeeming the past of a whole people is quite another, which is what Argentine historical films tried to do in the 1970s. One of the productions that took up historical themes was *Juan Moreira*, which portrayed the injustices caused by unfettered capitalism and the dire consequences it brought on poor Argentines, especially in the countryside. *Juan Moreira* was the screen adaptation of a police drama written by Eduardo Gutiérrez in 1879. The novella was serialized in the newspaper *La Patria Argentina* between the end of November 1879 and early January 1880. More than four years later, in July 1884, *Juan Moreira* was produced on the stage as a pantomime. It is based on a true story involving a gaucho, a cowboy who undergoes the travails of many of his countrymen throughout much of the nineteenth century. Gauchos came to represent in the last quarter of the nineteenth century two very different visions of the path taken to nation-building in the second half of the 1800s. For the governments of the era, all of which advanced the aspirations of a Europeanized elite, the gauchos represented the most dangerous obstacle to order and progress. Their far-flung mobility and their well-known disdain for institutional authority served to mark them as troublemakers, unreliable workers, and gullible followers of demagogic caudillos who through much of the century had thrown the country into anarchy and war. As such, gauchos suffered abuse and different forms of exploitation, including forcible recruitment into the military, often far away from home in the miserable conditions found along the Indian frontier.

By the 1880s, political, military, and economic conditions had served to neutralize the gauchos as a source of continuous concern for the authorities. The stiffening of official policies of social control blended with the equally effective forces of commercial capitalism and infrastructural investments to marginalize the gauchos as an identifiable group capable of mounting an organized threat to the prevailing order. A wide spectrum of Argentines, both in and out of government, considered the elimination of the gaucho danger to be a major achievement, the removal of a key obstacle to unlimited progress as European investors, especially from England, poured their capital into the country.

By contrast, a small but influential group of intellectuals and literary figures noted with melancholy and regret the virtual elimination of one of the country's most genuine and vital forces while the native traditions were undergoing dramatic and unwelcome change in the form of an increasingly materialistic and foreign culture. Massive waves of foreigners and foreign capital washed on Argentine shores. The most famous of these intellectuals and writers was José Hernández, who in 1872 published a highly praised epic poem, *Martín Fierro*. Its more than one thousand stanzas depict the human drama of a gaucho who was relentlessly pursued by the police and military authorities for wanting nothing more than to live free, while watching his beloved countryside, the pampas, turn into a land increasingly populated by European immigrants single-mindedly interested in making money. Eduardo Gutiérrez's choice of a gaucho for his serialized police novella, *Juan Moreira*, formed part of the development of a nationalist gauchesque literature that celebrated the purity of heart and simplicity of country folk while lamenting the demise of the old Argentina. This literature, in turn, echoed the sentiments of many who witnessed the country turning away from its Iberian traditions into an increasingly alien culture. In 1904, Lucio V. Mansilla reminisced in his *Mis memorias* with more than slight bitterness: "I have a modest aspiration, which I trust will be rewarded with some success. It consists in helping to prevent the complete death of the nation's traditions. This Argentine land of ours is transforming itself so much in its moral being and its physical shape, as is the appearance of its vastly distant regions spread in all directions. That symbol, the gaucho, is going, the deserted countryside is going, the village is disappearing, the locomotive's whistle replaces the wagon: in a word, they are changing our language, the country is rotting away."[10]

Mansilla was echoing the sentiments of other writers, such as Lucio V. López, who in the late 1880s struck a chord with his fellow *porteños* (residents of the city of Buenos Aires) when he published *La gran aldea* (The large village), a vehicle of reminiscences of the city before it became the bustling metropolis filled with immigrants, merchants, capitalists, and industrialists. These observers felt themselves becoming part of a nation increasingly disconnected from its religious habits and turning, instead, to a secular materialism that threatened class harmony.

Juan Moreira, as noted earlier, was adapted for the stage in the form of a pantomime. It opened in July 1884 to very few reviews, which ranged from mixed to hostile, and to general ridicule from the culturally sophisticated elite. A reviewer for the newspaper *El Diario* noted that with the production of *Juan Moreira* the national theater had been born, "but this newborn had emitted such weak cries that no one had taken notice. With the announcement of the pantomime of *Juan Moreira*, the intellectual aristocracy reacted with gestures of disdain, and the majority of the newspapers have ignored the event. They had laughed at *Juan Moreira* the novel. They continue to laugh at *Juan Moreira* the pantomime. They say: This is for the *plebe* (rabble)."[11] Thus, the social and political distances that had long separated the urban-based gentry from their countryside laborers had begun to take on more definitive cultural hues. The division between "civilization" and "barbarism"—the description first used in the 1840s by Domingo F. Sarmiento, the highly influential political intellectual and writer, to describe the two basic antagonistic forces in Latin America—would become part of the nation's literary legacy. In time, the published portrayals in the print medium of the powerful urban aristocrats and the lowly countryside laborers, along with their mutual distrust and antagonism, would be reconstituted in film.

The film version of *Juan Moreira*, colorfully and closely shot, represents the freedom-loving, nationalist gaucho driven into banditry by the forces of modernization funded at the initial stages of Argentina's fast-paced boom of the last third of the nineteenth century by foreign capital.[12] Gutiérrez described Moreira, who became a well-known cowboy bandit, perhaps in the style of Butch Cassidy, with considerable respect and even honor: "Moreira was like the majority of our gauchos: endowed with a strong soul and a generous heart, he would have been a source of glory for the motherland had he been sent down noble paths—such as, for example, at the head of a cavalry regiment; instead, he was pushed down the slope of criminal activity, having failed to recognize the limits of the savage instincts that had been awakened within him by the same hatred and fury with which he was pursued."[13]

By the 1970s, this portrayal had become prototypical of the consequences of authoritarianism and rapacious capitalism. A widely shared nationalist sentiment that joined with a partisan leftist interpretation of Peronism, these views telescoped into an explanation for the country's dependent relationship with the industrial West. The authoritarian nature of government officials underlies the film as much as it did the original text. The principal character,

Juan Moreira, is caught in the vise of corrupt politicians who joined with the landowning classes in furthering their own interests. Any attempt to free oneself from the grip of these authorities meant imprisonment or worse. "The gaucho," wrote Gutiérrez, "is a man for whom the law means nothing more than this great practical truth: that the justice of the peace in his district has the right to put him in chains and send him to the frontier to serve in the military's frontlines."[14] If those words represented the construction of the historical moments experienced by Gutiérrez in his own times, a century later they had become more widely representative of Argentine society.

These film productions reflected a hardening of attitudes and the narrowing of perspectives in an Argentina that would be plunged into years of political chaos. A series of military regimes, the last of which invited Juan Perón to return in the hopes of saving the nation from virtual civil war, was followed by no such miracle but rather by Perón's death in 1974. His departure opened the way for the remarkably inept administration of his widow (his second wife, not Evita)—voted into office through the Perón-Perón ticket of the previous year's election—and then the military coup of 1976, which ended the mockery of constitutional rule. Propelled by the violence of the extreme left, which the extreme right used as legitimator for its own violent practices, the years of authoritarianism culminated in the folly of the Falklands War against the British over the islands populated mostly by sheep. A gullible nation that had swallowed the story that its *desaparecidos* (disappeared persons) were largely the slanderous creation of the nation's enemies at home and abroad had come to believe that Argentina had brought the British to their knees. And then they literally awoke one morning in July 1982 to the news of the Argentine surrender. In the ensuing months, the performance of the armed forces, in particular the army, and the loss of over a thousand lives became the subjects of enraged public sentiment. Argentines had long ago stopped believing in the government's efficiency—inherent faith in official corruption and ineptitude is as common to Argentines as it is to many other people throughout Latin America and elsewhere. The new variant, however, was the establishment of a culture of distrust that seeped down to the roots of Argentina's epistemological structures.

Faith in the ability of military and authoritarian regimes to govern effectively had begun to slip by the early 1980s. The Falklands War transformed the relations of political forces in Argentina.[15]

Moreover, the sudden awakening to the truths regarding the miserable conduct of the war by inept and corrupt military officers occasioned a fundamental change among Argentines toward all forms of official information. It also served to undermine belief in the mechanisms of information transmission, including the mass media. If the official news had been manipulated for years, if the vast majority of the press had practiced self-censorship, what else had been falsified? In the end, loss of faith in the government spread and metastasized into a general disbelief in the wider array of accepted truths, including received opinion about past times. For our purposes, this stage was a cathartic one, which offered a momentous opening for an Argentine film industry that had been dormant for many years. To the extent that other stories could be disclosed and that other voices could present new stories, Argentine films found a public hungry for alternatives to the clichéd celluloid romances and cheap action films imported from Hong Kong, in the case of martial arts, and from Italy, in the form of "spaghetti Westerns."

Three basic changes are seen in films produced after the Falklands War. First, while the subject of social criticism resurfaces, the focus shifts to particular aspects of the Argentine experience instead of wondering about a generic malaise. Second, the fundamental story on film is told through more complex characters, who display more ambiguities, are more fully developed, and who receive more of the directors' and writers' attention. Third, the principal protagonists are likelier to be women who, seen through their familial interactions rather than as individuals, represent the principal vehicle for the story.

Families in Crisis: Two Case Studies

The two films treated here are representative of the family's centrality in a far wider scope than its productive and reproductive functions. They allow us to observe the effects brought about by the political culture on family members and their negotiations with the difficult choices it engendered. The family unit reflects an unsettling quality of challenge, the difficulties in withstanding the blows that emanate from both the external world and internal relations, and a hovering threat of extinction of family ties as they are historically understood. When the challenge to familial integrity arises, a female is presented as the foil. She represents the relentless force that will have its way regardless of consequences, and she is the agent of blows to the social conventions and the beliefs of her kin.

Oligarchical Folly

Miss Mary appeared on the heels of María Luisa Bemberg's international success, *Camila*. Bemberg died in Buenos Aires of cancer on May 7, 1995, at the age of seventy-three. By end of her career, she had been involved in numerous films as screenwriter, directorial assistant, and, finally, director in her own right. Her directorial debut took place in 1980, at the age of fifty-eight, with *Momentos*, the story of a woman from the high society of Buenos Aires suddenly left rudderless after her divorce. Four years and a film or two later, Bemberg came to the attention of audiences in Europe and the United States with *Camila*, set during the 1840s in the Argentina of Juan Manuel de Rosas. The film was nominated for an Oscar in the category of Best Foreign Film.

In 1986, Bemberg directed *Miss Mary*, which brought the British actress Julie Christie into a role made more demanding by the decreasingly clear definitions of status and power during the ominous 1940s, a period of transition from oligarchical to populist regimes. In 1990, Bemberg directed *Yo, la Peor de Todas* (*I, the Worst of All*), depicting the life of Sor Juana Inés de la Cruz (1651–1695), a nun in the Convent of San Jerónimo in Mexico City, who became the most renowned poet of the seventeenth century and one of the greatest intellectual figures of the colonial period.[16] Bemberg's last picture, *De Eso No Se Habla* (*I Don't Want to Talk about It*), starring Marcello Mastroianni, appeared in 1993 and is another period piece revolving around the 1940s.

Bemberg cowrote the screenplay of *Miss Mary* with Jorge Goldenberg, adapting it from an original story in the creation of which she also participated. The movie's cast may be seen as one more example of Bemberg's well-known and calculated barbs at Argentina's conservatism and its political culture: Julie Christie and, indeed, an Anglophile relationship soon after Argentina's defeat in the Falklands War; Nacha Guevara, who had been forced into exile after receiving anonymous death threats during the military rule; and Eduardo Pavlovsky, a frequent consultant for Bemberg on the psychological dimensions of her characters, and who, as a well-known psychoanalyst, would be considered a natural enemy of the anti-Freudian Catholic establishment.[17] The film is effortlessly bilingual, a linguistic representation of the easy communication that had long guided Anglo-Argentine relations.

Miss Mary picks up on the historical theme of authoritarianism in Argentina and, as a counterpart, borrows liberally from *Tea and Sympathy* in exploiting the tension between the preceptist woman—part mentor, part caretaker—and the teenager in love with the gentle image of authority. Yet it would be too confining to say that Bemberg views the authoritarian character as merely institutional in nature and political in manifestation, somehow independent of the social conditions and spiritual makeup of the society in which it flourishes. If, in *Camila*, Bemberg focuses on the casual acceptance of the violence of caudillos, even by those who would—in the end—fall victims to it, the case of *Miss Mary* depicts the modern variant of condoning the destructiveness of war and the political violence of Argentina in the interwar period. Furthermore, Bemberg's treatment of the past, whether dealing with the brutality of Buenos Aires in the 1840s or with the wholesale death witnessed during the Spanish civil war in the 1930s, maintains a critical view of the moral and political underpinnings of Catholic conservatism.

Through a series of flashbacks, not always successful in clarifying the political labyrinth that spans the period between September 6, 1930, and October 16, 1945, Mary Mulligan, the English governess hired by the Martínez-Bordagain family, takes us inside the world of an oligarchy too focused on international Jewish and Communist conspiracies to consider its own impending eclipse. The movie begins with the immediate aftermath of the military coup that brought down the second administration of President Hipólito Irigoyen in 1930 and ends on the eve of the massive demonstrations that brought Perón back from a brief term of incarceration and into the unquestioned leadership of the laboring masses in 1945.

The family includes two daughters and one son. The story begins with a sense of renewed confidence, shared by the parents. The children can resume their normal, happy lives now that Argentina has been made safe by General José Uriburu's successful conspiracy against Irigoyen's constitutional government. The parents are seen on their way to a white-tie affair to celebrate the event, a transparent allusion to the parties given in September 1973 by the Chilean military and the civilian supporters of the coup against President Salvador Allende. For its part, the Argentine military would once again interrupt the constitutional process on March 24, 1976, by deposing the remarkably inept government of Isabel Perón, the ill-equipped widow of the populist leader who had died in office in July 1974. Little resistance was registered to the military's move in 1976—less, in fact, than the minimal opposition that General Uriburu had faced in 1930. In an Argentina that, by the 1970s, had been rent by social and economic cleavages, populism would succumb "to the crossfire between society's demand for greater democratization and the exigencies of the Argentine political economy."[18]

The opening scene of *Miss Mary* shows the British governess putting the two young daughters to bed. The preparations call for tying together the ends of the long sleeves of one girl's nightgown to keep her from sucking her thumb. This ritual is performed with as much en passant matter-of-factness as is the search under their beds for any strangers, undoubtedly males. As this scene develops and the girls' parents set out for the ball, all is said in British-accented English. *Miss Mary* can easily be dismissed as a medium for a series of silly and arcane beliefs in old wives' tales or as a heavy-handed treatment of the Argentine oligarchy's delusion that desirable outcomes can simply be willed, aided by the vigilance and constricted behaviors of a long-dead Victorian era, now mimicked by a moribund generation emulating the best of British upbringing. We hear the voiced thoughts of Mary Mulligan as she finishes packing for her transatlantic voyage: "Perhaps you should have gone to India, Miss Mary, where at least you know who the natives are." Thus, the adults' behaviors and expectations form merely a part of a sense of order insisted upon by an oligarchy blind to the violent changes that will ultimately consume them. This self-delusion propels the oligarch's wife in 1938 to explain Hitler's true intentions to Miss Mary: "My husband believes that he'll only go after Jews and Communists." In this fashion, the sophisticated Argentine allays the English commoner's worries about British involvement in a war with Germany: it is all quite silly.

The Martínez-Bordagain clan displays the end of a multigenerational path toward moral decadence and political corruption. The wife's father—a member of the vaunted Generation of '80 responsible for the country's economic miracle—had lost his own fortune at the gambling tables of Monte Carlo. A marriage of financial calculation by his daughter with an estanciero husband was the only means of maintaining appearances and the appropriate life-style.

But the old man never recuperated from the shock: Grandpapa retains an aged and vacant look, and he never makes a sound. For her part, Grandmama's favorite activity involves separating photographs of the extensive family members into two piles: *muertos* and *vivos* (those dead and those alive).

Miss Mary Mulligan awaits her introduction to the Martínez-Bordagain family with apprehension. *Courtesy Museum of Modern Art*

The mother's odd behaviors include periodically locking herself into her "little crying room," less a shelter from melancholy than a space to revel in it. And the father appears as the ever-pragmatic and sardonic observer of a world that is slipping away from his authoritarian grasp. His son does not appear to have much interest in the estancia business; indeed, we never know what the young man seeks except, of course, Miss Mary. He is emotionally weak, indecisive, indolent, and has to be virtually dragged to a back-country bordello to lose his virginity. The younger daughter, by contrast, needs to be dragged away from losing hers, an activity to which she dedicates a strongly voluntaristic attitude and experimental approach even if, in the end, she cannot decide whether or not it was enjoyable.

The elder daughter, the most creative and energetic of all, enters into the world of narcotics and mental illness and is forced to suppress all her talents, adding to the apparent female conspiracy to bring down the family. And then there is the children's uncle, brother to the reclusive mother. An ardent nationalist and anti-Semite, he avidly scans the radio for news of the Spanish civil war, cheering every advance by General Francisco Franco's Fascists. This armchair general follows the action on a wall map dotted with flags organized into two sets—one of which displays the hammer and sickle—which he moves according to the reported military movements. Years later, in the tremulous political atmosphere of 1945 Buenos Aires, a Spaniard would boast to Miss Mary that none of the licentious demonstrators running freely throughout the city in support of Perón would have dared such antics if Franco had been in charge.

The film explodes the antinomies of asserted values and behavioral practices. This central opposition is manifested in various ways but always within the framework of ethical opposites, of morality and lasciviousness, of conservatism in public and licentiousness in private, of affinity for Fascist hierarchies in the thirties and support for liberal democracies in the forties. Bemberg explored these dyads through longitudinal portrayals of Argentine mores. Thus, the Fascist uncle sinks in mourning upon hearing of the suicide of Leopoldo Lugones, an intellectual who had broken with the Socialists to become the spiritual leader of Argentine and Latin American rightists.[19] And yet, while outwardly rigid and anti-Semitic, he is also assigned the family ritual of taking the young nephew to the nearby bordello to lose his virginity to a Jewish prostitute. By contrast, the loss of virginity by one of the girls through a completely unemotional sexual encounter with a member of a proper oligarchical family results in a scandal that explodes into significant consequences.

The father is portrayed as the only one who apprehends the environment of pervasive duplicity and hypocrisy. Bemberg uses him as the prophet of doom, a good-natured reminder of the bleak future that lies ahead. At the ball celebrating his daughter's wedding, the groom—portrayed as a dull and irate member of the oligarchy whose sexual passions required the loveless marriage—resolutely proclaims that negotiating with Perón would amount to treason. "Never fear," responds his newly acquired father-in-law, "we're not that smart. We'll fight him." It was the evening of October 16, 1945. The following day, tens of thousands of Argentines, mostly from the working classes, would descend on the capital city to embark on the journey that would bring to an end the era of oligarchical politics.[20] But none of this is shown; depicting political mobilization is not Bemberg's goal. Her approach is to pierce the political culture of the family. The film ends subtly: at dawn, we see Miss Mary's trunks hoisted by a crane onto the ship that will return her to England.

Middle-Class Awakenings

If *Miss Mary* portrays the past, *The Official Story* addresses its construction. The film can thus resonate with the historian to the extent that both seek to weave together the historical record from disparate parts. Yet the film evokes a very different empathetic chord from Argentines who lived through the Proceso of the 1970s and 1980s. The central preoccupation of *The Official Story* deals with the unfolding of layers designed to hide the historical truth. Much in the same way as the lead actress's hair unravels over the course of the film (in contrast to the tightly controlled bun she wears at the start), the official history of events in the Argentina of military governments unravels at the end, loosened from the weight of fear and political naïveté.

The movie, which won the 1985 Academy Award for Best Foreign Film, was produced in late 1982 and early 1983, only months after Argentina's surrender to Great Britain in the Falklands War. Directed by Luis Puenzo, the cast includes Norma Aleandro, Hugo Arana, and Hector Alterio. By then, Alterio had become typecast as an Argentine conservative and an authoritarian *padre de familia*. His role as the family patriarch in *Camila* established his scowl as the symbol of intolerance and of the smug disdain for anyone who disagreed with him and his like-minded peers. For Argentine authoritarians, individualists deserved personal scorn and required careful watching by the guardians of order. The disposition to questioning accepted historical truths occasioned in Argentina different forms of violence, most of which are delivered in *The Official Story* through sensory and emotional, rather than physical, ways. The very first sound effect is heard in the initial frames when the film's title is torn apart on screen and the crisp sound of shredded paper augurs the destruction of records and lives. We are immediately taken to a schoolyard where morning exercises are being held, centered on the singing of the national anthem.

Alicia Marnet de Ibañez, played by Norma Aleandro, is a teacher in a secondary school for boys. To her classes on Argentine history since 1810 she brings a dedication to achievement based on order, hierarchy, and established precepts. She introduces herself to her students on the first day of school, laying out her expectations and the course's objectives. Her demands, particularly in the context of classroom order and civility, are clear and absolute: *"La indisciplina no se aprende, ni se enseña"* (Lack of discipline is neither learned nor taught). In her view, the importance of her subject matter is overwhelming, for, as she tells her students, to be able to understand history is to be able to understand the world. The calling of the roll provides director Puenzo with the opportunity to point out the difficulties encountered on a daily basis by anyone not fully in step with the crowd. Failure to fit always carries a price, as shown in the case of the slightly effeminate Martin Cullen. His stylized response to the teacher's calling of his name generates the predictable jeers by the rest of the boys. We see the pranksterism of the students, which over time melds into the intolerance of a wide spectrum of Argentine society, ill disposed toward deviants of any sort, including, ultimately, the protesting Mothers of the Plaza de Mayo.

Their protests had been taking place since 1978, when the number of cases of men and women who had disappeared had grown into the thousands. In a bold move, imitated by few others, a group of women organized to petition the government to conduct an investigation into the whereabouts of their children. The lack of responsiveness by the government, the different branches of the military, and the police fueled the suspicions that the missing thousands had been abducted by the military regime or, at a minimum, that such abductions were countenanced by its highest officials. For their part, the prelates of the Catholic Church, especially in Buenos Aires, showed a calculated reluctance to become involved in the women's demands for an investigation.

Having nowhere else to turn, the women organized themselves into a small group that met to exchange any bit of information and to march quietly on Thursday afternoons around Buenos Aires's Plaza de Mayo, the central plaza facing the Pink House, seat of the executive branch of government. They marched in a circle, holding up signs showing pictures of their missing children and demanding that they be found. Derided at first by a public that believed in the government and its assertion that these women represented a front organization for the nation's enemies from within and from outside, the women were called the "Crazy Mothers of the Plaza." And yet they served as a weekly reminder that all was not well in Argentina, and, as time passed, they became an identifiable point of reference for human rights claims. The international community was by then increasing pressure on the military government to investigate and account for these cases. Demands came especially from France, Spain, and Italy, whose citizens had been among the disappeared. In addition, the administration of President Jimmy Carter was insisting that the Argentine military confront its human rights records, and the Canadian government was seeking the release of Argentines with connections to Canada.

Alicia, the schoolteacher, finds herself entering the self-questioning Argentine political and cultural realms in March 1983. By then, several critical episodes in the political realm, both internally and internationally, had taken their toll on the country, widening the schism between state and society. The war against the British over the Falklands had been launched by General Leopoldo Galtieri's military government on April 2, 1982. By mid-June, Argentine forces had surrendered in Port Stanley, victims of inept military leadership and self-delusional diplomacy combined with tragic performances on the battlefield. Only the air force had demonstrated professional abilities and daring; neither the navy nor the army could claim much glory or interservice coordination. Compounding the sense of popular outrage at the time of surrender was the belief that the war was going well, which was sustained up to the very last moment by news releases falsified by the government and sheepishly reported by the Argentine news media. Thus, the early morning announcement of surrender came as a complete surprise to virtually everyone. Any remaining trust in the efficacy of the government now disappeared, and the military prepared for its exit from power.

By March 1983 political parties were fully engaged in the campaigns that would culminate in the national elections scheduled for October 3. The level of public frustration with the political order and the depth of the skepticism over whether the national crisis would be solved are known from both empirical evidence and from the cinematic portrayal. Over 60 percent of the electorate reported in March 1983 that it was undecided as to which candidates it would support: the Radical Party was the choice of 14 percent of the survey respondents, while the Peronists achieved only a 21 percent voter preference.[21] More than any other single factor for indecision was the high level of uncertainty over received truths that Argentines had taken for granted. This skepticism was captured on film in the unconvinced expressions of the students when Profesora Marnet de Ibañez intones the clichés about history as a key to understanding the world.

The Ibañez family represents the prototype of the Buenos Aires upper middle class. Alicia and her husband, Roberto, live in a comfortable apartment with their five-year-old daughter, adopted at birth. Ibañez works for an important company of financial consultants that has at its disposal easy contacts with the military, both retired and on active duty. The film depicts a common practice during the era of military governments, whereby high-ranking military officers were recruited into private-sector firms immediately upon their retirement from the services. Such companies benefited either directly from government contracts or from inside information regarding financial projections based on the Central Bank's economic plans. Information was easily gathered thanks to the fluid nature of contacts between active and retired officers.

Firmas de asesoramiento (investment firms) had sprung up throughout the nation in response to the opportunities and challenges offered by a political economy that wavered from one minister of economics to another; moreover, the economy would reflect, in the end, the whims and exigencies of the military. Fortunes were made and lost during a period of dramatic financial oscillations. Only the foreign debt kept growing, achieving 60 percent of gross domestic product by 1982. In their attempts to curb inflation, government officials tightened credit and lowered tariffs. The overexposed private banking sector began its descent into near collapse in 1980; by midyear, capital flight in the hundreds of millions of dollars per month found landing spots in banks in Montevideo, New York, Miami, and London. With the advent of war over the Falklands, the neoliberal economic policies came to a sudden halt; credit from abroad, especially from the United States, dried up, and the war economy favored strategic industrial partners. Finally, military defeat and the collapse of what remained of the economy battered the population, swept away many people's savings, and brought the nation to a state of emergency.

A complex and obscure series of economic measures and mismanagement caused more than a few speculators to suffer the drastic consequences of uncertain times. Macci, an investor in Ibañez's firm, complained that his portfolio was not yielding the profits he had been promised by officials within the firm and in the government. "What promises, Macci?" responds a company officer. "We made no promises, we are only consultants. We can only advise."

While for Roberto Ibañez the potential for a disaster looms too far for him to discern or worry about, his wife faces a rapidly moving series of events that causes her to doubt the solidity of the world she has inhabited over the last half-dozen years. Ultimately, Alicia begins to inquire into her daughter's identity and the manner in which she came to be adopted. Her character is carefully developed to show someone who is comfortable with her beliefs and who does not come to doubt easily. But she is also portrayed as a highly tenacious person who, as she begins to suspect that all is not as it appears, pursues the truth with increasing determination. Her colleague, a teacher of Argentine literature with questionable ideological loyalties to the traditional sense of flag and country and who employs unorthodox teaching methods, initiates the process of breaking down Alicia's self-assured exterior and absolute comfort with received opinion. To be sure, he does not make a good impression at first: she disapproves of the theatrical manner in which he reads Gutiérrez's *Juan Moreira* to his class and of his lively engagement in the students' own learning process. How can such revisionists inspire confidence in this history teacher who venerates Argentine hagiography with dutiful obeisance?

Unlike her students and her colleague, Alicia is neither a natural skeptic nor an avid seeker of underlying reality. Her truths are of the more comfortable sort, such as those found in the received information of history textbooks. She is quick to show her disapproval to a student who dares to say that "history is written by the assassins." What proof does he have of this "fact"? What evidence can he bring to support such a statement? This teacher believes in the clarity of factual relationships as found in the documents; her student believes that the documents are themselves the results of historical struggles. Alicia represents the comfortable belief in official history, while her student knows that to the victor go the spoils. The matter underlying this rhetorical parrying is simple but crucial: who owns history?

In Alicia's world, only sinister minds would cast doubt on pristine truths, a concept echoed by her husband when he responds to her question as to why friends had been arrested and made to disappear years ago: "*Se los llevaron, por algo debe haber sido*" (They must have taken them away for a reason). Alicia's initial doubts about the origins of her adopted child arise from a luncheon at an exclusive Buenos Aires restaurant. The occasion is her annual re-union with her closest high-school classmates, only this time, one of them, Ana, reappears after years of absence. Afterward, during a long night of shared memories, drinks, and laughter, Ana describes her months of incarceration and torture, which were followed by exile without her husband, who disappeared forever. In the course of her anecdote, Ana also tells Alicia about the pregnant women who gave birth while in prison and whose babies were turned over by the authorities for adoption, their parents killed.

Putting the pieces together now takes up the rest of the film, and as Alicia enters the realm of researcher of an unwanted story, she also softens her rigid sense of order and acceptance of hierar-chy. In so doing, director Puenzo follows the new pattern of Argen-tine historical and self-critical cinema in that the central female character becomes the agent of the status quo's destruction. By the end of the film, Argentine history in the school—as researched and written by the students—is transformed into an exercise in inde-pendent thinking. Yet, if Argentine official history in schools is to undergo anything resembling what occurs to the Ibañez family, a great deal of destruction, both to the body politic and to the body of the family, looms ahead. Finally, Alicia is made to understand the flawed nature of her premises, the falsification of the evidence that had defined her, and thus the questionable nature of her sense of identity. Her marriage ends in shambles, and there is more con-cern for its reconfiguration than for its reintegration. After all, di-vorce is commonplace among middle-class Argentines, but the family's validity had not been questioned: now, the sense of be-trayal by the leadership of the family was replacing the historical sense of trust.

By the time that Alicia takes up the cause of the Mothers of the Plaza, she has become enlightened. The historical problem left un-resolved by the film, however, revolves around the concept of col-lective responsibilities. How was it possible that Alicia and her peers remained impervious for so many years to alternative interpreta-tions of the official storytellers' tales? In the context of the movie's temporal setting of March 1983, Alicia would have had several years during which to evaluate the domestic and international dimensions of Argentina's political environment. Yet she arrives at the start of her saga with a Lockeian tabula rasa that remains an unconvincing and elusive facet of Argentine history.

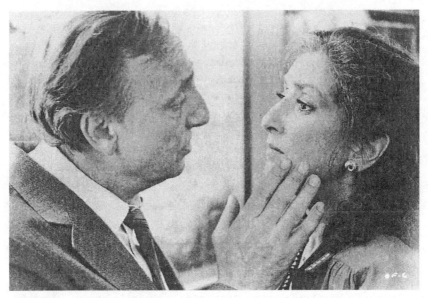

The need to understand the true story of her adopted daughter's birth drives Alicia into conflict with her husband. *Courtesy Museum of Modern Art*

Conclusion

The films discussed in this essay represent the power of cinema to reconstitute some of the vital issues in depicting the Argentine historical experience. By their very nature, these productions are not capable of presenting "better" or "clearer" views of the past: movies are subjected to important structural limitations such as length of time, budgets, and concerns for marketing. Still, they are better suited for portraying nuances than many history texts. The look that Alicia gives her husband toward the end of *The Official Story*, for example, speaks volumes about the bleakness of their situation and, indeed, of the nation's condition. Argentine history portrayed in cinema has succeeded to the extent that it has not been frivolous—that is, it has tackled issues deeply embedded in the national consciousness and in the historical debates.

Historical cinema joined the national debates that fueled the divisions of a country that in the 1970s and 1980s questioned authority as well as received historical truths. Films such as *Miss Mary* and *The Official Story* give us added dimensions to the observation and analysis of the Argentine past that go beyond traditionally bifurcated perspectives: liberalism-conservatism, nationalism-internationalism, federalism-centralism, and other historical antagonisms. At the same time, the nature of the medium itself—and the many commercial and financial considerations that go into the production of films—inhibit fuller explorations of historical phenomena and analyses of historical problematics. Like all matters related to human emotion and calculation, however, exploring the past can be done well or poorly, regardless of the medium. These productions are richer than texts but only in the context of their own confines, raising more questions than answers and serving to remind us that, as historians, we can still learn a thing or two about nuanced meanings.

Suggested Readings

As a distinct body of scholarship, the historical film in Argentina has received minimal treatment. Readers must therefore cull from different sources in order to construct an identifiable analytical structure. The titles of works listed here are merely suggestive of the variety of historical, political, and literary modes of inquiry that have informed Argentine historical filmmaking.

For the conventional treatment of the Latin American past by elite writers of the nineteenth and early twentieth century, see E. Bradford Burns, *The Poverty of Progress: Latin America in the 19th Century* (Berkeley: University of California Press, 1980); and Burns, "Ideology in Nineteenth-Century Latin American Historiography," *Hispanic American Historical Review* 58 (August 1978): 409–31. A good example of the Argentine hagiographic approach is seen in Bartolomé Mitre, *Historia de San Martín* (Buenos Aires: "La Nación," 1888). For an overview of Argentine historical revisionism, see Tulio Halperín Donghi, "El revisionismo histórico argentino como visión decadentista de la historia nacional," *Punto de Vista*, April 23, 1985; and Halperín Donghi, *El espejo de la historia: Problemas argentinos y perspectivas latinoamericanas* (Buenos Aires: Editorial Sudamericana, 1987). The literary treatment of the gauchesque is introduced and explored as a nationalistic leitmotif in Nicolas Shumway's *The Invention of Argentina* (Berkeley: University of California Press, 1991). Examples of the genre include *Juan Moreira* by Eduardo Gutiérrez (Buenos Aires: EUDEBA, 1965); and the epic poem by José Hernández, *Martín Fierro*. Also see Angel Mazzei, comp., *Dramaturgos post-románticos* (Buenos Aires: Ministerio de Cultura y Educación, 1970). The gendered perspective of historical nationalism in Argentina is carefully explored in Francine Masiello, *Between Civilization and Barbarism: Women, Nation, and Literary Culture in Modern Argentina* (Lincoln: University of Nebraska Press, 1992).

Miss Mary treats the period following the military coup that deposed President Hipólito Irigoyen, leader of the Reformist Party's Unión Cívica Radical. One of the most comprehensive studies of Irigoyen and Radicalism can be found in David Rock, *Politics in Argentina, 1890–1930: The Rise and Fall of Radicalism* (Cambridge, England: Cambridge University Press, 1975). Rock provides the most recent treatment of right-wing ideologies in his *Authoritarian Argentina: The Nationalistic Movement, Its History and Its Impact* (Berkeley: University of California Press, 1993). In addition, a helpful array of approaches to Argentine rightist thought is presented in Sandra McGee Deutsch and Ronald H. Dolkart, eds., *The Argentine Right: Its History and Intellectual Origins, 1910 to the Present* (Wilmington, DE: Scholarly Resources, 1993). Different views of the Anglo-Argentine relationship are available in A. G. Ford, "British Investment and Argentine Economic Development, 1880–1914," in *Argentina in the Twentieth Century*, ed. David Rock, 12–40 (Pittsburgh: University of Pittsburgh Press, 1975). A nationalist and critical perspective on Britain's role in Argentine development is offered by Julio Irazusta, *Influencia económica británica en el Río de la Plata* (Buenos Aires: Editorial Universitaria de Córdoba, 1968).

The Perón period contains an extraordinary amount of literature, not all of the highest caliber. Among the better treatments of the period immediately preceding Perón's first presidential term in 1946 is Gustavo Sosa-Pujato, "Popular Culture," in *Prologue to Perón: Argentina in Depression and War, 1930–1943*, ed. Mark Falcoff and Ronald H. Dolkart, 136–63 (Berkeley: University of California Press, 1975); and Félix Luna's detailed *El 45. Buenos Aires: Crónica de un año decisivo* (Buenos Aires: Editorial J. Alvarez, 1969). The days of mid-October 1945, which are referred to in *Miss Mary* as auguring the Perón era, are carefully analyzed by Daniel James, "October 17th and 18th, 1945: Mass Protest, Peronism, and the Argentine Working Class," *Journal of Social History* 21 (Spring 1988): 441–61.

The Official Story references the years of the military dictatorship that began in 1976 and lasted until 1983. The analysis of this period draws significantly from the fields of political science and economics. For the historical background to military governments prior to the 1976 coup, see Marvin Goldwert, *Democracy, Militarism, and Nationalism in Argentina, 1930–1966: An Interpretation* (Austin: University of Texas Press, 1972); and Rubén M. Perina, "The Performance and Consequences of Military Rule in Argentina, 1966–1973" (Ph.D. diss., University of Pennsylvania, 1981). Finally, one of the most respected historical treatments of the military in Argentina is offered in a three-volume study by Robert M. Potash, *The Army and Politics in Argentina*, Vol. 1, *1928–1945, Yrigoyen to Perón*; Vol. 2, *1945–1962, Perón to Frondizi*; and Vol. 3, *1962–1973, From Frondizi to the Peronist Restoration* (Stanford: Stanford University Press, 1969–1980). In political sociology, the classic study analyzing the intricate relationships that governed Argentina's political and economic realms is Guillermo A. O'Donnell, *Modernization and Bureaucratic-Authoritarianism: Studies in South American Politics* (Berkeley: University of California Press, 1973). Also from the domain of political sociology, but with a greater sensitivity to the cultural elements undergirding Argentine political movements, is Carlos H. Waisman, *Reversal of Development in Argentina: Postwar Counterrevolutionary Policies and Their Structural Consequences* (Princeton: Princeton University Press, 1987). The political economy in the twentieth century is explored in William C. Smith, *Authoritarianism and the Crisis of the Argentine Political Economy* (Stanford: Stanford University Press, 1991). The coalition of forces that restored constitutional government following the military's exit from government is explained in Manuel Mora y Araujo, "La naturaleza de la coalición alfonsinista," in *La Argentina electoral*, ed. Natalio R. Botana et al., 89–97 (Buenos Aires: Editorial Sudamericana, 1985).

Two works provide scholarly treatments of the Mothers of the Plaza de Mayo: Marguerite Guzman Bouvard, *Revolutionizing Motherhood: The Mothers of the Plaza de Mayo* (Wilmington, DE: Scholarly Resources, 1994); and Marysa Navarro, "The Personal Is Political: Las Madres de Plaza de Mayo," in *Power and Popular Protest: Latin American Social Movements*, ed. Susan Eckstein, 241–58 (Berkeley: University of California Press, 1989). After the fall of the military government, Argentina's civilian government created the Comisión Nacional Sobre la Desaparición de Personas (headed by noted novelist Ernesto Sábato), which investigated the disappearance and torture of prisoners. Their report has been published in English as *Nunca Más: The Report of the Argentine National Commission on the Disappeared* (New York: Farrar, Straus, and Giroux, 1986).

CHAPTER TWELVE

Pixote
Fiction and Reality in Brazilian Life

ROBERT M. LEVINE

Pixote, A Lei dos Mais Fracos *(1980), or* Pixote; *produced by Silvia B. Naves; directed by Héctor Babenco; written by Héctor Babenco and Jorge Duran based on the book* A infancia dos mortos *by José Louzeiro; color; 127 minutes; Unifilm/Embrafilme. Using both professional actors and real children from the slums of Brazilian cities, this shocking and important film follows the desperate lives and criminal activities of abandoned children who live in the streets of contemporary São Paulo and Rio de Janeiro. As the film begins, the title character, Pixote (Fernando Ramos da Silva), is a young boy remanded to the custody of juvenile authorities in São Paulo, when police round up all the children near the scene of a mugging that ended in the death of a judge.*

*P*ixote depicts the violent world of abandoned and outlaw children in Brazil's cities and the failure of the system to offer any remedies. It became the third-most commercially successful Brazilian film up to that time. The other two—*Dona Flor and Her Two Husbands* and *Bye Bye, Brazil*—were lighthearted and fanciful in contrast to the brutality of *Pixote* (pronounced "pee-*shoat*," loosely translated as "Peewee"). This essay discusses *Pixote* in the social and political context of the period and offers parallels between the fictional world of the film's script and the reality of life in the streets. The first part discusses the movie; the remainder then considers the fate of its child star in the context of Brazil during the early 1980s.

Héctor Babenco, the director and writer, was born in Argentina, the son of Russian and Polish Jews who had fled nazism in the 1930s. After spending some time in Europe during the early 1970s, he moved to Brazil, where he started to make films. His first feature, *The King of the Night*, opened in 1975. It depicted the relationship between a hypocritical womanizing businessman and a prostitute. Three years later, his second feature film, *Lúcio Flávio: The Passenger of Agony*, became an enormous box office hit in Brazil. Using the narrative line of a newsreel, *Lúcio Flávio* was the biography of an infamous bank robber and professional criminal whose conscience led him to denounce a secret police death squad and who was stabbed to death in Rio de Janeiro's Hélio Gomes penitentiary in January 1975.[1] When he negotiated with the military censors before starting filming, Babenco had to promise never to show uniformed policemen involved in death-squad activities, nor to use official police vans or squad cars in such acts, and to add a written disclaimer at the end of the film saying, "All the policemen involved in the Lúcio Flávio affair were expelled from the police force and punished." This was a lie, of course, and audiences laughed when they read the message on the screen. He also changed the ending so that Lúcio Flávio's death in prison would not be shown and used fictitious names for the policemen who had been involved. Eight million Brazilians saw the film in the first four months of its run. The man who was hired by the police for five dollars to murder Flávio was murdered himself in prison the day before the movie opened in Rio de Janeiro.[2]

Babenco then attempted to produce a documentary about Brazil's urban juvenile detention centers. These were stark state institutions housing orphans and street children, both hardened criminals and scruffy kids randomly picked up in periodic dragnets. Babenco started to work on his documentary, but officials abruptly and without explanation withdrew their permission to film at the reformatory after he had made ten or twelve visits. He and Jorge Duran then bought the rights to a *romance-reportagem* novel about the same subject, journalist José Louzeiro's *A infancia dos mortos*, although in the end they wrote an original script about street youths, using only a small part of Louzeiro's narrative. *Pixote* was the result, in Babenco's words, "a *Lúcio Flávio* in short pants."[3]

Both films, the neonaturalist *Pixote* and *Lúcio Flávio*, were inspired by works of documentary fiction (*romances-reportagem*), devices used during the military dictatorship in part to avoid the censors when dealing with issues of authoritarianism and violence.[4] Following in the tradition of Luis Buñuel and Vittorio de Sica, writer-director Babenco used seven real street urchins in his cast. Fernando Ramos da Silva, the eleven-year-old boy who played the title role, grew up in abject poverty in São Paulo's gritty industrial district of Diadema, although he still had a family, unlike Pixote.[5] When the film opened, Rio de Janeiro's chief Youth Court judge sought Babenco's indictment under the National Security Law "for inciting corruption of minors, advocating drug usage, and undermining social institutions."[6]

Babenco trained each child from scratch, thereby avoiding the stereotypical mannerisms that likely would have come from using professional child actors. The resulting performances, although minimal, emerged expressive and graphic, above all spontaneous. At the same time, they were complemented by the mature performances of the film's professional actors, notably Marília Pera, usually cast as a comedienne, who played Sueli, a bitter, aging whore. Director Babenco revealed later that the children taught him so much about street life that he invited them to change the script as they worked through it. He estimated that, in the end, perhaps 40 percent of the original script was rewritten. Every day, Babenco held a workshop on the day's shooting, and everyone improvised. An assistant, a prison therapist, talked with the children every morning to help them relax and to discuss the things that they had to do in front of the cameras. At one point, Babenco piled the kids into his car and took them to a Moviola studio so that they could see how editing worked and thus would not complain so much about having to retake scenes over and over. The shooting took sixteen weeks, and the film cost twice as much as budgeted. Babenco never relinquished control. His imprint remains indelible throughout *Pixote*. Some of the story's violence is quick and brutal, while other scenes are choreographed like a soccer play; when the kids rob a pedestrian, the camera pulls back, giving us a view of the whole area, so that we "get the social picture."[7]

In *Pixote*'s opening scene, Babenco introduces the eleven-year-old Fernando with his real mother in front of their shack. Babenco looks strikingly like a grown-up version of Fernando, but one gets the idea quickly that the boy from the slums will never make it to the director's age. Babenco tells the audience that "Brazil has 120 million people of which approximately 50 percent are under 21 years of age. About 28 million children have a lower standard of living than that stipulated in the UN's Children's Rights Declaration. Almost 3 million are homeless and have no real family." But it is important to know that the people who live in a slum work. Babenco points out that he is standing in "a working-class neighborhood in São Paulo, the great industrial center of Latin America, responsible for 60 to 70 percent of the gross national product of Brazil. . . . Typically, both parents work and the children stay home. Usually the elder sister babysits, or a neighbor, who is paid. Fernando, the star of the film, lives with his mother and nine brothers and sisters in this house. The whole film is acted by children who have this common background." The camera then shifts to Fernando, who becomes Pixote, a fictional wide-eyed and apprehensive new inmate of the juvenile center. In a police sweep of street kids (*tromba-dinhos*), he is brought in following the death of a prominent judge who died after being pushed in front of a moving car during a mugging. Pixote is "a little camera taking it all in."[8] He is quick: he learns that you keep your mouth shut, you do whatever stronger people tell you to do, and you watch out for yourself.

In the hellish, Dickensian juvenile center, Pixote witnesses a homosexual gang rape and other sordid scenes culminating in the killing of one of his comrades. He and several other suspects are singled out and taken to a city jail, where two are murdered. On their return to the juvenile center, they are confined to sleeping naked under a stairway. The prison and the detention center are nearly exclusively male worlds; the women who appear briefly are caring and helpful, but these interludes are very short. During one lyrical scene a kind teacher helps Pixote learn to write, but the movie shrugs off sentimentality. Throughout the film, the police are depicted as arrogant, corrupt, violent, and accountable to no one—a wholly accurate portrayal, despite the official line defending them as enforcers of law and order. Babenco conveys this mood astutely by shooting mostly at night in confined spaces, casting a feeling of unrelieved, ominous gloom. The detention center—one of its pavilions named for the eminent writer Euclides da Cunha—is unerringly accurate in the way it is shown.

Pixote intersperses shocking images relieved occasionally by fleeting moments of tenderness dashed by the intrusion of sordid reality. When brief scenes of tragicomic adventures occur, they are followed by events that take the children deeper into the world of alienation and pathos. The first part of the film, set in the institution and in the adult prison to which some of the children are taken, is brutal and violent. The storyline demonstrates in short order how the children are doomed. They school themselves in the ways of the street, play at robberies, teach one another how to react under police interrogation, smoke marijuana and sniff glue to bring on hallucinations, play soccer, and form a kind of family unit.[9]

Pixote and his friends play at bank robbery. *Courtesy Museum of Modern Art*

An ineffective investigation by a police official whose superiors are leaning on him to find a scapegoat leads to the savage beating death of Fumaça, one of the youths implicated in the crime that had led to the roundup. After Fumaça's body is found in a city dump, a television newscast blames his death on Diego, one of the older adolescents in the detention center. When the rest of the boys learn that Diego has been beaten to death by the authorities, they riot, wreck their dormitory, and escape. The breakout is accompanied by an abrupt change in mood. Visually, after the harrowing and dark opening part, the film becomes suffused in pale, dawnlike hues; at night the pastel-colored light gives way to garish, raw neon red, pink, and orange. The scene changes to the street, although its freedom becomes as confining as the detention center. Pixote joins with three other boys for solidarity and protection.

Each of the film's child characters is a stereotype. There is Lilica, the seventeen-year-old transvestite ringleader, or "queen";

Chico, an abandoned street kid; seventeen-year-old Dito, a black kid the police are waiting for when he turns eighteen (sensitive and searching, he is Lilica's lover); and Pixote, babylike and vulnerable.[10] They snatch purses and pick pockets, philosophize about life, and eventually travel to a grayish Rio de Janeiro, where they become involved in selling cocaine. They are soon enticed into a drug deal but are ripped off.[11] By the end of film, Pixote has killed three people, run drugs, and pimped, but he remains a child.[12] He murders one of his victims by sticking a knife into her. He had wanted her money, not to kill her. The argument between the woman and the child is just like a kindergarten fight, Babenco recalls. " 'Give me my pocketbook.' 'I don't want to give it to you.' 'Please give it to me.' Whap."[13]

Although Pixote and his friends escape, they remain confined to a prison of degradation. Eventually the boys buy the "rights" to the alcoholic whore Sueli, using her as a decoy to rob her clients. One of the schemes goes sour, and Pixote shoots both Dito and an American businessman who has come to Sueli's flat. Sueli, who had earlier aborted her fetus with a knitting needle, briefly comforts Pixote by taking him to her breast, but then, after thinking about escaping with him to the country to pose as mother and son, she pushes him away. The film ends with the boy walking impassively down a railroad track, kicking cans, with a gun in his pocket, heading for trouble. His friends have been killed, he has been rejected by his mother figure, he is dazed by what he has seen, and he is destined for a violent end himself. *Pixote* succeeds because it never holds back its strength of feeling, it does not go in for cheap moralizing, and it manages to invoke images of loyalty, honor, love, and even the absurd, in the most tragic of circumstances.[14]

Pixote is not a political film because it does not point fingers in any specific way. Unlike Costa-Gavras, for example, or Oliver Stone, Babenco brings to his films no particular ideology. It is telling that *Pixote* was not invited to the annual film festival in Havana. Both left-wingers and right-wingers washed their hands of Babenco: the leftists for his showing the evils of society without offering a solution, the rightists for his suggesting that society's ills breed crime and depravity. The Cubans also dismissed Babenco's film because they said it had "too much immorality and that homosexuality is a sickness."[15] Instead, *Pixote* is more of a psychological tragedy, pointedly showing the range of differences among the children, from the soulful Lilica to Pixote, whose soul has not yet been awakened, and to Sueli, who casts off Pixote after briefly comforting him. Babenco's point was that outsiders, the marginal people, are always innocent, and society eventually kills their innocence.

Brazilian audiences reacted ambivalently. This response was less in reaction to the film's shocking themes—other movies had depicted violence, homosexuality, and brutality—than to the fact that its indictment of Brazilian institutions made viewers feel self-conscious and defensive.[16] *Pixote* premiered in São Paulo in September 1980 and in Rio de Janeiro a month later. The country was emerging from almost two decades of harsh military rule, and some critics complained that the film was too unrelenting in its sordidness. In all, it did moderately well at the box office, mostly after it started to win prizes abroad.[17]

In contrast to the film's modest reception in Brazil, in North America and Europe it caused a sensation. Rave reviews alluded to Babenco's refusal to sentimentalize or moralize and lauded its tender portrayal of the children drawn into the corrosive life of the streets. *Pixote* spurred a new wave of interest in Brazilian cinema, reminiscent of the early 1960s, when the Cinema Novo caught the attention of critics in Europe and in North America. In 1981, after *Pixote*'s initial success, Brazilian films won twenty-one international prizes. Only one of these films was not coproduced by the Brazilian counterpart of the Canadian Film Board, Embrafilme, which had provided 30 percent of the money to make *Pixote*. Some British critics, however, were negative. One, the *New Statesman*'s John Coleman, panned *Pixote* as sleazy and manipulative, and the film journal *Screen*, in an otherwise sympathetic review, lamented that it offered "a characteristically exoticised view of Third World poverty . . . rather than a broader perspective on the economic and political relations which create that poverty."[18]

Overall, however, the foreign reaction was extremely positive. After *Pixote* screened at the Museum of Modern Art's New Directors/New Films series in New York in April 1981, it ran for a year at the Quad Art Cinema. It was named best foreign film by both the New York Film Critics and the Los Angeles Film Critics but was declared ineligible for an Academy Award because of the timing of its opening. It received a nomination for the Golden Globe award for best foreign film. Judy Stone of the *San Francisco Chronicle* called it "a classic," on the same level as Luis Buñuel's *Los Olvidados* and François Truffaut's *The 400 Blows*. The film won the Silver Leopard at Locarno, the Critics' Prize at San Sebastian, and a third award at Biarritz. Virtually every leading newspaper and newsmagazine listed it in their top ten films of the year. Vincent Canby declared in the *New York Times* that Fernando Ramos da Silva had "one of the most eloquent faces ever seen on the screen. It's not actually bruised, but it looks battered. The eyes don't match, as if one eye were attending to immediate events and the other were considering escape routes. It's a face full of life and expression."[19]

~

The single most tragic by-product of the film was the fate of its lead actor. After his fame from the film had subsided, Fernando drifted into petty crime and was arrested twice for minor offenses. He complained that the police were out to get him, that they could not distinguish him from his role in the movie. At the age of nineteen, in August 1987, the boy who had been selected out of thirteen hundred applicants to play the title role of the thieving street kid was shot to death by the police.

Fernando was born on November 29, 1967, the sixth of ten children, into a family whose poverty deepened when the father, João Alves, died when Fernando was eight. His parents were peasants from the northern state of Pará who had migrated to the coffee fields of Paraná before moving on to the city of São Paulo, where they hoped they could find more reliable work. His mother, Josefa Carvalho da Silva, received a pension of less that ten dollars per month; to survive, she and all of her children sold lottery tickets in the city streets. They were light-skinned and therefore did not face racial discrimination, but their status as rural migrants marked them as outcasts. Fernando attended grade school but did not learn to read or write very well; at seven he won a small part in a play put on by a theater group. He had no record of delinquency as a child.

The movie's national and international success came when Fernando was twelve, a year after the movie was made. *Pixote* was seen by an estimated 2.5 million people in twenty countries, mostly in art cinemas. After his acting success, Fernando was signed to a one-year contract by TV Globo to play a small part in a prime-time soap opera, and he was cast in the role of an errand boy in Bruno Barreto's film of Jorge Amado's novel, *Gabriela, Clove and Cinnamon*. Globo dropped him for being lazy and because he could not read his lines, although his clumsy mannerisms and street vocabulary likely made people afraid of him. He was hired briefly to advertise UNICEF Christmas cards on Brazilian television. Moved by Fernando's story, the mayor of Duque de Caixias, a depressed-income city on the outskirts of Rio de Janeiro, gave him a house there and a scholarship to an acting school, but his mother and other family members moved back to Diadema some months later. He dropped out of the acting school after two days. "I don't think he truly wanted to be an actor, a job that requires a lot of dedication and patience," the actress Fernanda Montenegro was quoted as saying. In 1984 he was arrested on robbery charges in his old neighborhood. After his second arrest, in 1985, he told a reporter that he wanted the public to forget his image as Pixote. "I want a chance to live as a man, without being persecuted," he said. "They created a Pixote, but they did not know how to prepare him for life." He pleaded with José Louzeiro to write a sequel to his *romance-reportagem* in which Pixote would be redeemed. The request was not considered viable, however. "I pulled him out of this absurd dream, to wake him up for other projects, but he didn't seem to believe me," Louzeiro said in response.[20]

His brothers and sisters said that Fernando felt persecuted by being typecast as Pixote and wanted to play romantic roles. In 1985, now nineteen with two tattoos on his arms and a sparse beard, he married a sixteen-year-old girl from a family of migrants from the interior of Minas Gerais, Cida Venâncio da Silva. Fernando settled down to an ordered life after the birth of their daughter, Jacqueline. His wife later said that Fernando always had two personalities: the aggressive and self-sufficient character of Pixote and a more emotional, romantic, and sensitive face, which she called the "real Fernando."[21] His last job was in the Northeast, where he had been acting in a play, "Atalpia My Love," in the part of a hired assassin.

When he returned to his family, he was playing cards in a neighborhood tenement when he learned that the military police were conducting raids in the area, looking for criminals. Fearing that he would be harmed, he fled unarmed to another house. The police found out about his flight and, although they had no formal charge against him or any warrant, pursued him and dragged him out from under a bed where he was hiding. He pleaded with his captors not to harm him; he was overheard by several residents of the tenement as saying that he was the father of a small daughter whom he had to raise. But he was shot to death. The official police report claimed that on August 25, Fernando and a young boy were caught trying to hold up a pedestrian on a street near Diadema, and that in the ensuing chase he opened fire on his pursuers with a .32-caliber revolver. His family vigorously denied this version of events and produced witnesses to swear that he was not involved in the street mugging. Virtually no one believed the official story.

His mother and wife cried to reporters that the shooting had been a police execution. The body had seven bullet holes in it, two in the right arm, five more in the chest. A forensic examination revealed that on the basis of the powder burns on his white cotton shirt the youth had been shot with the gun virtually touching him while he was lying on the ground, but the official police report blandly stated that he had died while resisting arrest.[22] Police spokesmen, attempting damage control, rationalized Fernando's violent end by emphasizing that he was a known bandit and that he had used his fame as Pixote to demand clemency when he was caught. "Every time he was detained," claimed Mario Miguel Bittar, the police officer who first arrested him, "[he] promised to straighten out, and he cried a lot."[23] What Bittar did not mention was that each time that Fernando was arrested the boy had been tortured with electric shocks and that the police had treated him more roughly than other youths in their custody because of his fame.[24] Fernando's death caused an outcry across Brazil, although it quickly subsided. A thin paperback book authored by Cida, Fernando's widow (skillfully edited, presumably by a professional), appeared, blaming the military police for murdering him.[25] The three policemen who had killed him were dismissed from the force. One dropped out of sight, but the other two started a lucrative private security firm in Diadema, accusing the left-wing media of trumping up the charges against them.[26]

On the one hand, then, the outcry against what had happened suggested that people did care, that the success of *Pixote* and the publicly expressed sympathy at what had happened to the film's baby-faced title actor was a positive sign. On the other hand, the fact was that nothing changed. Two of Fernando's own brothers died violent deaths without public outcry; they were, of course, unimportant marginals without the aura of film stardom. Six months before Fernando's murder, his older brother, Paulo, age twenty, was lynched by a crowd of more than fifty people who left the body so badly mutilated that it took days to identify it. The motive for the lynching is not known, although Paulo had a reputation for womanizing. Three years later, another brother, Waldemar, was shot to death. Two of the surviving three brothers fled Diadema in fear of being killed as well. Of the seven child actors in *Pixote*, only the

boy who played the androgynous Lilica, Jorge Julião, briefly succeeded in an acting career. All the rest dropped back into their lives
in poverty.

~

Pixote, appearing as it did during the shaky midpoint of Brazil's
transition to democratic rule, unequivocally claimed to tell the truth
about the sordid underside of urban life. Contemporary research by
Brazilian and foreign sociologists and others clearly confirms that
nothing in the film was far-fetched. A Brazilian journalist, Caco
Barcellos, who exposed citizen murders by police in São Paulo (including the execution of Fernando Ramos da Silva) in a book named
after one of the most violent vigilante squads, *Rota 66*, had his life
threatened until he sought refuge in the United States. Martha K.
Huggins of Union College has written extensively on police violence, corruption, and death-squad activity directed against reputed
criminals, including street children. Paulo Sérgio Pinheiro, a courageous political scientist, heads an institute at the University of
São Paulo that monitors abuses of human rights.[27]

A few years after the execution of Fernando, on July 23, 1993,
six police vigilantes killed homeless children sleeping on cardboard
mats near the entrance to Rio de Janeiro's floodlit Candelaria Church
and three others sleeping in front of the Modern Art Museum about
a mile away.[28] The findings of the social science literature emphasize the fact that the victims of the police are invariably street punks
and petty criminals—never the wealthy and successful drug and
crime kingpins widely believed to have bought protection from the
police and politicians. With lawlessness a raging epidemic in Brazilian cities, officials have permitted law enforcement agents to go
far beyond their legally mandated limits, an inheritance of the war
against urban guerrillas during the early 1970s. There is an obsession with putting more police on the streets, Pinheiro observes, to
"let the ruling classes know that the police are at their service."[29]

When asked about *Pixote*, many Brazilians say that the situation is much worse today. Pixote and the other social misfits in the
film were exceptions, different from the rest. Slang words for child
muggers had not yet entered the vocabulary. The uncontrolled
sweeps by mobs of *favela* (slum) youths through Rio's beach zones
had not yet occurred. Today, Brazilians say with sadness, in many
cities there are so many delinquent and homeless street children
that their experience is common, almost the norm, and drugs and
deepening crime have far worsened the hopelessness of slum life.

The actor who played Pixote, as we have seen, died as violently as most of the fictional characters in the film, a metaphor for the fact that society rejects these stories; there is no follow-up. The children die, and their story stops.

Despite its success in movie theaters, Babenco's film avoids making any global statement about Brazilian society, unlike most other films of the Cinema Novo. Rather, in some ways it blames institutions—notably the juvenile detention centers, the ineffective social work apparatus, and the police—as if they are part of a ghettoized system of local abuse.[30] *Pixote*, if anything, is too uncritical of the children portrayed in the film, giving the impression that the system dooms all who pass through it to a life of lost hope. Those (the doctor, the social worker, the teacher) who attempt to help, as Robert Stam reminds us, are one-dimensional stereotypes, incapable of offering real assistance. The film, he concludes, "forces us to see the institution critically, but not ourselves. The emotional impact leaves little analytical residue in its wake."[31]

Still, *Pixote* is a commercial movie, not a celluloid doctoral dissertation. It is a historical film insofar as it depicts accurately the harrowing side of Brazilian urban life that has grown measurably worse since it was released in 1981.[32] It punctures stereotypes, portraying the nation's biggest cities as grimy places of alienation. It does not preach, however; it simply presents its case. Its documentary edge gives it the weight of a sociological report. *Pixote* shocked most viewers, but Brazilian audiences knew that the depiction of reformatory life and the ineffectiveness of the social welfare system were chillingly accurate. Moreover, the film reliably captured the growing street violence of Brazilian cities during the tense transitory evolution from dictatorship to civilian government as well as the sense of helplessness. A decade and a half later, Brazil was convulsed by the forced resignation of its first democratically elected president, the abysmally corrupt Fernando Collor de Mello. The political events overshadowed a deepening drug problem, military occupation of some of Rio de Janeiro's worst slums, and the rising spiral of violent crime caused by unchecked population migrations and poverty at the margins of urban life. The inauguration of the capable Fernando Henrique Cardoso in 1995 restored a good measure of confidence, and the country was buoyed by the achievement of relative monetary stability and a turn to a free-market system under which billions of dollars in foreign investment poured in. However, despite the administration's sincere desire to tackle the underlying social causes of marginality and crime, Brazil remained as segregated as ever, the affluent protected by layers of private armed and electronic security and the poor left to fend for themselves.

The government's stance toward Babenco and his work was telling as well. In 1972 the Ministry of Education and Culture tried to prevent politically conscious producers from making pictures about contemporary ills by offering an annual prize for films adapted from literary works by "dead authors," a crude effort to encourage "safe" costume dramas.[33] Producers were permitted, for the first time, to add erotic content to their films; violence was tolerated as well, as long as the films were not explicitly political. TV Globo, the dominant television network, also came into the picture by hiring Cinema Novo filmmakers to produce dramas and documentaries that were considered safe. TV Globo, relying on slick, expensively produced prime-time soap operas, won more than 70 percent of the national viewing market, thus relegating Brazilian-made films to a relatively small audience of intellectuals.

Television's impact grew even greater with the establishment of national hookups made possible by communications satellites during the late 1970s. Brazilian-made films for the most part were limited to soft-core *pornochanchadas* (porno melodramas) or other low-budget, low-quality movies produced in a few weeks. The military government continued to pressure filmmakers to avoid controversial themes. Nonetheless, astute directors such as Babenco, Roberto Farias, Jorge Bodánsky, and others were able to fool the government, which was not very capable of understanding nuanced meanings. Still, director Babenco had been forced to stop filming his documentary on reform schools and had to re-create the detention center by renting an old military barracks. Throughout the early 1980s the government continued to censor some films, using the threat of their being banned upon completion, a potent weapon to force filmmakers to censor themselves or risk economic disaster.

We know that one of the most blurred of boundaries lies precisely between fiction and nonfiction.[34] In April 1982, a year after *Pixote* premiered, authorities banned Farias's *Onwards Brazil*, a film about terrorism, repression, and police brutality during the worst years of the dictatorship, from 1969 to 1974. When the president of the state film industry protested, he was dismissed.[35] Police death squads and other vigilante groups still carry out violence. Censorship is no longer an issue, but almost no Brazilian films like Babenco's or Farias's have appeared in recent years.

Suggested Readings

Arruda, Rinaldo Sérgio Vieira. *Pequenos bandidos.* São Paulo: Global Editora, 1983. A sociological study of children who commit street crimes in São Paulo.

Babenco, Héctor. Interview by George Csicsery. "Individual Solutions: An Interview with Hector Babenco." *Film Quarterly* 36, no. 1 (Fall 1982): 2–17. A searching interview with the Argentine-born producer that addresses the plight of Brazil's legions of abandoned children.

Barcellos, Caco. *Rota 66.* 19th ed. São Paulo: Editora Globo, 1993. Courageous denunciation of police vigilantism by a journalist forced to leave Brazil owing to death threats against him.

Bicudo, Hélio Pereira. *Meu depoimento sobre a esquadrão da morte.* 3d ed. São Paulo: Pontífica Comissão de Justiça e Paz de São Paulo, 1976. Excerpts from the transcripts of the official investigation into police vigilante violence, most notably the notorious death squads.

Dassin, Joan. "Fear and the Armed Struggle in Brazil: Political Memoirs of the Generation of '68." Paper presented at Social Science Research Council Seminar on "The Culture of Fear," Buenos Aires, May 30–June 1, 1985. Examines the atmosphere of repression and civil rights violations that accompanied Brazil's so-called economic miracle during the years of the military dictatorship from 1964 to 1978.

Huggins, Martha K., ed. *Vigilantism and the State in Modern Latin America.* New York: Praeger, 1991. A sociological analysis of police violence and the weakness of civil society in several Latin American countries, with strong coverage of the Brazilian case.

Levine, Robert M., and José Carlos Sebe Bom Meihy. *The Life and Death of Carolina Maria de Jesus.* Albuquerque: University of New Mexico Press, 1995. Examines the plight of the black diarist whose book became Brazil's all-time best-seller in 1960 but who died in poverty seventeen years later. Raises questions about gender, class, race, and poverty in Brazilian life.

Pinheiro, Paulo Sérgio. "Police and Political Crisis: The Case of the Military Police," in *Vigilantism and the State in Modern Latin America,* ed. Martha K. Huggins, 167–88. An analysis by one of Brazil's leading proponents of civil society. Pinheiro heads the watchdog Institute for the Study of Violence in Brazilian Life.

Notes

Chapter 1, Stevens, Never Read History Again? pp. 1–11

1. D. W. Griffith interviewed by Richard Barry, "Five-Dollar Movies Prophesied: D. W. Griffith Says They Are Sure to Come with the Remarkable Advance in Film Productions," *New York Times Magazine*, March 28, 1915, 16.

2. For the professionalization of history and its idea of "objectivity," see Peter Novick, *That Noble Dream: The "Objectivity" Question and the American Historical Profession* (Cambridge, England: Cambridge University Press, 1988). Ranke's words, in the original German, were *"wie es eigentlich gewesen."* See p. 28 for discussion of whether the phrase should be translated "as it really was" or "as it essentially was." The difference is significant. On the development of photography, see Robert Taft, *Photography and the American Scene: A Social History, 1839–1889* (New York: Dover Publications, 1964, 1938).

3. Griffith quoted by Barry, "Five-Dollar Movies," 16.

4. Allan R. Millet and Peter Maslowski, *For the Common Defense: A Military History of the United States of America* (New York: Free Press, 1984), 553. I am grateful to Dr. J. Walter High for locating this citation for me.

5. Leon F. Litwack has written that *"The Birth of a Nation* molded and reinforced racial stereotypes, distorting the physical appearance of black men and women, making a mockery of their lives and aspirations, and fixing in the public mind the image of a race of inferiors—sometimes amusing and comical, sometimes brutal and subhuman, but in either case less than white men and women." Litwack, *"The Birth of a Nation,"* in *Past Imperfect: History According to the Movies*, ed. Mark C. Carnes (New York: Henry Holt, 1995), 140–41.

6. On the popular reception of this film and its technical innovations, see Everett Carter, "Cultural History Written with Lightning: The Significance of *The Birth of a Nation* (1915)," in *Hollywood as Historian: American Film in a Cultural Context*, ed. Peter C. Rollins (Lexington: University Press of Kentucky, 1983), 9–19; and William Hughes, "The Evaluation of Film as Evidence," in *The Historian and Film*, ed. Paul Smith (Cambridge, England: Cambridge University Press, 1976), 72.

7. John E. O'Connor, "History in Images/Images in History: Reflections on the Importance of Film and Television Study for an Understanding of the Past," *American Historical Review* 93, no. 5 (December 1988): 1201.

8. Paraphrased by E. Bradford Burns, *Latin American Cinema: Film and History* (Los Angeles: UCLA Latin American Center, University of California, 1975), 14.

9. An intellectual apparatus to describe and analyze historical film has developed slowly over the last thirty years. Film is taken more seriously today than it was even a few decades ago. The Historians' Film Committee was formed in 1970 and has published the journal *Film & History* continuously since 1971. Even the *American Historical Review* now regularly includes reviews of films of

historical interest. Much of this activity has focused on the history of the film industry. For Latin America, see John King, *Magical Reels: A History of Cinema in Latin America* (London: Verso, 1990); and Jorge A. Schnitman, *Film Industries in Latin America: Dependency and Development* (Norwood, NJ: Ablex, 1984). Robert A. Rosenstone has proposed a new direction: films "can be a unique way of rendering and interpreting the past." See Rosenstone, ed., *Revisioning History: Film and the Construction of a New Past* (Princeton: Princeton University Press, 1995), 4.

10. Robert A. Rosenstone, "History in Images/History in Words: Reflections on the Possibility of Really Putting History onto Film," *American Historical Review* 93, no. 5 (December 1988): 1178–79.

11. Robert Brent Toplin, "The Filmmaker as Historian," *American Historical Review* 93, no. 5 (December 1988): 1227.

12. O'Connor, "History in Images/Images in History," 1204.

13. As Rosenstone pointed out: "When we historians explore the historical film, it is 'history' as practiced by others. Which raises an ominous question: By what right do filmmakers speak of the past, by what right do they do 'history'? The answer is liberating or frightening, depending on your point of view. Filmmakers speak of the past because, for whatever reasons—personal, artistic, political, monetary—they choose to speak. They speak the way historians did before the era of professional training in history, before history was a 'discipline.' " Robert A. Rosenstone, "The Historical Film as Real History," *Film-Historia* 5, no. 1 (1995): 15.

14. See Robert Sklar, "*Oh! Althusser!* Historiography and the Rise of Cinema Studies," in *Resisting Images: Essays on Cinema and History*, ed. Robert Sklar and Charles Musser (Philadelphia: Temple University Press, 1990), 12. Note that all of the contributors to this volume are associated with film studies or communications rather than traditional history departments.

15. Films were expensive, even to rent. Showing them required a considerable investment in equipment that was difficult to operate and maintain, and screenings usually took place in less than ideal circumstances. Finding suitable films required a great deal of time and effort. The improvements that Burns expected in 1974 to make access to them cheaper and less technically complex were rather slow in coming. See Burns, *Latin American Cinema*, 4–5; Bryan Haworth, "Film in the Classroom," in *The Historian and Film*, ed. Paul Smith (Cambridge, England: Cambridge University Press, 1976), 157–68.

Many older films and many more of recent vintage are conveniently available for rental and purchase at prices far below what it used to cost to use 35- or 16-mm films. Domestic productions are still easier to find than those made in Latin America. Videocassette players are ubiquitous and knowledge of how to run tapes is child's play (even if setting the clock and recording broadcast programs still elude the abilities of many adults in our much-ballyhooed technological culture). Videotape is inferior to film in some significant ways (lower contrast, decreased definition, and a different frame that usually means parts of the film are lopped off), but video gives us greater control. We can now manipulate the films more easily, stop and study the images, take them home, and play them over again. Skipping from one part to another is not as easy on video as it is with a book, but it is much easier than with a film projector. Video disks are even easier to manipulate, but they remain relatively expensive and uncommon. Perhaps this situation will further improve as computers become more adept at storing and replaying visual material.

16. Rosenstone, "Historical Film as Real History," 5.

17. Compare Natalie Zemon Davis, " 'Any Resemblance to Persons Living or Dead': Film and the Challenge of Authenticity," *Historical Journal of Film, Radio, and Television* 8, no. 3 (1988): 269–83.

18. Davis and Rosenstone each have worked closely with filmmakers. Each is a strong proponent of the use of film in history but naturally not without some reservations.

19. See the remarks of Davis in Ed Benson, "*Martin Guerre*, the Historian and the Filmmakers: An Interview with Natalie Zemon Davis," *Film & History* 13, no. 3 (September 1983): 49–65, especially 62.

20. Hayden White, "Historiography and Historiophoty," *American Historical Review* 93, no. 5 (December 1988): 1194.

21. Burns, *Latin American Cinema*, 6.

22. Historians will probably always be at odds with postmodern literary theory. "History is crucially distinguished from fiction by curiosity about what actually happened in the past. Beyond the self—outside the realm of the imagination—lies a landscape cluttered with the detritus of past living, a mélange of clues and codes informative of a moment as real as this present one." Joyce Appleby, Lynn Hunt, and Margaret Jacob, *Telling the Truth about History* (New York: W. W. Norton and Co., 1994), 259.

23. Robin W. Winks portrays the historian as "like Sergeant Friday, he only wants to get the facts." Nevertheless, the stories he excerpts of searches for manuscripts also show that success requires imagination and even luck. See Robin W. Winks, ed., *The Historian as Detective: Essays on Evidence* (New York: Harper and Row, 1968).

24. Natalie Zemon Davis, *The Return of Martin Guerre* (Cambridge, MA: Harvard University Press, 1983), viii.

25. Quoted in Barbara Abrash and Janet Sternburg, eds., *Historians & Filmmakers: Toward Collaboration; A Roundtable Held at the New York Institute for the Humanities, New York University, October 30, 1982* (New York: Institute for Research in History, 1983), 12.

26. Burns, *Latin American Cinema*, 7–13; Pierre Sorlin, "Historical Films as Tools for Historians," in *Image as Artifact: The Historical Analysis of Film and Television*, ed. John E. O'Connor (Malabar, FL: R. E. Krieger, 1990), 42–68.

27. Bill Nichols argues that "the categories and boundaries surrounding documentary and reality, fact and fiction, defy hard and fast definition." See Nichols, *Blurred Boundaries: Questions of Meaning in Contemporary Culture* (Bloomington: Indiana University Press, 1994), xiii.

28. Taft, *Photography*, 310, 347.

29. The photograph that I have in mind is number 86 in Anita Brenner's *The Wind That Swept Mexico: The History of the Mexican Revolution, 1910–1942* (Austin: University of Texas Press, 1943, 1971); number 31 in Aurelio de los Reyes, *Con Villa en México: Testimonios sobre camarógrafos norteamericanos en la revolutión, 1911–1916* (Mexico: Universidad Nacional Autónoma de México, 1985); and Kevin Brownlow, *The War, the West, and the Wilderness* (New York: Alfred A. Knopf, 1979), 88–89. I am grateful for the observations of Dr. Friedrich Katz on Villa's relationship to the film industry.

30. Robert M. Levine, *Images of History: Nineteenth- and Early Twentieth-Century Latin American Photographs as Documents* (Durham, NC: Duke University Press, 1989), 9, 184–85. See also Robert M. Levine, ed., *Windows on*

Latin America: Understanding Society through Photographs (Miami: North-South Center, 1987).

31. See Alan Trachtenberg, "Albums of War: On Reading Civil War Photographs," *Representations* 9 (Winter 1985): 1–32. Nancy Leys Stepan, "Portraits of a Possible Nation: Photographing Medicine in Brazil," *Bulletin of the History of Medicine* 68, no.1 (Spring 1994): 136–49, finds certain uncaptioned Brazilian photographs mute. As Stepan is an expert on race, she comes to the altogether unsurprising conclusion that the photographs speak to that issue.

32. See the essay by Donald F. Stevens in this volume.

33. Julianne Burton, "Toward a History of Social Documentary in Latin America," in *The Social Documentary in Latin America*, ed. Burton (Pittsburgh: University of Pittsburgh Press, 1990), 21.

34. John Mraz, "Memories of Underdevelopment: Bourgeois Consciousness/Revolutionary Context," in *Revisioning History: Film and the Construction of a New Past* (Princeton: Princeton University Press, 1995), 102–14, especially 107.

35. See Burton, "Toward a History of Social Documentary in Latin America," 13.

36. Sklar, quoted in *Historians & Filmmakers*, 10.

37. The ideal of "objectivity" has been contested within the historical profession since the First World War. Novick, *That Noble Dream*, chap. 5.

38. Quoted in Burns, *Latin American Cinema*, 16–17. Burns cites the 1964 publication but the first edition of Gottschalk's *Understanding History* appeared in 1950.

Chapter 2, Lipsett-Rivera and Rivera Ayala, 1492: The Conquest of Paradise, pp. 13–28

1. Notice, for example, the use of props such as oranges and bananas in the Caribbean (these fruits were not indigenous to the Americas) and the smoking of cigars in a dinner scene upon Columbus's return to Spain (Columbus ignored tobacco).

2. David P. Henige, *In Search of Columbus: The Sources for the First Voyage* (Tucson: University of Arizona Press, 1991), has painstakingly analyzed the logbook to determine where Las Casas may have altered the contents. A good source for the published documents by Columbus is Consuelo Varela, *Cristóbal Colón. Textos y documentos completos. Relaciones de viajes, cartas y memoriales* (Madrid: Alianza, 1982). An English version of Columbus's logbook of the first voyage is available in *The Voyages of Christopher Columbus*, trans. Cecil Jane (London: Argonaut Press, 1930). See also *The Life of the Admiral Christopher Columbus by His Son Ferdinand*, trans. Benjamin Keen (New Brunswick, NJ: Rutgers University Press, 1992).

3. For a historiographical review of this literature in English, see Claudia Bushman, *America Discovers Columbus: How an Italian Explorer Became an American Hero* (Hanover, NH: University Press of New England, 1992), 22–40, 152–57. A more recent example of a positive interpretation of Columbus can be found in Salvador de Madariaga, *Christopher Columbus: Being the Life of the Very Magnificent Lord Don Cristobal Colon* (London: Hollis and Carter, 1949).

4. Hans Koning, *Columbus: His Enterprise* (New York: Monthly Review Press, 1976), is a good example. For a more scholarly attempt at a revisionist

history of Columbus, see Kirkpatrick Sale, *The Conquest of Paradise* (New York: Alfred A. Knopf, 1990).

5. See, for example, David Stannard, *American Holocaust: Columbus and the Conquest of the New World* (New York: Oxford University Press, 1992).

6. See, for example, Mario Vargas Llosa, "Questions of Conquest," *Harper's* (December 1990): 45–83.

7. See Bushman, *America Discovers Columbus*, 98–107.

8. Thomas Schlereth, "Columbia, Columbus, and Columbianism," *Journal of American History* 79, no. 3 (December 1992): 937–68; Bushman, *America Discovers Columbus*, 40–53, 107–26; Washington Irving, *The Life and Voyages of Christopher Columbus* (Boston: Twayne Publishers, 1981).

9. Jeffrey Burton Russell, *Inventing the Flat Earth: Columbus and Modern Historians* (New York: Praeger, 1991), chap. 3; Schlereth, "Columbia, Columbus, and Columbianism," 955–57.

10. For example, the myth that Queen Isabela pawned her jewels to finance the first voyage.

11. This presentation is not entirely new. Samuel Eliot Morison, *Admiral of the Ocean Sea: A Life of Christopher Columbus* (Boston: Little, Brown and Co., 1942), asks, "Was he not *Christoferens*, the chosen instrument of divine providence to illuminate these dark heathen countries with the Light of the World?" (403).

12. Martin Behaim constructed the first globe in 1492.

13. Russell, *Inventing the Flat Earth*, chaps. 2 and 3.

14. Carl Ortwin Sauer, *The Early Spanish Main* (Berkeley: University of California Press, 1966), 15.

15. There is a considerable literature on the Spanish Inquisition. For a general introduction, see Henry Kamen, *The Spanish Inquisition* (London: Weidenfeld and Nicolson, 1965), and his updated version of the same, *Inquisition and Society in Spain in the Sixteenth and Seventeenth Centuries* (London: Weidenfeld and Nicolson, 1985). For a review of historiography and accounts of Spanish resistance to the Inquisition, see Stephen Haliczer, *Inquisition and Society in the Kingdom of Valencia, 1478–1834* (Berkeley: University of California Press, 1990).

16. According to the psychoanalytic theories of cinema, the film is like a mirror in which the spectator can find him or herself on the screen through an identification with the character of the film. The spectator recognizes his or her likeness on the screen as a pure act of perception. See Christian Metz, *The Imaginary Signifier: Psychoanalysis and the Cinema*, trans. Celia Britton, Annwyl Williams, Ben Brewster, and Alfred Guzzetti (Bloomington: Indiana University Press, 1977), 42–57.

17. William D. Phillips, Jr., and Carla Rahn Phillips, *The Worlds of Christopher Columbus* (New York: Cambridge University Press, 1992), 100, 110.

18. Russell, *Inventing the Flat Earth*, 51–56; Morison, *Admiral of the Ocean Sea*, 89. "What a striking spectacle must the hall of the old convent have presented at this memorable conference! A simple mariner, standing forth in the midst of an imposing array of professors, friars, and dignitaries of the church; maintaining his theory with natural eloquence, and, as it were, pleading the cause of the new world. We are told that when he began to state the grounds of his belief, the friars of St. Stephen alone paid attention. . . . The others appear to have entrenched themselves behind one dogged position." Irving, *Life and Voyages*, 49.

19. Kamen, *The Spanish Inquisition*, 194, states that the burning at the stake of heretics was not only rare but also was usually undertaken outside the city limits apart from the main auto-da-fé.

20. Morison, *Admiral of the Ocean Sea*, 215–21, provides an interesting discussion of this debate and the evidence.

21. Phillips and Phillips, *Worlds of Christopher Columbus*, 147–48; Sauer, *Early Spanish Main*, 20; Sale, *Conquest of Paradise*, 48–50.

22. Phillips and Phillips, *Worlds of Christopher Columbus*, 152–53.

23. Margarita Zamora, *Reading Columbus* (Berkeley: University of California Press, 1993); José Rabasa, *Inventing America: Spanish Historiography and the Formation of Eurocentrism* (Norman: University of Oklahoma Press, 1993).

24. Although his account is faulty in many regards, Tzvetan Todorov, *The Conquest of America: The Question of the Other*, trans. Richard Howard (New York: Harper and Row, 1984), provides an interesting analysis of the "communication" between Columbus and the natives.

25. Robert Stam, "Rewriting 1492: Cinema and the Columbus Debate," *Cineaste* 19, no. 4 (1993): 66–71, provides not only an interesting critique of the film but also an overview of previous Hollywood attempts and Latin American films which, while not precisely on Columbus, give an alternative interpretation of conquest and colonialism.

26. There were actually several native societies in the Caribbean: the Arawak (also sometimes called the Taino), the Caribs, and the Siboney. A number of books focus on these cultures: Sauer, *Early Spanish Main*, chap. 3 in particular; William Keegan, *The People Who Discovered Columbus: The Prehistory of the Bahamas* (Gainesville: University Press of Florida, 1992); Irving Rouse, *The Tainos: Rise and Decline of the People Who Greeted Columbus* (New Haven: Yale University Press, 1992); and Samuel M. Wilson, *Hispaniola: Caribbean Chiefdoms in the Age of Columbus* (Tuscaloosa: University of Alabama Press, 1990).

27. Also, the horses shipped over to the Caribbean on this trip were nags. Thus, Moxica would be hard put to perform such feats of horsemanship. Morison, *Admiral of the Ocean Sea*, 390, 423–24. The prancing of the horse in this scene is reminiscent of a famous painting by Velásquez and thus appears authentic.

28. Varela, *Cristóbal Colón*, 245, see n. 7. Morison, *Admiral of the Ocean Sea*, 570, mentions a Moxica in reference to this same letter.

29. Morison, *Admiral of the Ocean Sea*, 486–87, comments on Columbus's involvement in the slave trade of Hispaniola.

30. This scene evokes memories of the etchings of Theodore de Bry, which are constantly used to illustrate the atrocities of Spanish colonialism in textbooks and other volumes.

31. Sauer, *Early Spanish Main*, 85; Morison, *Admiral of the Ocean Sea*, 443, 483.

32. This scene provides one of the only mentions of the abuse of Arawak women by the Spanish. Women, in fact, are notably absent from this film, and all, even Queen Isabela, fall into subservient if not adoring roles.

Chapter 3, Holloway, Aguirre, the Wrath of God, pp. 29–46

1. Quoted in S. S. Prawer, *Caligari's Children: The Film as Tale of Terror* (New York: Oxford University Press, 1980), 19.

2. Elena Mampel González and Neus Escandell Tur, *Lope de Aguirre: Crónicas, 1559–1561* (Barcelona: 7 1/2, 1981), is an indispensable compilation of the accounts of Gonzalo de Zúñiga, Toribio de Hortiguera, Pedro de Monguia, Custodio Hernández, Vásquez and Almesto, and an unidentified chronicler.

3. This question is raised by Luisela Alvaray in "Filming the 'Discovery' of America: How and Whose History Is Being Told," *Film-Historia* 5, no. 1 (1995). 37.

4. This summary is drawn from the secondary literature and the chronicles and documents related to the case listed in "Suggested Readings." The most complete modern compilation of contemporary documents is Mampel González and Escandell Tur, *Crónicas*.

5. An extensive review of the El Dorado legends and efforts to confirm them, including the involvement of Sir Walter Raleigh in South America, is Demetrio Ramos Pérez, *El mito del Dorado: Su genesis y proceso* (Caracas: Academia Nacional de la Historia, 1973; 2d ed. enlarged, Madrid: Ediciones Istmo, 1988). Playing on the Spanish explorers' manifest desire for precious metals, indigenous informants apparently concluded that they could be rid of passing bands of Europeans by spinning tales of gold for the taking in some far-off location. An ethnographic basis for the legends involved rituals among indigenous peoples of the northern Andes in which a priest or prince periodically applied gold dust to his body and swam in a sacred lake, into which other gold offerings were tossed. Lake Guatavita, not far from Bogotá, Colombia, has been identified as one site of such rituals. These legends emerged during the first Spanish forays into South America in the 1520s and persisted well into the seventeenth century.

6. The Montesinos letter is reproduced in several studies, including Mampel González and Escandell Tur, *Crónicas*, 285–86.

7. Emiliano Jos, *La expedición de Ursúa al Dorado y la rebelión de Lope de Aguirre y el itinerario de los "Marañones," según los documentos de Archivo de Indias y varios manuscritos inéditos* (Huesca, Spain: V. Campo, 1927), 111.

8. For a detailed reconstruction of the world of the conquistadors, see two works by James Lockhart, *Spanish Peru, 1532–1560* (Madison: University of Wisconsin Press, 1968), and *The Men of Cajamarca* (Austin: University of Texas Press, 1972), the latter a collective biography of the 167 men who shared in the ransom of the Inca emperor Atahualpa. A good overview of the era is John Hemming, *The Conquest of the Incas* (New York: Harcourt, Brace, Jovanovich, 1970).

9. This translation is by Thomas Holloway of the version published in A. Arellano Moreno, comp., *Documentos para la historia económica de Venezuela* (Caracas: Instituto de Antropología e Historia, Facultad de Humanidades y Educación, Universidad Central de Venezuela, 1961), 291–97, which in turn is from that published in Casto Fulgencio López, *Lope de Aguirre, el Peregrino: Primer caudillo de América* (Madrid: Plon, 1977), 234–40, after Jos, *La expedición de Ursúa al Dorado*, 196–200, and checked against the versions in the Vázquez and Almesto chronicle (Mampel González and Escandell Tur, *Crónicas*, 255–59) and the Aguilar y de Córdova version in the British Museum, dated 1578. All these versions differ only slightly from one another, not in ways that add or subtract sections or change the thrust of the document.

Chapter 4, Ramírez, I, the Worst of All, pp. 47–62

1. Octavio Paz, *Sor Juana, or, The Traps of Faith* (Cambridge, MA: Belknap Press, Harvard University, 1988). Paz is a celebrated author, philosopher, poet,

and winner of the Nobel Prize for literature in 1990. One of his most famous works is *Labyrinth of Solitude*. Bemberg was a scriptwriter and director, who also brought to the screen *Momentos* (1981), *Señora de Nadie* (1981), and such perennial favorites as *Camila* (1984) and *Miss Mary* (1987). She made *Yo, la Peor de Todas* in 1990. Bemberg was born in Buenos Aires in 1925. Her first screenplay, *Cronica de una señora*, dates from 1971.

2. Paz, *Sor Juana*, 109; but Paz says later (123) that she was self-taught.

3. Dorothy Schons, "Some Obscure Points in the Life of Sor Juana Inés de la Cruz," in *Feminist Perspectives on Sor Juana Inés de la Cruz*, ed. Stephanie Merrim (Detroit: Wayne State University Press, 1991), 39; Schons says that she was not quite sixteen when she professed.

4. Paz, *Sor Juana*, 248, reports that the number may be exaggerated. He concludes that it is impossible to know the true number of the volumes in her personal library.

5. Cloister also refers to the enclosed part of a religious house where none but the religious themselves may enter. The rules of cloister or enclosure restrict the entry of outsiders to maintain religious retirements and to prevent unnecessary worldly distractions. Violation of strict cloister results in automatic excommunication.

6. The marquis de la Laguna was named viceroy in a decree on August 8, 1680; he arrived in Mexico in November. He took possession on November 7, 1680, and passed on the staff of authority on November 30, 1686 (Paz, *Sor Juana*, 147, 191, 265).

7. Her confessor helped pay other expenses, for clothes, the purchase of a cell, as well as provision for slaves or servants. Asunción Lavrin, "Unlike Sor Juana? The Model Nun in the Religious Literature of Colonial Mexico," *University of Dayton Review* 16, no. 2 (Spring 1983): 75.

8. Her poems are silent, with one exception, about the next viceroy, don Melchor Portocarrero y Lasso de la Vega, conde de Monclova, who remained in office from 1686 to 1688, when he was transferred to Peru. His replacement, don Gaspar de Sandoval Cerda Silva y Mendoza, conde de Galve (September 1688 to February 1696 [Paz, *Sor Juana*, 269]), was part of a faction opposed to the duque de Medinaceli. Although on friendly terms with the conde, Sor Juana dedicated only a few poems to him and his wife (Schons, "Some Obscure Points," 47). None of these men seems to have played as prominent a role as protector as the marqués de la Laguna.

9. Paz, *Sor Juana*, 266.

10. Irving A. Leonard believes that legislation limiting the circulation of certain books in New Spain was only enforced at the end of the seventeenth century (Paz, *Sor Juana*, 248). Schons, "Some Obscure Points," in contrast, talks of "strict censorship on books that existed in New Spain" (49; see also her footnote 28, 59).

11. Paz, *Sor Juana*, 403.

12. Schons, "Some Obscure Points," 52, characterized it as "a defense of the rights of women, a memorable document in the history of feminism."

13. As quoted in Lavrin, "Unlike Sor Juana?" 86.

14. See Paz, *Sor Juana*, 450–70.

15. Ibid., 461–62.

16. The phrase "the worst of all" was used commonly by the religious—both male and female—of her time. Its source is biblical, from Paul's first epistle to Timothy: "Christ Jesus came into the world to save sinners, of whom I am the

worst of all" (1 Timothy 1:15). Sor Juana wrote the phrase in the margins of her books (Paz, *Sor Juana*, 448). She also actually signed her name below a statement in the Book of Professions (*Libro de profesiones*) that read: "Here above the day, month and year of my death shall be recorded. I beg, for the love of God and of his Purest Mother, my beloved religious sisters, . . . to entrust me to God, . . . I have been and am the worst of all. To all I ask pardon for the love of God and of his Mother. I, the worst one of the world."

Paz believes that she wrote these words months before her death. Ezequiel Chávez believes that this statement was not written by Sor Juana but only signed by her (Lavrin, "Unlike Sor Juana?" 81; Paz, *Sor Juana*, 464–65). The *Libro de profesiones* was purchased by Schons and is today in the library of the University of Texas at Austin.

17. Paz, *Sor Juana*, 102; Lavrin, "Unlike Sor Juana?" 78.

18. Josefina Ludmer, "Tricks of the Weak," in *Feminist Perspectives*, 88; Jean Franco, *Plotting Women: Gender and Representation in Mexico* (New York: Columbia University Press, 1989), 24, 27.

19. Paz, *Sor Juana*, 101. See also Schons, "Some Obscure Points," 39.

20. Paz, *Sor Juana*, 110. See his wider discussion of the question from 100–11.

21. For the complete text of *Hombres necios*, see Sor Juana's *Sor Juana Inés de la Cruz: Sus mejores poesías* (Mexico: Gómez Hermanos Editores, 1980), 57–59.

22. Paz, *Sor Juana*, 219. See the rest of Paz's chap. 15, "Religious Fires," for his interpretation of Sor Juana's love.

23. Ibid., 201, 202.

24. Ibid., 199.

25. Ibid., 101–2. For more on this topic, see Paz, pt. 4, chap. 14.

26. See also Stephanie Merrim, "Toward a Feminist Reading of Sor Juana Inés de la Cruz: Past, Present, and Future Directions in Sor Juana Criticism," in *Feminist Perspectives on Sor Juana Inés de la Cruz*, ed. Stephanie Merrim (Detroit: Wayne State University Press, 1991), 18, on this issue.

27. Paz, *Sor Juana*, 423.

28. Ibid., 304.

29. Ibid., 300.

30. Lavrin, "Unlike Sor Juana?" 77.

31. Kathleen A. Myers, "The Addressee Determines the Discourse: The Role of the Confessor in the Spiritual Autobiography of Madre María de San Joseph (1656–1719)," *Bulletin of Hispanic Studies* 69, no. 1 (January–March 1992): 39–47.

32. Lavrin, "Unlike Sor Juana?" 84.

33. Ibid., 85.

34. Ibid., 81.

35. Schons, "Some Obscure Points," 56.

36. Paz, *Sor Juana*, 77. These were words used by Sor Juana to describe the pythoness of Delphi in "El epinicio al conde de Galve."

Chapter 5, Saeger, The Mission, pp. 63–84

1. Clarence Haring, *The Spanish Empire in America* (New York: Oxford University Press, 1947; reprint ed., Gloucester, MA: P. Smith, 1973), 184–89;

Charles Gibson, *Spain in America* (New York: Harper and Row, 1966), 81–83; James Lockhart and Stuart B. Schwartz, *Early Latin America: A History of Colonial Spanish America and Brazil* (New York: Cambridge University Press, 1984), 260–65; and Lyle N. McAlister, *Spain and Portugal in the New World, 1492–1700* (Minneapolis: University of Minnesota Press, 1984), 320, 366.

2. Herbert E. Bolton, *The Mission as a Frontier Institution in the Spanish-American Colonies* (El Paso: Texas Western College Press, 1962; reprinted from *American Historical Review* 23 (October 1917): 1; Peter Masten Dunne, S.J., *Pioneer Jesuits in Northern Mexico* (Berkeley: University of California Press, 1944); and John Francis Bannon, S.J., *The Mission Frontier in Sonora, 1620–1687* (New York: U.S. Catholic Historical Society, 1955).

3. Philip Caraman, S.J., *The Lost Paradise: The Jesuit Republic in South America* (New York: Seabury Press, 1975; New York: Dorset Press, 1990). The film credits Caraman as a technical adviser but does not mention *Lost Paradise*.

4. Father Daniel Berrigan, actor and technical adviser for *The Mission*, acknowledges that the missions of the film never existed, except as the filmmakers imagined them. See Daniel Berrigan, S.J., *The Mission: A Film Journal* (San Francisco: Harper and Row, 1986), 4. Berrigan knows little about Native Americans. See his comments on the Onanís, 64. Born in Sale, Manchester, England, in 1924, Robert Bolt attended the University of Manchester and taught English. Of his many plays, the best known in the United States is "A Man for All Seasons," a sympathetic portrayal of Sir Thomas More. Bolt also wrote screenplays for *Lawrence of Arabia* and *Dr. Zhivago*. Director Roland Joffé, born in London in 1945, also attended Manchester University. His first film was *The Killing Fields* (1984).

5. Guillermo Furlong [Cardiff], *Misiones y sus pueblos de guaraníes* (Buenos Aires: n.p., 1962; Posadas, Argentina: Lumicop, 1978), 646–56.

6. The seven rebel missions were San Nicolás, San Luis, Santo Angel, San Lorenzo, San Borja, San Juan, and San Miguel; Guaranis and Jesuits settled them in the 1600s; Furlong, *Misiones*, 656.

7. Ibid., 102–7, 117–32.

8. *The Mission* was filmed mostly in Colombia, although a few exteriors were shot in Argentina at Iguasú Falls. The film's flaws, though, arise from insensitivity to Native Americans and ideological confusion, not from erroneous geography.

9. Branislava Susnik, *El rol de los indígenas en la formación y en la vivencia del Paraguay*, 2 vols. (Asunción: Instituto Paraguayo de Estudios Nacionales, 1982–83), 1:33–56.

10. Ibid.

11. Margarita Durán Estrago, *Presencia franciscana en el Paraguay* (Asunción: Universidad Católica, 1987), 93–101.

12. The word "reduction" and the word "mission" can be used interchangeably.

13. Durán Estrago, *Presencia franciscana*, 99–164, 201.

14. Branislava Susnik, "Etnohistoria de Paraguay," *América Indígena* 49, no. 3 (July–September 1989): 472.

15. Luis G. Benítez, *Historia del Paraguay: Epoca colonial* (Asunción: Imprenta Comuneros, 1985), 100–111; Harris G. Warren, *Paraguay: An Informal History* (Norman: University of Oklahoma Press, 1949), 81–100; and Caraman, *Lost Paradise*, 79–81.

16. Father Gabriel's arduous, lonely voyage upriver in 1750 lacks authenticity. Guaranis accompanied historical Jesuits to help found new missions, and Jesuits expected Indians to work. Showing a lonely Father Gabriel paddling his own canoe alters the nature of the historical Guarani-Jesuit relationship. See Florian Paucke, *Hacia allá y para acá (una estada entre los indios Mocobíes, 1749–1767)*, 4 vols. (Tucumán-Buenos Aires: n.p., 1942–1944), 1, Lámina XI (opposite p. 164); and James S. Saeger, "Eighteenth-Century Guaycuruan Missions in Paraguay," in *Indian-Religious Relations in Colonial Spanish America*, ed. Susan E. Ramírez (Syracuse, NY: Maxwell School of Citizenship and Public Affairs, Syracuse University, 1989), 61.

17. When this essay was presented as a paper at the 1991 Latin American Studies Association meeting in Washington, DC, Professor Murdo MacLeod asked of Father Gabriel's ascent, "Why didn't he go around?" The question remains.

18. *Lost Paradise*, 212–14.

19. In fact, Guaranis in Guairá liked European music, but they joined missions for hand-held metal hatchets, which replaced tools of wood, bone, and stone; Susnik, *El rol de los indígenas* 1:138–39.

20. I cannot imagine what a "mercenary" did or who would have paid for his services in colonial Paraguay, a poor frontier province with no standing army and no paid force. The crown repeatedly rejected Paraguayan requests for a salaried military. See, for example, Informe del gobernador Agustín Fernando de Pinedo al rey, Asunción, January 29, 1777, Archivo Nacional de Asunción (hereafter ANA), Sección Historia, vol. 142, no. 4. The movie Mendoza is apparently Paraguayan, but Robert Bolt's novel *The Mission* (Harmondsworth, England: Penguin, 1986), published with the film's release, says that he is from Cadiz, Spain. Ignorant of things Hispanic, Bolt demeans Spanish culture more in the novel than on the screen. Indian laborers in Paraguay in the novel are "encomiendaros," not "encomendados," as they should be. One character is named Gaspachio. A Guarani slave sells for "three quarters of a dinero."

21. The Jesuits' "Spiritual Conquest" of the Guaranis embraced several strategies for gaining converts, most involving nonviolent persuasion. Nevertheless, one Jesuit method of recruiting Indians for missions was to hunt them, as they did, for example, with Guayakíes, whom they then sent to Guarani missions. Susnik, *El rol de los indígenas*, 2:27.

22. Ramón Gutiérrez, *When Jesus Came, the Corn Mothers Went Away: Marriage, Sexuality, and Power in New Mexico, 1500–1846* (Stanford, CA: Stanford University Press, 1991), 149–56, 180–90; Gastón Gabriel Doucet, "Sobre cautivos de guerra y esclavos indios en el Tucumán; Notas en torno a un fichero documental salteño del siglo XVIII," *Revista de Historia del Derecho* (Buenos Aires) 16 (1988): 59–152; and James Schofield Saeger, "Survival and Abolition: The Eighteenth-Century Paraguayan Encomienda," *The Americas* 38 (July 1981): 59–85.

23. Like the Franciscans in Yucatán, Paraguayan Jesuits denied their interest in Indian labor. Only they were disinterested; others were greedy; Inga Clendinnen, *Ambivalent Conquests: Spaniard and Maya in Yucatán, 1517–1570* (New York: Cambridge University Press, 1987).

24. In the 1620s and 1630s, Jesuits Roque González de Santa Cruz, Alonso Rodríguez, Juan de Castillo, and Cristóbal de Mendoza lost their lives while laboring among the Guarani. Martin Dobrizhoffer, *An Account of the Abipones: An Equestrian People of Paraguay*, 3 vols. (London: J. Murray, 1822; reprint ed., New York: Johnson Reprint Corp., 1970), 3:413–14.

25. San Miguel had 6,954 inhabitants in 1751. Santo Angel had 5,186; San Nicolás, 4,453; San Luis, 3,653; San Borja, 3,550; San Juan, 3,560; and San Lorenzo, 1,835; Furlong, *Misiones*, 674.

26. Ibid., 649–51; and Caraman, *Lost Paradise*, 236–42.

27. The historical San Carlos, located in the very heart of the missions between the Paraná and the Uruguay rivers, was founded not around 1750 but in 1631, and it did not rebel; Furlong, *Misiones*, 114.

28. Dobrizhoffer, *Abipones*, 2:127–28.

29. We will know better the degree of Guarani acceptance of Christianity after the rising generation writes ethnohistories of missions. Frequently cited in this essay, Furlong's *Misiones* is the best traditional survey of the reductions, but the author's paternalistic attitude toward Guaranis and emphasis on Jesuits need ethnohistorical revision. The recent *Estrategías de desarrollo rural en los pueblos guaraníes (1609–1767)* (Barcelona: A. Bosch, 1992), by Rafael Carbonell de Masy, S.J., is an excellent macroeconomic study of the missions' economy. It contains great insight into Guarani life. Told from a Jesuit point of view, it supplements but does not replace Furlong's survey.

30. See Robert F. Berkhofer, Jr., *The White Man's Indian: Images of the American Indian from Columbus to the Present* (New York: Alfred A. Knopf, 1978), 3–31.

31. Susnik, *El rol de los indígenas*, 1:106–7; Furlong, *Misiones*, 114.

32. Caraman, *Lost Paradise*, 214.

33. Haring, *Spanish Empire in America*, 41–57; and Lewis Hanke, *The Spanish Struggle for Justice in the Conquest of America* (Philadelphia: University of Pennsylvania Press, 1949; reprint ed., Boston: Little, Brown and Co., 1965), 91–95; and José L. Mora Mérida, *Historia social de Paraguay, 1600–1650* (Seville: Consejo Superior de Investigaciones Científicas. Escuela de Estudios Hispano-Americanos, 1973), 164–84.

34. Susnik, *El rol de los indígenas*, 1:133; and Caraman, *Lost Paradise*, 157–58.

35. One finds this idea in Caraman, *Lost Paradise*, 41. Caraman cites Bartolomé Meliá, S.J., an anthropologist at the Catholic University in Asunción, who, unlike the English author, knows and respects Native Americans.

36. Fathers Dobrizhoffer and Paucke condemned infanticide in their chronicles of missions cited above.

37. Branislava Susnik, *Los aborígenes del Paraguay*, 7 vols. (Asunción: Museo Etnografico Andres Barbero, 1978–1986), vol. 5, *Ciclo vital y estructura social*, 16.

38. Much of the work of the Jesuit hacienda at Paraguarí, for example, was done by Jesuit-owned, Afro-Paraguayan chattel slaves. Missions also invested in slaves. The filmmakers dissemble when they have Jesuits denounce slavery. Jesuits in fact had little objection to the slavery of Africans, but accuracy would require slave-owning Jesuits with whom contemporary audiences would not sympathize.

39. Susnik, "Etnohistoria," 473–80; Caraman, *Lost Paradise*, 163; and Furlong, *Misiones*, 372–75.

40. See Nicholas Cushner, *Jesuit Ranches and the Agrarian Development of Colonial Argentina, 1650–1767* (Albany: State University of New York Press, 1983).

41. Susnik, "Etnohistoria," 478–79.

42. Ibid., 472.

43. In the Paraguayan *mitaria*, males owed two months' labor a year to their encomendero. Females also contributed by spinning, performing domestic service, and sometimes going to the fields. Men in the pueblos also grew subsistence and cash crops for the community. Another labor obligation, the levy (*leva*), was owed to the crown; officials used Guarani labor to build and repair forts. Susnik, *El rol de los indígenas*.

44. In 1754 the seven rebellious missions owned about 600,000 head of cattle and 500,000 horses and mules; Furlong, *Misiones*, 652; Robert Southey, *History of Brazil*, 3 vols. (London: Longman, Hurst, Rees, and Orme, 1810–1819; reprint ed., New York: Greenwood Press, 1969), 2:356–62; Adalberto López, *The Revolt of the Comuñeros, 1721–1735: A Study in the Colonial History of Paraguay* (Cambridge, MA: Schenkman Publishing, 1976), 24–29; Magnus Mörner, *Actividades políticas y económicas de los Jesuítas en el Río de la Plata: La era de los Habsburgos* (Buenos Aires: Paidos, 1968); Caraman, *Lost Paradise*, 121; on the yerba trade, see Thomas Whigham, *The Politics of River Trade: Tradition and Development in the Upper Plata, 1780–1870* (Albuquerque: University of New Mexico Press, 1991), 3, 10–13, 107–32.

45. Dobrizhoffer, *Abipones*, 1:31.

46. Susnik, *Rol de los indígenas*, 2:22.

47. The Onaní actors, of course, spoke no Guarani, a language familiar to virtually all Paraguayans.

48. Susnik, "Etnohistoria," 477.

49. This thought certainly comes from *The Uruguay* (Canto II), a poem written in 1769 by the Brazilian José Basilio da Gama. I am grateful to Professor Stuart B. Schwartz for calling it to my attention.

50. Southey, *History of Brazil*, 2:328–32; and Caraman, *Lost Paradise*, 69–81. The eight-day battle of Mbororé in 1641 had naval and land engagements. Its resemblance to the conflict that brings *The Mission* to a climax cannot be coincidental. Guaranis, however, won at Mbororé; Furlong, *Misiones*, 126–27.

51. Scholars have generally understood that urban riots in Spain in 1766, not events in Paraguay in the 1750s, sparked Charles III's decision to expel the Order. Other explanations include the conflict between the nationalism of the Spanish crown and the ultra-Montanism of the Jesuits, royal desire to acquire Jesuit wealth, Spanish regalism, and several conspiracy theories. Yet the monarch was provoked by such intransigence as movie Jesuits display. See Magnus Mörner, ed., *The Expulsion of the Jesuits from Latin America* (New York: Alfred A. Knopf, 1965); and Pablo Hernández, *El extrañamiento de los Jesuítas del Río de la Plata y de las misiones del Paraguay por decreto de Carlos III* (Madrid: V. Suarez, 1908).

52. Susnik, *El rol de los indígenas*, 1:181–96.

53. Dobrizhoffer, *Abipones*, 2:57, 67.

54. In Bolt's novel, Gabriel is Irish, but Irons plays the part without hinting that he was Irish. Thus, three of four Jesuit resistance leaders of the movie are English. Only a few English Jesuits came as missionaries to Paraguay. Peter Poole, for example, was miserable as he assisted Father Paucke in the Mocobí mission of San Javier, and Thomas Falkner's labors in Patagonia are well known. Pedro Polo, S.J., al visitador Nicolás Contucci, S.J., San Javier, April 28, 1762, Archivo General de la Nación (hereafter AGN), Buenos Aires, Argentina, Sala 9, 6-10-5; and Thomas Falkner, *A Description of Patagonia and the Adjoining Parts of South America* (Hereford, England: C. Pugh, T. Lewis, 1774; reprint ed., Chicago: Armann and Armann, 1935). Despite the movie's fascination with English

missionaries, however, most priests in Paraguayan missions were Spanish. Foreigners were more often Italian or German than English; see Padres, curas, y compañeros de las nuevas reducciones del Chaco en la frontera de Tucumán . . . July, 1765, AGN, Buenos Aires, Argentina, Sala 9, 6-10-6.

55. At this point, the movie becomes even more confused. Exactly how many movie missions Spain trades to Portugal is unclear. The Asunción debate is about the fate of missions "above the falls," but the great mission of San Miguel was never there.

56. Other Jesuits, including Father Sebastian (Berrigan), return to Asunción.

57. Furlong, *Misiones*, 383–90.

58. How Mendoza's sword avoided rust the filmmakers let the viewer wonder. Weapons deteriorated quickly in the subtropical Platine climate.

59. John Hemming, *Red Gold: The Conquest of the Brazilian Indians* (Cambridge, MA: Harvard University Press, 1978), 469–74; Furlong, *Misiones*, 659–63; and Dobrizhoffer, *Abipones*, 1:27–33.

60. Pedro de Cevallos, the governor of Buenos Aires who ordered an investigation, found no direct Jesuit participation.

61. Hemming, *Red Gold*, 470; and Dobrizhoffer, *Abipones*, 1:23.

62. Casualty figures in the most important historical battles were overwhelming. Thousands of Guaranis died; almost no Spaniards did. Drawing on the "Diario da expedição de Gomes Freire de Andrada ás Missoes do Uruguay pelo Capitão Jacinto Rodrigues da Cunha (1756)," *Revista do Instituto Histórico e Geographico Brasileiro* 16 (1853): 139–328, John Hemming reports that at the battle of Caaibaté on February 10, 1756, Guarani forces lost 1,400 dead and 127 captives to the allied armies, whose casualties were only 3 dead and 26 wounded; *Red Gold*, 472–73. Furlong says that 1,511 Guaranis and only 3 Spaniards and 2 Portuguese died; *Misiones*, 669.

63. In fact, Guarani guerrillas, not European troops, first practiced the scorched-earth policy.

64. Although the Academy of Motion Picture Arts and Sciences chose *The Mission* as a finalist for best picture, the only important Oscar that it received was the award to Chris Menges for best cinematography.

65. Descendants of Guaranis in the 1860s and 1930s fought two of the bloodiest wars in the history of South America.

66. Susnik, "Etnohistoria," 480.

67. Bolton, *The Mission as a Frontier Institution*, 1.

68. Ibid., 2, 6, 18.

69. David J. Weber, "John Francis Bannon and the Historiography of the Spanish Borderlands: Retrospect and Prospect," *Journal of the Southwest* 29, no. 4 (Winter 1987): 336.

70. When filming in Argentina, Berrigan drove to the booming border city then named for the Paraguayan tyrant, General Stroessner. Although many Paraguayans and Brazilians there were improving their standard of living, the Jesuit says, "The atmosphere here turns one into swine. One should snoop about on all fours, going 'oink, oink.' " Berrigan thus sullies all Paraguayans in the city. *The Mission*, 141.

71. See Robert F. Berkhofer, Jr., "Cultural Pluralism versus Ethnocentrism in the New Indian History," in *The American Indian and the Problem of History*, ed. Calvin Martin (New York: Oxford University Press, 1987), 35–45; Neal Salisbury, "American Indians and American History," ibid., 46–54; and Calvin

Martin, "Ethnohistory: A Better Way to Write Indian History," *Western Historical Quarterly* 9 (January 1978): 41–56.

72. For suggestions about how Spanish sources can yield Native American reality, see Clendinnen, *Ambivalent Conquests*, 131–38.

73. Robert F. Berkhofer, Jr., doubts that we can "throw out the ethnocentric bath water of Indian history without also tossing out the baby. . . . While cultural pluralism expanded the horizons of traditional history . . . it also placed certain conceptual constraints upon its transformation. History-as-understanding and history-writing are parts of specific cultures, hence ethnocentric in their presuppositions about the nature and ordering of the past-as-lived. Without these constraints, there can be no formal history-as-now-understood." "Cultural Pluralism versus Ethnocentrism," 44.

74. Susnik's treatment of religion shows why her indispensable books invite historians to study Guarani missions. Although she compares Guarani and Catholic ideology to explain how fundamentally aboriginal Guarani beliefs in missions remained, her chronology is casual. She neglects, for example, the two centuries from 1640 to 1848, and her primary sources are inadequate. Although she investigates manuscript sources in Asunción for the Paraguayan *tava*, she generally ignores archival sources on the missions, most of which are outside Paraguay. See *El rol de los indígenas*, esp. 1:181 ff.

75. Census information is found in ANA, Sección Nueva Encuadernación, vols. 166, 143, 16, 14, 61, 1145, 1784, and 1785. See Presentación del gobernador a María Isabel Cavallero, Asunción, November 10, 1772, ANA, Sección Nueva Encuadernación, vol. 9.

76. Letters of Francisco Oliden to Governor Ribera, October 30, 1797, and from Ribera to the administrators of Ytá, Guarambaré, and Yaguarón, November 8, 1797, cited in Jerry W. Cooney, *Economía y sociedad en la intendencia del Paraguay* (Asunción: Centro Paraguayo de Estudios Sociologicos, 1990), 103–4.

77. Ernest J. A. Maeder, "Las fuentes de información sobre las misiones jesuíticas de Guaraníes," *Teología* (Buenos Aires) 24, no. 2 (1987): 143–63.

78. Dobrizhoffer, *Abipones*. See also Felix Becker, *Un mito jesuítico: Nicolás I, Rey del Paraguay: Aportación al estudio del ocaso del poderío de la Compañía de Jesús en el siglo XVIII* (Asunción: C. Schauman Editor, 1987), versión castellana por Lorenzo N. Liveres Banks y María Jesús Rodero.

79. Dobrizhoffer, *Abipones*, 1:22–40.

80. Paucke, *Hacia allá*, 2:18, 31–38, 66; Dobrizhoffer, *Abipones*, 2:1117–18.

81. José Sánchez Labrador, *El Paraguay católico, homenaje de la Universidad Nacional de La Plata al XVII Congreso Internacional de los Americanistas en su reunión de Buenos Aires, en mayo 16 a 21 de 1910*, 2 vols. (Buenos Aires: Imprenta de Coni Hermanos, 1910) 1:295–98.

Chapter 6, Stevens, Camila, pp. 85–102

1. More than two million people saw the film in Argentina alone, by far the largest attendance of any Argentine film of the 1980s. See Alberto Ciria, *Más allá de la pantalla: Cine argentino, historia y política* (Buenos Aires: Ediciones de la Flor, 1995), 192.

2. Caleb Bach, "María Luisa Bemberg Tells the Untold: Interview," *The Americas* 46, no. 2 (March 1994): 20–27; Carrie Rickey, " 'Camila': Argentina's Forbidden Story," *New York Times*, April 7, 1985.

3. Bach, "Bemberg."

4. Quoted in Rickey, " 'Camila.' "

5. " 'If I had not my own money I never would have made movies,' she once said," as quoted in her obituary in *The Times* (London), May 19, 1995; Rickey, " 'Camila.' " Estela Dos Santos, *El cine nacional* (Buenos Aires: Centro Editor de América Latina, 1971), 13.

6. Kevin Thomas, " 'Camila': Argentina's Star-Crossed Lovers," *Los Angeles Times*, April 25, 1985; "María Luisa Bemberg," *The Times* (London), May 19, 1995.

7. "Pride and Prejudice: María Luisa Bemberg," interview by Sheila Whitaker in *The Garden of Forking Paths: Argentine Cinema,* ed. John King and Nissa Torrents (London: British Film Institute, 1988), 117.

8. Vincent Canby, " 'Camila': Story of Love in Argentina," *New York Times*, March 15, 1985; David Beard, "New Vitality in Argentina's Film Industry," *Chicago Tribune*, July 12, 1985; Paul Attanasio, "Doomed 'Camila,' " *Washington Post*, May 3, 1985; John Simon, "Moving Picture Reviews," *National Review*, May 17, 1985.

9. Bradley Graham, "In Argentina, Cinema's Time to Shine: After Censorship, a Filmmaking Boom," *Washington Post*, May 4, 1986.

10. Manuel de Vizoso Gorostiaga, *Camila O'Gorman y su época, La tragedia mas dolorosa ocurrida durante el gobierno del "Restaurador de las Leyes" estudiada a base de documentación y con opiniones de sus contemporaneos* (Santa Fe, Argentina: Talleres Gráficos Castellvi, 1943), 32, 73,n. 60.

11. For a transcript of this letter see Manuel Bilbao, ed., *Vindicación y memorias de Don Antonino Reyes* (Buenos Aires: Imprenta del "Porvenir," 1883), 348–53; or Natalio Kisnerman, *Camila O'Gorman: El hecho histórico y su proyección literaria* (Buenos Aires: Universidad de Buenos Aires, Instituto de Literatura Argentina "Ricardo Rojas," 1973), 14–17.

12. John Lynch, *Argentine Dictator: Juan Manuel de Rosas, 1829–1852* (Oxford: Clarendon Press, 1981), 185–86.

13. Bilbao, *Vindicación y memorias*, 345–46. This and all subsequent translations from the Spanish are mine, unless otherwise noted.

14. Bilbao, *Vindicación y memorias*, 361–62.

15. Ibid., 363.

16. Attanasio, "Doomed 'Camila.' "

17. Transcriptions of the original appear in Julio Llanos, *Camila O'Gorman* (Buenos Aires: La Patria Argentina, 1883), 121; and Kisnerman, *Camila O'Gorman*, 5–6.

18. Llanos, *Camila*, 121.

19. Lynch, *Argentine Dictator*, 119–24

20. See the transcript of this letter in Llanos, *Camila*, 122; or Kisnerman, *Camila O'Gorman*, 7–8.

21. Bilbao, *Vindicación y memorias*, 355–56.

22. Bemberg's script quotes this fragment but changes the chronology, moving it from shortly after the lovers fled Buenos Aires to eight months later after the pair had been arrested and returned to Buenos Aires to await their punishment.

23. Ann Twinam, "Honor, Sexuality, and Illegitimacy in Colonial Spanish America," in *Sexuality and Marriage in Colonial Latin America*, ed. Asuncion Lavrin (Lincoln: University of Nebraska Press, 1989), 118–55.

24. Bilbao, *Vindicación y memorias*, 357.

25. Lynch, *Argentine Dictator*, 169.

26. Ibid., 178.

27. Ibid., 177–79.

28. Ibid., 125.

29. Ibid., 179.

30. Mark D. Szuchman, "A Challenge to the Patriarchs: Love among the Youth in Nineteenth-Century Argentina," in *The Middle Period in Latin America: Values and Attitudes in the 18th–19th Centuries*, ed. Mark D. Szuchman (Boulder, CO: Lynne Rienner Publishers, 1989), 141–65.

31. I am not aware of any documentation proving that Camila's father approved of her execution, although the accusation that he suggested it to Rosas appears in a number of works.

32. Lynch, *Argentine Dictator*, 240.

33. Bilbao, *Vindicación y memorias*, 364–66.

34. The story that Camila was eight months pregnant seems to have circulated at the time of her death in 1848. Juan Manuel Beruti recorded it in his diary, which was published as *Memorias curiosas*, in the series Senado de la Nación, *Biblioteca de Mayo* (Buenos Aires: Senado de la Nación, 1950), 4:4076–77. One of the earliest published descriptions of Camila as eight months pregnant and the "federalist baptism" is Hilario Ascasubi, *Trobas y lamentos de Donato Jurao, soldado Argentino, a la muerte de la infeliz Da. Camila Ogorman [sic] que en compañia del desgraciado Cura Gutiérrez fueron ferozmente asesinados en Buenos Aires por órden del famoso y cobarde carnicero Juan Manuel Rosas titulado Gefe Supremo* (Uruguay: Imprenta del Colejio, 1851[?]), 37, 39.

35. Bilbao, *Vindicación y memorias*, 367.

36. Translated by Donald F. Stevens from the Spanish version published in Llanos, *Camila*, 271. The Spanish text also appears in Kisnerman, *Camila O'Gorman*, 5–6.

Chapter 7, Mraz, The Other Francisco *and* The Last Supper, *pp. 103–22*

1. Julianne Burton and Gary Crowdus, "Cuban Cinema and the Afro-Cuban Heritage: An Interview with Sergio Giral," *The Black Scholar* 8, nos. 8–10 (Summer 1977): 67–68.

2. Manuel Moreno Fraginals, *The Sugarmill: The Socioeconomic Complex of Sugar in Cuba, 1760–1860*, trans. Cedric Belfrage (New York: Monthly Review Press, 1976), 53–54.

3. Tomás Gutiérrez Alea, cited in John Mraz, "Absolved by History: On the Aesthetics and Ideology of History in the Cuban Film Institute," *Film-Historia* (Barcelona) 3, no. 3 (1993): 401–2.

4. Robert A. Rosenstone, "The Historical Film as Real History," *Film-Historia* 5, no. 1 (1995): 18.

5. Franklin Knight, *Slave Society in Cuba during the Nineteenth Century* (Madison: University of Wisconsin Press, 1970), 6.

6. Moreno Fraginals, *Sugarmill*, 18.

7. Ibid., 106, 144; Hugh Thomas, *Cuba: The Pursuit of Freedom* (New York: Harper and Row, 1971), 176.

8. Moreno Fraginals, *Sugarmill*, 38.

9. Knight, *Slave Society*, 112.

10. Thomas, *Cuba*, 151.

11. J. Pérez de la Riva, *El barracón y otros ensayos* (Havana: Editorial de Ciencias Sociales, 1975), 41.

12. Fernando Ortiz, *Los negros esclavos* (Havana: Editorial de Ciencias Sociales, 1975), 182, 334; Thomas, *Cuba*, 182.

13. Thomas, *Cuba*, 171.

14. Herbert Klein, *Slavery in the Americas: A Comparative Study of Virginia and Cuba* (Chicago: University of Chicago Press, 1967), 104.

15. Knight, *Slave Society*, 136.

16. Ortiz, *Negros esclavos*, 284; Thomas, *Cuba*, 180.

17. Knight, *Slave Society*, 64; Ortiz, *Negros esclavos*, 284; Thomas, *Cuba*, 183.

18. Esteban Montejo, *The Autobiography of a Runaway Slave*, ed. Miguel Barnet (New York: World Publishing Co., 1969), 40; Ortiz, *Negros esclavos*, 230.

19. Ortiz, *Negros esclavos*, 237, 366, 368.

20. Moreno Fraginals, *Sugarmill*, 148; Orlando Patterson, *The Sociology of Slavery: An Analysis of the Origins, Development, and Structure of Negro Slave Society in Jamaica* (Rutherford, NJ: Fairleigh Dickinson University Press, 1967), 69; Thomas, *Cuba*, 174.

21. Ortiz, *Negros esclavos*, 149.

22. Moreno Fraginals, *Sugarmill*, 25.

23. Ibid., 152, 31; Ortiz, *Negros esclavos*, 38.

24. Ortiz, *Negros esclavos*, 215.

25. Ibid., 215; Pérez de la Riva, *El barracón*, 39; Thomas, *Cuba*, 177.

26. Knight, *Slave Society*, 76; Moreno Fraginals, *Sugarmill*, 142; Hubert Aimes, *A History of Slavery in Cuba, 1511–1868* (New York: G. P. Putnam's Sons, 1907), 68; Thomas, *Cuba*, 170–71.

27. Ortiz, *Negros esclavos*, 257; Knight, *Slave Society*, 78; Moreno Fraginals, *Sugarmill*, 143.

28. Patterson, *Sociology of Slavery*, 106.

29. Ortiz, *Negros esclavos*, 359; Knight, *Slave Society*, 78.

30. Knight, *Slave Society*, 79.

31. Thomas, *Cuba*, 1472.

32. Moreno Fraginals, *Sugarmill*, 87; Knight, *Slave Society*, 78.

33. Moreno Fraginals, *Sugarmill*, 39.

34. Ortiz, *Negros esclavos*, 388.

35. Moreno Fraginals, *Sugarmill*, 136.

36. Ortiz, *Negros esclavos*, 389.

37. Knight, *Slave Society*, 191.

38. Edwin F. Atkins, *Sixty Years in Cuba* (Cambridge, MA: Private printing at the Riverside Press, 1926).

Chapter 8, Weinstein, Lucía, pp. 123–42

1. For a study of Cuban cinema that focuses on these two films, see Michael Myerson, *Memories of Underdevelopment: The Revolutionary Films of Cuba* (New

York: Grossman Publishers, 1973). Pat Aufderheide observes that these films "became the darlings of international festivals as well as box office hits at home." "Cuba Vision: Three Decades of Cuban Film," in *The Cuba Reader*, ed. Philip Brenner et al. (New York: Grove Press, 1989), 498.

2. Gutiérrez Alea's first postrevolutionary feature film, *Histórias de la Revolución* (1960), adopted this same format.

3. E. Bradford Burns, *Latin American Cinema: Film and History* (Los Angeles: UCLA Latin American Center, University of California, 1975), 23. For a brief but insightful summary of the film, see Peter B. Schumann, *Historia del cine latinoamericana* (Buenos Aires: Editorial Legasa, 1987), 165. For an alternative view—that the film is not truly feminist—see Anne Marie Taylor, "Lucía," *Film Quarterly* 28, no. 2 (Winter 1974–75): 53–59.

4. In 1985 I visited a block meeting of the FMC in Cienfuegos as part of a delegation of women's studies scholars. Soon after we arrived, a local woman stood up and recited for us a brief biography of Ana Betancourt de Mora, acknowledged by all those present as the foremother of women's emancipation in Cuba.

5. Alfred Padula and Lois Smith, "Women in Socialist Cuba, 1959–84," in *Cuba: Twenty-five Years of Revolution*, ed. Sandor Halebsky and John M. Kirk (New York: Praeger, 1985), 83; Marifeli Pérez-Stable, *The Cuban Revolution: Origins, Course, and Legacy* (New York: Oxford University Press, 1993), 108.

6. This dismissal was made more credible by the relative decline of the feminist movement after the legal successes of 1934 and 1940. By far the best study of pre-1959 Cuban feminism is K. Lynn Stoner, *From the House to the Streets: The Cuban Women's Movement for Legal Reform, 1898–1940* (Durham, NC: Duke University Press, 1993).

7. Joel C. Edelstein, "Economic Policy and Development Models," in *Cuba: Twenty-five Years of Revolution*, ed. Sandor Halebsky and John M. Kirk (New York: Praeger, 1985), 181–87.

8. On the surge in women's employment, see Padula and Smith, "Women in Socialist Cuba," 84.

9. For an early discussion of such issues, see Gerda Lerner, "New Approaches to the Study of Women in American History," *Journal of Social History* 3, no. 1 (Fall 1969): 53–62; and "Placing Women in History: Definitions and Challenges," *Feminist Studies* 3, no. 1/2 (Fall 1975): 1–14. In the latter article, Lerner argues that "the history of notable women is the history of exceptional, even deviant women, and does not describe the experience and history of the mass of women."

10. For a pathbreaking formulation of this argument, see Joan Kelly-Gadol, "Did Women Have a Renaissance?" in *Becoming Visible: Women in European History*, ed. Renate Bridenthal and Claudia Koonz (Boston: Houghton Mifflin, 1977), 137–64. According to Kelly-Gadol, "One of the tasks of women's history is to call into question accepted schemes of periodization. To take the emancipation of women as a vantage point is to discover that events that further the historical development of men . . . have quite different, even opposite, effects upon women" (139).

11. The foregoing account of women's role in the Cuban independence movement is based on Stoner, *From the House to the Streets*, 13–33.

12. This neglect of the film's "middle child" may be partly due to the more obscure political events being chronicled. And Solas makes matters worse by providing little historical context for the anti-Machado movement. See Taylor, "Lucía," 57.

13. Indeed, Lucía number two performs the roles outlined for the (male) guerrilla's companion by Ernesto "Che" Guevara, in his *Guerilla Warfare*. See Francesca Miller, *Latin American Women and the Search for Social Justice* (Hanover, NH: University Press of New England, 1991), 146–47.

14. Stoner, *From the House to the Streets*, 116–26.

15. Ibid., 122.

16. See, for example, Muriel Nazzari, "The 'Woman Question' in Cuba: An Analysis of Material Constraints on Its Solution," *Signs* 9, no. 2 (Winter 1983): 246–63.

17. This depiction contrasts with two later films that focus on women in revolutionary Cuba—Pastor Vega's *Portrait of Teresa* (1979) and Gutiérrez Alea's *Up to a Certain Point* (1983)—both of which portray *machismo* as a more pervasive problem.

18. The women at the FMC meeting (n. 4) were very insistent that domestic violence was not a problem in revolutionary Cuba because couples were under so much public scrutiny (in other words, socialism had erased the boundaries between public and private). Interestingly, they also claimed that it had not been much of a problem in prerevolutionary Cuba, either.

19. Schumann, *Historia del cine*, 165.

20. Another early debate in the field of women's history was over whether scholars should emphasize the distinctive experiences of women from different social classes or whether the common aspects of their gender position should be stressed. While Solas would certainly advocate the first position, the film contains a few moments that show gender transcending class. On this debate, see Berenice A. Carroll, ed., *Liberating Women's History* (Urbana: University of Illinois Press, 1976), 347.

21. This point is significant because governments, in moments of emergency, have portrayed women's work as socially desirable but also have implied that, once the emergency has passed, women will want to return to the "comfort" of their homes.

22. During my brief 1985 tour of Cuba with a women's studies group, the only time a Cuban official admitted "defiance" of a legal regulation was when a male politician jocularly informed us that he would divorce his wife rather than cook. On paper, the Cuban Family Code of 1975 required all couples to share household tasks, but the state made no serious effort to enforce it. Pérez-Stable, *The Cuban Revolution*, 141–42.

Chapter 9, Henderson, Gabriela, pp. 143–55

1. Those who use this film in the classroom should discuss it thoroughly beforehand. They should be especially careful to forewarn students that it contains a number of sex scenes of the "R" variety (described by one reviewer as "explicit almost to the point of soft porn"). The present writer offers his students an alternative but similar film assignment that can be completed in the library, should one or more of them feel that their sensibilities might be offended by the movie. Thus forewarned, college students appear to take *Gabriela*'s sex scenes in stride and do not seem to find them especially scandalous.

The question of lawsuits arising from films used in the classroom is treated in Eugene C. Bjorklun, "Regulating the Use of Theatrical Movies in the Classroom: Academic Freedom Issues," *West's Education Law Reporter* 25, no. 12 (July 13, 1995): 1–13.

2. Jorge Amado, *The Violent Land*, trans. Samuel Putnam (New York: Alfred A. Knopf, 1945; rev. ed., 1965).

3. Jorge Amado, *Gabriela, cravo e canela, cronica de uma cidade do interior; romance* (São Paulo: Martins, 1958); *Gabriela, Clove and Cinnamon* (New York: Alfred A. Knopf, 1962).

4. Bruno Barreto is one of the generation of Brazilian filmmakers who emerged during the 1970s. Trained by Cinema Novo pioneers Nelson Pereira dos Santos, Anselmo Duarte, and Glauber Rocha, Barreto achieved fame by directing the film adaptation of Amado's *Dona Flor and Her Two Husbands* (1976). *Dona Flor* became an international hit.

5. Amado, *Gabriela*, epilogue.

6. Examples from the year 1995 include the use in general circulation Latin American news magazines of a U.S. courtroom scene in which John Wayne Bobbitt's lawyer points to an enlarged photograph of his client's severed penis; another photo, taken by someone apparently crouching under a speaker's platform on which Brazilian president Fernando Henrique Cardoso stood alongside a movie starlet, explicitly reveals the mini-skirted young woman not to be wearing underpants. Photographs of human genitalia are not lightly published in U.S. news magazines.

7. Sonia Braga's starring roles in *Dona Flor* and *Gabriela* earned her international fame and subsequent parts in *Kiss of the Spider Woman* (1985), *Moon over Parador* (1988), *The Milagro Beanfield War* (1988), and *The Rookie* (1990).

8. Those who wish to highlight gender issues through Brazilian film might show *Gabriela* in conjunction with Suzana Amaral's brilliant *Hour of the Star* (1977). While both dwell heavily on the subject of male-female relations, and while the protagonist of each film is a young female refugee from Brazil's impoverished Northeast, the two could scarcely be more dissimilar.

9. Quoted in Ed Scheff, "Jorge Amado," *Contemporary Authors*, 35 New Revision Series (Detroit: Gale Research, 1992), 17.

Chapter 10, *Tenenbaum*, Like Water for Chocolate, pp. 157–72

1. It is well to keep in mind that even duds like *Waterworld* routinely gross over $100 million.

2. Victor Zamudio-Taylor and Inma Guiu, "Criss-Crossing Texts: Reading Images in *Like Water for Chocolate*," in *The Mexican Cinema Project*, ed. Chon A. Noriega and Steven Ricci (Los Angeles: UCLA Film and Television Archive, Research and Study Center, 1994), 45–51.

3. Laura Esquivel, *Like Water for Chocolate: A Novel in Monthly Installments, with Recipes, Romances, and Home Remedies*, trans. Carol and Thomas Christensen (New York: Doubleday, 1992), 151. Quotations without footnotes come directly from the movie itself.

4. For more on this subject, see Barbara A. Tenenbaum, "Streetwise History: The Paseo de la Reforma and the Porfirian State, 1876–1910," in *Rituals of Rule, Rituals of Resistance: Public Celebrations and Popular Culture in Mexico*, ed.

William H. Beezley, Cheryl English Martin, and William E. French (Wilmington, DE: Scholarly Resources, 1994), 127–50.

5. Thomas C. Tirado, *Celsa's World: Conversations with a Mexican Peasant Woman* (Tempe, AZ: Center for Latin American Studies, Arizona State University at Tempe, 1991), 25.

6. See Esquivel, *Chocolate*, 136–38, 180.

7. For more on this, see William E. French, "Rapto and Estupro in Porfirian and Revolutionary Chihuahua," in *Reconstructing Criminality in Latin America*, ed. Robert Buffington and Carlos Aguirre (Wilmington, DE: Scholarly Resources, forthcoming).

8. Tirado, *Celsa*, 59.

9. Alma Guillermoprieto, *The Heart That Bleeds: Latin America Now* (New York: Alfred A. Knopf, 1994), 237.

10. *Comida familiar en el Estado de Coahuila* (Mexico: Voluntario Nacional, Banrural, 1988).

11. See Stafford Poole, *Our Lady of Guadalupe: The Origins and Sources of a Mexican National Symbol, 1531–1797* (Tucson: University of Arizona Press, 1995).

12. Edith O'Shaughnessy, *A Diplomat's Wife in Mexico* (New York: Harper and Brothers, 1916).

13. Tirado, *Celsa*, 84.

14. Frances Toor, *A Treasury of Mexican Folkways: The Customs, Myths, Folklore, Traditions, Beliefs, Fiestas, Dances, and Songs of the Mexican People* (New York: Crown Publishers, 1947), 236–40.

Chapter 11, Szuchman, Miss Mary *and* The Official Story, *pp. 173–200*

1. Anthony Pagden, *Spanish Imperialism and the Political Imagination: Studies in European and Spanish-American Social and Political Theory, 1513–1830* (New Haven: Yale University Press, 1990), 92–93. A wider hagiographic array may be found in David A. Brading, *The First America: The Spanish Monarchy, Creole Patriots, and the Liberal State, 1492–1867* (New York: Cambridge University Press, 1991).

2. E. Bradford Burns, *The Poverty of Progress: Latin America in the 19th Century* (Berkeley: University of California Press, 1980); idem, "Ideology in Nineteenth-Century Latin American Historiography," *Hispanic American Historical Review* 58, no. 3 (August 1978): 409–31; John R. Fisher, "Royalism, Regionalism, and Rebellion in Colonial Peru, 1808–1815," *Hispanic American Historical Review* 59, no. 2 (May 1979): 232–57.

3. Bartolomé Mitre, *Historia de San Martín y de la emancipación sudamericana (segun nuevos documentos)*, 3 vols. (Buenos Aires: "La Nación," 1888). In similar fashion, the treatment of Moreno's life shows him to have been a complex man, "fascinating, contradictory, and considerably less saintly than Mitre suggests." Nicolas Shumway, *The Invention of Argentina* (Berkeley: University of California Press, 1991), 25.

4. Doris Sommer, "*Amalia*: Homebodies as Heroes" (unpublished paper presented at Latin American Studies Association Meeting, New Orleans, 1988), 9.

5. Gustavo Sosa-Pujato, "Popular Culture," in *Prologue to Perón: Argentina in Depression and War, 1930–1943*, ed. Mark Falcoff and Ronald H. Dolkart (Berkeley: University of California Press, 1975), 152.

6. Ibid., 153–57.

7. Ibid., 163.

8. Shumway, *Invention of Argentina*, 112.

9. Ricardo Talesnik, *Teatro: La fiaca. Cien veces no debo*, ed. Miguel Angel Giella and Peter Roster (Ottawa: Girol Books, 1980).

10. Lucio V. Mansilla, *Mis memorias* (Buenos Aires: Editorial Universitaria de Buenos Aires, 1966), 20–21.

11. Bernardo Verbitsky, "Prologue" to *Juan Moreira* by Eduardo Gutiérrez (Buenos Aires: Editorial Universitaria de Buenos Aires, 1965), 5–6.

12. Angel Mazzei, comp., *Dramaturgos post-románticos* (Buenos Aires: Ministerio de Cultura y Educación, 1970).

13. Eduardo Gutiérrez, *Juan Moreira* (Buenos Aires: EUDEBA, 1965), 15.

14. Ibid., 226.

15. William C. Smith, *Authoritarianism and the Crisis of the Argentine Political Economy* (Stanford, CA: Stanford University Press, 1991), 257.

16. For a brief review of the life of Sor Juana Inés de la Cruz, see Irving A. Leonard, *Baroque Times in Old Mexico: Seventeenth-Century Persons, Places, and Practices* (Ann Arbor: University of Michigan Press, 1959); and Octavio Paz, *Sor Juana, or, The Traps of Faith*, trans. Margaret Sayers Peden (Cambridge, MA: Harvard University Press, 1988).

17. The military government that seized power in 1976 undertook several measures aimed at inhibiting the clinical practices of psychologists and psychiatrists, especially in Buenos Aires. Overtones of anti-Semitism were discerned in these measures, which were accompanied by frequent references to the disproportionately Jewish constituency of the mental health professionals. The triumvirate of Trotsky, Marx, and Freud was mentioned as a single unit, a metaphor for Jewish internationalism and the antifamily stand of Freudians.

18. Smith, *Authoritarianism*, 227–31. The progressive National Council of Brazilian Bishops founded the construction of a shelter for children in need, naming it "Pixote House."

19. Richard J. Walter, *The Socialist Party of Argentina, 1890–1930* (Austin: Institute of Latin American Studies, University of Texas at Austin, 1977), 33–34; David Rock, *Authoritarian Argentina: The Nationalistic Movement, Its History and Its Impact* (Berkeley: University of California Press), 1993.

20. A sophisticated portrayal and analysis of the events of October 17 is given in Daniel James, "October 17th and 18th, 1945: Mass Protest, Peronism, and the Argentine Working Class," *Journal of Social History* 21 (Spring 1988): 441–61. See also Félix Luna, *El 45. Buenos Aires: Crónica de un año decisivo* (Buenos Aires: Editorial J. Alvarez, 1969).

21. Manuel Mora y Araujo, "La naturaleza de la coalición alfonsinista," *La Argentina electoral*, ed. Natalio R. Botana et al. (Buenos Aires: Editorial Sudamericana, 1985), 89–97.

Chapter 12, Levine, Pixote, pp. 201–14

1. He was stabbed nineteen times. See John Mosier, "Pixote," *Américas* 34, no. 2 (March–April 1982): 61.

2. Héctor Babenco, interview by George Csicsery, "Individual Solutions: An Interview with Héctor Babenco," *Film Quarterly* 36, no. 1 (Fall 1982): 2–17. See also Martha K. Huggins, ed., *Vigilantism and the State in Modern Latin America: Essays on Extralegal Violence* (New York: Praeger, 1991).

3. Sylvia Bahiense Naves et al., "Héctor Babenco (Entrevista)," *Cinema* (Fund. Cinemateca Brasileira) 5 (Spring 1980): 9–22, cited by Randal Johnson, "The *Romance-Reportagem* and the Cinema: Babenco's *Lúcio Flávio* and *Pixote*," *Luso-Brazilian Review* 24, no. 2 (Winter 1987): 38. In Louzeiro's book, "Pichote" was gunned down in the first chapter after trying to flee through a cemetery to avoid being abused by pimps and drug pushers.

4. See Johnson, "The *Romance-Reportagem* and the Cinema," 35–48.

5. Alan Riding, obituary of Fernando Ramos da Silva, *New York Times*, August 27, 1987; *Magill's Survey of Cinema*, file 299 (Englewood Cliffs, NJ: Salem Press, 1995). Diadema is the fourth of the so-called ABCD towns ringing São Paulo: Santo André, São Bernardo, São Caetano, and Diadema.

6. Johnson, "The *Romance-Reportagem* and the Cinema," 39.

7. Pauline Kael, "Current Cinema," *New Yorker* (November 9, 1981): 170–77, esp. 172.

8. Ibid., 170.

9. *Magill's Survey of Cinema*, file 299, abstract and review of *Pixote*.

10. Robert Stam, review in *Cineaste* 12, no. 3 (1983): 44–45.

11. Babenco, interview by Csicsery, "Individual Solutions," 2; William R. Long, "The Short Life and Bitter Death of Pixote," *Los Angeles Times*, September 4, 1987; *Magill's Survey of Cinema*, file 299.

12. Johnson, "The *Romance-Reportagem* and the Cinema," 44.

13. Babenco, interview by Csicsery, "Individual Solutions," 8.

14. Ibid., 2–3.

15. Ibid., 10.

16. It is a characteristic of Brazil that books and films deemed too critical, even if accurate, are not welcomed. Other examples are the cases of Carolina Maria de Jesus, the black diarist whose book became an international best-seller during the 1960s but who was disparaged in Brazil by intellectuals; and Francisco (Chico) Mendes, the Amazonian labor organizer who became an international hero after his murder but who in Brazil was the target of criticism as well as respect. See Robert M. Levine and José Carlos Sebe Bom Meihy, *The Life and Death of Carolina Maria de Jesus* (Albuquerque: University of New Mexico Press, 1995), and Robert M. Levine, *Brazilian Legacies* (Armonk, NY: M. E. Sharpe, 1997), 96–97.

17. Janet Hawken and Chaim Litewski, "Exploitation for Profit," *Screen* (London) 24, no. 2 (March–April 1983): 69.

18. John Coleman, *New Statesman* (London), April 8, 1983; Hawken and Litewski, "Exploitation for Profit," 70.

19. Vincent Canby, *New York Times*, May 5, 1981.

20. Quoted by Long, "Short Life and Bitter Death," 1.

21. Maria Aparecida Venâncio da Silva, quoted in Alan Riding, *New York Times*, August 27, 1987.

22. Caco Barcellos, *Rota 66*, 19th ed. (São Paulo: Editora Globo, 1993), 227–29.

23. Quoted in Long, "Short Life and Bitter Death," 1.

24. Barcelos, *Rota 66*, 241.

25. Cida Venâncio da Silva, *Pixote: Nunca mais! A vida verdadeira de Fernando Ramos da Silva* (São Paulo: Global Editora, 1988).

26. Barcellos, *Rota 66*, 229, 242.

27. Huggins, *Vigilantism and the State*. See also Hélio Pereira Bicudo, *Meu depoimento sobre a esquadrão da morte*, 3d ed. (São Paulo: Pontífica Comissão de Justiça e Paz de São Paulo, 1976); and Rinaldo Sérgio Vieira Arruda, *Pequenos bandidos* (São Paulo: Global Editora, 1983); Barcellos, *Rota 66*; and Paulo Sérgio Pinheiro, "Police and Political Crisis: The Case of the Military Police," in Huggins, *Vigilantism and the State*, 167–88.

28. See Joseph A. Page, *The Brazilians* (Reading, MA: Addison-Wesley, 1995), 259.

29. Pinheiro, in Huggins, *Vigilantism and the State*, 174–80.

30. This point is made by Stam in his review in *Cineaste*, 44–45.

31. Ibid., 44.

32. See Robert A. Rosenstone, "Introduction," in *Revisioning History: Film and the Construction of a New Past*, ed. Robert A. Rosenstone (Princeton: Princeton University Press, 1995), esp. 4.

33. Hawken and Litewski, "Exploitation for Profit," 66–67.

34. Bill Nichols, *Blurred Boundaries: Questions of Meaning in Contemporary Culture* (Bloomington: Indiana University Press, 1995), x.

35. *Veja* (São Paulo), April 14, 1982.

About the Editor and Contributors

The Editor

DONALD F. STEVENS received his doctorate in history from the University of Chicago and is associate professsor of history at Drexel University. Author of *Origins of Instability in Early Republican Mexico* (Durham, NC, 1991), Stevens has long been fascinated by nineteenth-century history. He is currently at work on a study of marriage and sexuality during cholera epidemics with the support of the National Endowment for the Humanities, the Social Science Research Council, and the American Council of Learned Societies.

The Contributors

JAMES D. HENDERSON received his doctorate in history from Texas Christian University and teaches at Coastal Carolina University. His publications include *When Colombia Bled: A History of the Violencia in Tolima* (University, AL, 1985), and *Conservative Thought in Twentieth-Century Latin America: The Ideas of Laureano Gómez* (Athens, OH, 1988).

THOMAS H. HOLLOWAY, professor of Latin American history at Cornell University, received his doctorate from the University of Wisconsin, Madison. He first came across Aguirre's letter to King Philip II while teaching Spanish-American history as a Fulbright visiting professor in Brazil. His publications include *Immigrants on the Land* (Chapel Hill, 1980) and *Policing Rio de Janeiro* (Stanford, CA, 1993).

ROBERT M. LEVINE, professor of history, University of Miami, Coral Gables, received his doctorate in history from Princeton University. Among his most recent works are *Father of the Poor?* (Cambridge, England, 1997), and *Brazilian Legacies* (Armonk, NY,

1997). He has also produced a videotaped documentary, "Brazil in the 1940s," on photography during the Estado Novo.

Sonya Lipsett-Rivera, associate professor of history at Carleton University in Ottawa, Ontario, received her Ph.D. in history from Tulane University, and her work was given the Tibesar Award in 1992. Her most recent publication is "La violencia dentro de las familias formal e informal," in *Familia y vida privada en la historia de Iberoamérica: Seminario de historia de la familia* (Mexico, 1996).

John Mraz is Senior Research Fellow, Instituto de Ciencias Sociales y Humanidades, Universidad Autónoma de Puebla, Mexico, and associate editor of *Film Historia* (Barcelona). Among his recent books are *La mirada inquieta: Nuevo fotoperiodismo mexicano, 1976–1996* (Mexico, 1996) and *Uprooted: Braceros in the Hermanos Mayo Lens* (Houston, 1996). He also has directed the award-winning documentary videos "Innovating Nicaragua" and "Made on Rails: A History of the Mexican Railroad Workers." He received his Ph.D. in history from the University of California, Santa Cruz.

Susan E. Ramírez, professor of history at DePaul University, received her doctorate from the University of Wisconsin, Madison. She has written extensively on colonial Spanish-American history. Her most recent publication is *The World Upside Down: Cross-Cultural Contact and Conflict in Sixteenth-Century Peru* (Stanford, CA, 1996).

Sergio Rivera Ayala is a doctoral candidate in Spanish literature at Syracuse University and professor at the Escuela de Extensión of the Universidad Nacional Autónoma de México in Hull, Quebec. His most recent publication is "Lewd Songs and Dances from the Streets of Eighteenth-Century New Spain," in William H. Beezley, Cheryl English Martin, and William E. French, eds., *Rituals of Rule, Rituals of Resistance: Public Celebrations and Popular Culture in Mexico* (Wilmington, DE, 1994).

James Schofield Saeger, professor of history at Lehigh University, received his Ph.D. in history from Ohio State University. He is the author of the chapter on the aboriginal inhabitants of colonial Paraguay and the Gran Chaco for the *Cambridge History of Native Peoples of the Americas* (Cambridge, England, 1977) and recently completed a book manuscript entitled *The Chaco Mission Frontier: The Guaycuruan Experience, 1700–1800.* His research has been supported by grants from the Organization of American States, the Fulbright Commission, and the National Endowment for the Humanities.

MARK D. SZUCHMAN, professor of Latin American history at Florida International University, received his doctorate from the University of Texas at Austin. He is the recipient of several grants (including the Doherty Foundation, Fulbright, Social Science Research Council, and National Endowment for the Humanities) and the author of numerous articles on nineteenth- and twentieth-century Argentina. His books include *Mobility and Integration in Urban Argentina: Córdoba in the Liberal Era* (Austin, TX, 1980); *Order, Family, and Community in Buenos Aires, 1810–1860* (Stanford, CA, 1988); *The Middle Period in Latin America: Values and Attitudes in the 18th–19th Centuries* (Boulder, CO, 1989); *Revolution and Restoration: The Rearrangement of Power in Argentina, 1776–1860* (Lincoln, NE, 1994, with Jonathan C. Brown); and *I Saw a City Invincible: Urban Portraits of Latin America* (Wilmington, DE, 1996, with Gilbert M. Joseph).

BARBARA A. TENENBAUM is the first specialist in Mexican culture in the Hispanic Division of the Library of Congress, Washington, DC. She is the editor-in-chief of the *Encyclopedia of Latin American History and Culture* (New York, 1996) and recently coedited *Liberals, Politics, and Power: State Formation in Nineteenth-Century Latin America* (Athens, GA, 1996). She is currently working on a book on the development of Mexico City from 1867 to 1910. She received her Ph.D. in history from Harvard University.

BARBARA WEINSTEIN, associate professor of history and former director of women's studies at the State University of New York at Stony Brook, received her doctorate in history from Yale University. Her most recent publication is *For Social Peace in Brazil: Industrialists and the Remaking of the Working Class in São Paulo, 1920–1964* (Chapel Hill, NC, 1996). She is currently doing research on regional identity and nationalism in twentieth-century Brazil.

Latin American Silhouettes
Studies in History and Culture

William H. Beezley and
Judith Ewell
Editors

Volumes Published

William H. Beezley, Cheryl English Martin, and William E. French, eds., *Rituals of Rule, Rituals of Resistance: Public Celebrations and Popular Culture in Mexico* (1994). Cloth ISBN 0-8420-2416-6 Paper ISBN 0-8420-2417-4

Stephen R. Niblo, *War, Diplomacy, and Development: The United States and Mexico, 1938–1954* (1995). ISBN 0-8420-2550-2

G. Harvey Summ, ed., *Brazilian Mosaic: Portraits of a Diverse People and Culture* (1995). Cloth ISBN 0-8420-2491-3 Paper ISBN 0-8420-2492-1

N. Patrick Peritore and Ana Karina Galve-Peritore, eds., *Biotechnology in Latin America: Politics, Impacts, and Risks* (1995). Cloth ISBN 0-8420-2556-1 Paper ISBN 0-8420-2557-X

Silvia Marina Arrom and Servando Ortoll, eds., *Riots in the Cities: Popular Politics and the Urban Poor in Latin America, 1765–1910* (1996). Cloth ISBN 0-8420-2580-4 Paper ISBN 0-8420-2581-2

Roderic Ai Camp, ed., *Polling for Democracy: Public Opinion and Political Liberalization in Mexico* (1996). ISBN 0-8420-2583-9

Brian Loveman and Thomas M. Davies, Jr., eds., *The Politics of Antipolitics: The Military in Latin America*, 3d ed., revised and updated (1996). Cloth ISBN 0-8420-2609-6 Paper ISBN 0-8420-2611-8

Joseph S. Tulchin, Andrés Serbín, and Rafael Hernández, eds., *Cuba and the Caribbean: Regional Issues and Trends in the Post-Cold War Era* (1997). ISBN 0-8420-2652-5

Thomas W. Walker, ed., *Nicaragua without Illusions: Regime Transition and Structural Adjustment in the 1990s* (1997). Cloth ISBN 0-8420-2578-2 Paper ISBN 0-8420-2579-0

Dianne Walta Hart, *Undocumented in L.A.: An Immigrant's Story* (1997). Cloth ISBN 0-8420-2648-7 Paper ISBN 0-8420-2649-5

Jaime E. Rodríguez O. and Kathryn Vincent, eds., *Myths, Misdeeds, and Misunderstandings: The Roots of Conflict in U.S.-Mexican Relations* (1997). ISBN 0-8420-2662-2

Jaime E. Rodríguez O. and Kathryn Vincent, eds., *Common Border, Uncommon Paths: Race, Culture, and National Identity in U.S.-Mexican Relations* (1997). ISBN 0-8420-2673-8

William H. Beezley and Judith Ewell, eds., *The Human Tradition in Modern Latin America* (1997). Cloth ISBN 0-8420-2612-6 Paper ISBN 0-8420-2613-4

Donald F. Stevens, ed., *Based on a True Story: Latin American History at the Movies* (1997). ISBN 0-8420-2582-0

Jaime E. Rodríguez O., ed., *The Origins of Mexican National Politics, 1808–1847* (1997). Paper ISBN 0-8420-2723-8

Che Guevara, *Guerrilla Warfare*, with revised and updated introduction and case studies by Brian Loveman and Thomas M. Davies, Jr., 3d ed. (1997). Cloth ISBN 0-8420-2677-0 Paper ISBN 0-8420-2678-9

Adrian A. Bantjes, *As If Jesus Walked on Earth: Cardenismo, Sonora, and the Mexican Revolution* (1998). ISBN 0-8420-2653-3

Henry A. Dietz and Gil Shidlo, eds., *Urban Elections in Democratic Latin America* (1998). Cloth ISBN 0-8420-2627-4 Paper ISBN 0-8420-2628-2

A. Kim Clark, *The Redemptive Work: Railway and Nation in Ecuador, 1895–1930* (1998). ISBN 0-8420-2674-6

Joseph S. Tulchin, ed., with Allison M. Garland, *Argentina: The Challenges of Modernization* (1998). ISBN 0-8420-2721-1

Louis A. Pérez, Jr., ed., *Impressions of Cuba in the Nineteenth Century: The Travel Diary of Joseph J. Dimock* (1998). Cloth ISBN 0-8420-2657-6 Paper ISBN 0-8420-2658-4

Guy P. C. Thomson, *Patriotism, Politics, and Popular Liberalism in Nineteenth-Century Mexico: Juan Francisco Lucas and the Puebla Sierra* (1998). ISBN 0-8420-2683-5